You Don't Know Me

The Musical Memoir of Stormin' Norman Seldin

You Don't Know Me:
The Musical Memoir of Stormin' Norman Seldin

You Don't Know Me

The Musical Memoir of Stormin' Norman Seldin

by Norman Seldin
as told to Charlie Horner

Edited by Pamela Horner, Don Stine
and Douglas E. Friedman

Classic Urban Harmony® Press, Somerset, NJ

ISBN: 978-1-7329650-3-4

Cover Design:
Susan R. Wacker-Donle, SusanWackerDonle.com

Cover photo Credits:
Estelle Massry

Library of Congress Control Number: 2021918818

Published by Classic Urban Harmony Press
210 Sherwood Court
Somerset, NJ 08873
www.ClassicUrbanHarmony.net

Printed in the United States

First Edition

This book, "You Don't Know Me," is dedicated
to my mother Helen Seldin
who was the driving force behind my music,
my wife Jamey Seldin of thirty years
who literally saved my life and career when we met,
my daughter Melody who chose to live with me,
and the many music educators who didn't live to see
how I turned out from their teaching.
- Norman Seldin

Contents

Preface

This book answers the inquiries of hundreds of curious fans about how a three-year-old child could start formal piano lessons and practice eight hours a day until it was perfect. They didn't know how at fifteen I could have owned my own record label, promoted shows, managed black groups, composed and performed - all at the same time!

I was always taught to trust no one until it felt right. I had no fear of anything I was about to do. The words "I can't do that" or "it's impossible" didn't exist in my thoughts - ever. When I was a little four- or five-year-old, I heard an amazing classical artist named Dinu Lipatti who played the most beautiful Chopin you could ever imagine. He passed away at the age of 32. After reading his story, I felt that nothing was impossible! My mother always encouraged me to follow my dreams. She had a beautiful soprano voice but her father refused to pay for her to attend college. He felt women should cook and have children! I guess that's why she wanted me to live up to and beyond my potential. Nothing was normal in my life.

About five years ago, Bill Handelman of the *Asbury Park Press* started interviewing me for two hours, twice a week, for my life story. Six months into this intense venture, he developed cancer and shortly after passed away. I was stunned and again didn't trust anyone for years. Then I found a true music historian in Charlie Horner. With the COVID-19 pandemic closing in on us, Charlie jumped on the opportunity to co-write my autobiography. Little did I know, Charlie had already been following my career quite closely. Charlie is an authority on many black artists who were never really acknowledged and with my R&B background we made a perfect fit for a book. I don't think Charlie ever expected all the wild stories I was telling him would be backed up by his research, but he found it was all true!

Being taught the right way to book and manage honestly by veteran musician and agent Jimmy Lamare helped my career as both an agent and promoter. Working in the same office with comedian Myron Cohen gave me many more thoughts about what I was doing and where I was going. Even at the early age of 16, I was booking name acts like Tony Orlando, Larry Chance & The Earls, The Duprees, Randy & the Rainbows, Johnny Thunder, The Four Evers and many others from Arnold Klein in New York City. I was also doing some Brill Building work with publicity agent Jim McCarthy, the agent for Peter Duchin, owner Johnson Records and manager of The Shells and The Dubs. The one thing everyone kept telling me was, "Norman, you're as good or better than many performers. Why aren't you out there with your band?" The everyday lessons were being thrown at me left and right. I ended up at that young age recording with Pat Jacques at Broadway Recording Studios in the Ed Sullivan Theater building. That made me part of the R&B market and surrounded with now my longtime friend and world-renowned drummer Bernard "Pretty" Purdie along with Eric Gayle and Cornell Dupree. Richard Tee would come into Studio B and teach this little white kid the right way to play a B3 Hammond organ and special changes on the Fender Rhodes piano. Many more things happened including some great and some very bad situations that I had to overcome. I'm leaving all of that until you read this life story.

I do want to mention some people who are very special to me. Of course, my wife Jamey who saved my life and career. Over the years, I kept my favorite female vocalist Pam McCoy by my side and hope I helped advance her career. More recently, a bright young pianist half my age, Ryan Gregg, seemed to be the perfect fit to sit next to me during live performances and in the studio. You'll be hearing more on him in the near future.

I wanted to write about the immense help that Butch Gregoria put into making sure I arrived on time with my performance pianos ready to go. Butch would check the sound twice around to make sure it was right and represented "my sound!" If anyone had a question or request for me while I was performing, it was always directed to Butch. He took care of it. My longtime friend has more musical talent than many of the performers out there. He has an amazing ear. While other band members suffer trying to play Keith Emerson or Rick Wakeman, what Butch does by ear far surpasses them. There's one thing I will never do for Butch. He wants me to teach him which is impossible because he doesn't like to practice. I even put a 6'9" grand piano of mine in his home but he still won't practice! A more dependable friend like him is rare and hard to find. If you don't find Butch before a show of mine, the chances are that I won't be there! My special thanks to Terri Celendano Cuomo who has given such love and care to my wife Jamey while taking care of her during some difficult times.

During the past 16 years, after some life-threatening issues put me into a world that I had left a long time ago, I've been representing Steinway & Sons pianos. Jacobs Music Company is one of the oldest and most respected firms. You'll read about them. I became close friends with the most talented music educators I had ever heard or seen. Just to mention a few - Ingrid Clarfield and Marvin Blickenstaff always reminded me and so many others that if you don't learn something new every day you're not going anywhere. Even though I had left the classical field and had gone into New Orleans Blues/ Mississippi Stride Piano/vocals, I used the old techniques to blaze new fresh notes into my style and that only improved it

My experiences in my family's jewelry store and my own jewelry store chain taught me that I could sell anything. I'd promoted so many concerts that selling pianos came naturally to me. Learning the insides of the piano was the only thing I needed to do With the help of many of the finest experts at Steinway & Sons in Queens, New York, and the input of Al Rinaldi of Jacobs Music, those things also became second nature.

After completing this book with dozens of true good, bad, and ugly stories, I did finally realize that my best friend from the young age of three until now is still is a Steinway & Sons piano. You'll read about how it was my only savior when times were really tough. It most likely saved the sanity of a very small boy wanting to be much older and it has gotten me there. All I can say is thank you to everyone involved in my life. I think that practicing six to eight hours a day from the age of three has paid off!

Norman Seldin, September 16, 2021

Acknowledgments

The authors want to express our sincere gratitude to the people who helped us with this book. Editing was done by Pamela Horner, Don Stine and Douglas Friedman. The fabulous cover design is courtesy of Susan Wacker-Donle. Back cover blurbs were written by friends Larry Chance, Vini Lopez, Bernard Purdie, Doc Holiday and Jean Mikle.

First, a few words about the many photos in this book. Just about all of the early photos of me [Norman] and the groups I was promoting were taken by Earl Stout. When I was very young my mother, Helen Seldin, always had pictures taken of me at the piano and used our family friend and photographer Earl Stout. Earl worked for Dorn's Photography, the best photography studio in Red Bank, but when he took photos for me he was freelancing. When I was 13 or 14, I told Mr. Stout that I planned on performing with and promoting bands and groups. I wanted to hire him to take pictures for me.

What I didn't plan on was an education that has stayed with me to this day. Mr. Stout said to come back at the end of the week because he wanted to show me something and talk with me. When I came back, he asked me to sit down. I didn't know what a lesson I was in for as I was only asking for someone to take pictures! Mr. Stout said that there were many parts to taking a picture and started by saying there are the poses/stills of your groups, action photos that sometimes you give a photographer a heads up on when to shoot, and then there is that rare one or few pictures that last almost forever. Then are the ones that you take where you had no choice but to shoot. He opened the personal book he held in his hands and told me he was the lead photographer during the war with Nazi Germany. He was the first photographer to enter in the Auschwitz concentration camp and with tears in his eyes said, "These are the horrors that I never expected to see as a photographer with thousands of bodies of all ages stacked upon each other everywhere I took shots. This is part of being a real photographer, the good, the bad, the smiles, the tears, the ugly, along with the beautiful. If you remember, pass this along when you grow up. There will be many photographers who will want to take photos of you and your groups so make sure to know what you're looking for!"

Danny Sanchez' brilliant original publicity photos of me are still making their way around the world. I knew right away why all the TV and movie stars would arrive in limos at his little Red Bank, New Jersey, studio. They wanted those Danny Sanchez shots. To all of the wonderfully talented photographers who have credits in my true life story book, I find it necessary to send this message. Earl Stout always said that a great picture speaks a thousand words so make sure it sends the right message to everyone!

Every effort has been made to properly credit photographs and use with the owners' permissions. Most come from the archives of Stormin' Norman Productions. Some of the original copies of Earl Stout photos have been lost to time and newspaper copies had to be substituted. While the resolution of these may not be clear, they are the best copies we could obtain. Some older publicity photos are from the Classic Urban Harmony Archives and fall under the category of public domain. Thanks also for select images from Dorn's Classic Images and Madonna Carter Jackson for use of an image by her father, Joseph A. Carter Sr.

Many thanks to my many photographer friends, Danny Sanchez, Katie Murphy, Rick Verso, Nick Mead, John Cavanaugh and my wife Jamey Seldin. The brilliant photographer Estelle Massry who took my cover shots for "You Don't Know Me." It took hundreds of shots to get the perfect one. My thanks to all of you and especially the late Earl Stout who taught me the real meaning of photography and what it takes.

I'd like to thank the Rinaldi family and owners of Jacobs Music Company for always making sure that I had beautiful Steinway & Sons concert pianos at my shows and venues. They made sure that I was able to appear at every event and played a major part in making sure I was always performing on the best pianos in the world. Thank you Gabrielle, Bob, Chris and the late Al Rinaldi who made it happen for me.

Thanks to B&N Pianos and owner Dennis Borcky who made sure every Steinway & Sons Model D concert grand piano was delivered on stage for all of my shows. They also do all of the piano moving for Jacobs Music Company.

Thank you Vaune Peck, Director of the Pollak Theater at Monmouth University in West Long Branch, New Jersey, for having the vision to put not just the Stormin' Norman Seldin's "Dueling Pianos" on stage, but to allow me to bring in sensational young classical trained students and performers to open the show. Many saw how great it could be for their own children to be studying piano and add some musical culture to their lives.

Thank you to all of the great musicians and singers who performed with me throughout the years. There are too many of you to list here but I've written about you in this book. Most of all, thanks to all of my thousands of fans for your support. I hope you enjoy the book.

Stormin' Norman Seldin
July 15, 2021

Introduction

In my 50-plus years in the music business, I've come to know hundreds, if not thousands, of entertainers. Many displayed incredible talent as musicians or vocalists. Some showed amazing skill at songwriting or producing recordings. Others worked behind the scenes managing and promoting entertainers or producing concerts. But of all the music people I've met, I can probably count on one hand those who excelled in all of these vocations and even then, I'd still have a couple fingers left over. The ability to simultaneously handle all of these undertakings is the mark of a true music industry genius. Norman Seldin has excelled as a musician, singer, bandleader, songwriter, arranger, producer, promoter, manager, music director and record label owner. Incredibly, he has done so in such diverse music genres as classical, stride piano, jazz, blues, rhythm & blues, rock & roll, doo wop, soul, rock and pop music, to name a few.

Norman's influence on popular music is significant. As a teenage dance and concert promoter he brought together many of the early bands whose musicians gave rise to the Jersey Shore Rock scene of the 1970's. Groups like the Castiles, Motifs, DuCanes, Sonny & the Starfires and Jaywalkers produced rock luminaries like Bruce Springsteen, Vini Lopez, Doc Holiday, Billy Ryan, Mickey Holiday, Vinnie Roslin and a host of others. Norman hired Clarence Clemons and recorded with him prior to the E Street Band. In the area of soul music, Norman discovered Harry Ray prior to Ray Goodman & Brown and recorded members of the Broadways while they were still the Uniques. In the field of doo wop music, Norman managed acts like Larry Chance & the Earls and produced numerous dances and concerts by Nicky Addeo, Vito & the Salutations, Shells, Duprees, Bobbettes, Danny & the Juniors, Belmonts, Olympics and countless others. He recorded doo wop groups like the Darchaes, Uniques and Shondelles. These accomplishments of course, barely scratch the surface of a career that went from New Jersey to Mississippi to Florida and back.

But accomplishments alone don't make for a great read. There has to be a storyline that draws a reader in. You'll find that while music is woven through the fabric of every paragraph, this book is not really about music. It's about one man's determination to overcome adversity while living on his own terms. Whether it was racing horses, surviving health crises or fighting discrimination, Norman Seldin "stormed" his way through each situation. This book is the life story of Stormin' Norman Seldin. Music is just Norman's companion. Norman found early on that in an imperfect world, real music is pure. In a world full of discord, Norman found harmony.

- Charlie Horner, June 30, 2021

CHAPTER ONE

THEY CALL ME STORMIN' NORMAN

My fans call me "Stormin' Norman." Some people know me as a musician and bandleader. Some know me as a songwriter and arranger. Others know me as a manager, booking agent and concert promoter. Still others know me as a record producer and label owner. My involvement in music runs from classical to jazz, Harlem stride, rhythm & blues, rock & roll, doo wop, soul, garage and rock genres, to name a few. I recorded Clarence Clemons before he joined Springsteen and Harry Ray before Ray, Goodman & Brown. While many people know me for different segments of my music career, few know my whole life story and it's a fascinating one. Nevertheless, this book is more than just my autobiography. It's an inside look at how the Jersey Shore r&b and rock music scene developed, as seen through the eyes of someone who was there and helped shape it. But if you think that's all this book is about, then, as the Ray Charles song says, "you don't know me." So lets go back to the beginning.

Photo by Nick Mead

The story of the Seldin family in the United States began in 1909 when my grandfather, Max L. Seldin, emigrated Russia for the United States. He was part of a large number of Jewish people who fled Russia to escape the violent uprisings against them in the late 1800s and early 1900s. I'm told my grandfather walked halfway across Russia to escape so things must have been very bad. Initially he settled in Newark, New Jersey, but after serving in the U.S. Army during World War I he moved to Red Bank in 1920. There he married my grandmother, Ethel Cohen, who was also an immigrant from Russia. Actually, the two had known each other in Russia and when grandfather left to come here, he feared he'd never see her again. They were reunited in the United States.

Red Bank was then, and still is, a small town of about 11,000 in central New Jersey. It's on the banks of the Navesink River. Red Bank is about ten miles north of Asbury Park. The greater Red Bank area includes the surrounding communities of Fair Haven, Rumson and Little Silver. The Shrewsbury Avenue neighborhood my grandparents lived in then was a diverse community of European immigrants and African Americans.

At first, my grandfather operated a meat market and grocery at 222 Shrewsbury Avenue which he sold in 1923. From there, he went into the dry goods business, eventually operating a department store next to the family home at 184 Shrewsbury Avenue. My grandfather also dabbled in buying and selling real estate. My grandparents had three sons - my father Paul was the oldest, followed by my uncles Raymond and Harold.

My father, Paul Seldin, was born in 1921. Even at a young age, my father was a talented musician. While attending Red Bank High School, he played bass viol with both the school orchestra and marching band. (For non-musicians, the bass viol is an upright bowed string instrument.) In fact, he was selected to play in the New Jersey All-State

Red Bank High School Orchestra, 1939. Paul Seldin, second row, far left.

School Symphony Orchestra, the only student in his class to be so honored. The Orchestra played concerts in Newark and Atlantic City. At the same time he played in the Marlboro State Hospital Concert Orchestra.

After graduation in June 1939, my father played with the Rumson Symphonic Society, a group of local musicians directed by noted New York City conductor, Walter Pfeiffer. My uncle Raymond played violin for them as well. My father also played for the Spring Lake Sinfonietta. Before joining the Navy during World War II, my father was connected to the Columbia Music Festival in Columbia, South Carolina, but I'm not sure of the details. That was before I came to be.

In the service, from what I understand, my father never went to boot camp. He ended up stationed in Key West, Florida, at an admiral's house as his personal musician. He worked on the admiral's boats and other things. While my father was in the service in Florida, he met my mother. I was told my father was thrown in the brig one time for holding her hand instead of saluting an officer. He said that he didn't salute the officer because no one ever told him he should. I think that he got a night in the brig for that.

My mother, Helen Pollack Seldin, had a beautiful soprano voice. She actually was a voice scholarship winner to Julliard School of Music. She was accepted there but her father refused to pay for an additional $75 or $100 needed because he believed that women should only have children and cook. My mother's father was originally from the Bahamas where he was a jeweler. He even had a 120-foot yacht. He brought his family to Dothan, Alabama, and opened a jewelry store there. While stationed in Florida, my father learned the jewelry trade from his father-in-law.

After the war, my grandfather, Max Seldin, gave each one of his three sons four or five thousand dollars towards buying their first house or starting a business. My uncle Raymond went to NYU and became a public accountant. My uncle Harold became a civil engineer. My father and mother took the money and opened a jewelry store. So, Seldin's Quality Jewelers opened at 60 Monmouth Street in Red Bank in October, 1945. At the same time, my father assembled his own orchestra and began playing weddings and social functions.

I came into this world on April 26, 1947. I was born in Riverview Hospital in Red Bank. It's now the huge Riverview Medical Center but when I was born it wasn't much bigger than a large house. That's also where my father and my uncles were born.

When I was a baby we lived in an apartment on Leroy Place in Red Bank. Then my parents built a home on a big inexpensive piece of property on Harrison Avenue in Fair Haven. Harrison Avenue is kind of on the border between Fair Haven and Red Bank. I found out later that our house at 122 Harrison was only about eight blocks from where William "Count" Basie was born. But when I was growing up, between the Seldins and the Cohens, almost everyone in our two- or three-block area was related.

My godfather was Nat Daniel who would go on to be the inventor and owner of Danelectro Guitars. Danelectro Guitars was founded in Red Bank, New Jersey. They also made Silvertone guitars for Sears. That was the same guitar as the Danelectro, just with the Silvertone label on it. My aunt became Nat Daniel's bookkeeper.

I had a strange childhood. I was probably the only child whose first word ever spoken was "hotdog." It was not "Mama," "Ma," or "Dada" or anything like that. We had a friend who was painting the house and every time he'd go by my the crib he would say "hotdog." And that's what I said for weeks after my first words. All I said was "hotdog." It was just an unusual childhood. You had to have been there.

With my father being a musician, I was always exposed to music. At the time, my father was part of the National Orchestral Association and my parents took me to the orchestra rehearsals and recitals. They said that when I was two-and-a-half, I walked out from the front row during the orchestra rehearsal, went behind famed conductor Leon Barzin, and started conducting behind him with my hands. I think that they knew then I might want to be a leader of something musical. There's a picture of that somewhere. I remember seeing it. I might have come up to his knees and I was waving my arms conducting in back of him which everybody thought was hysterical.

While both my father and mother were musically inclined, my grandfather, Max Seldin, did not share that interest. My grandfather was quite religious. I spent pretty much most weekends at my grandfather's house. My grandfather believed that pro wrestling was real and we'd watched every match on TV. I can remember it well even though it was a long time ago. There were wrestlers like Yukon Eric, Killer Kowalski and Ricky Starr. We watched it every Friday night and grandfather would jump up and down in his chair. He was from Russia and to him it was real. We went to a couple wrestling matches when I was young and watched all the crazy people with the chairs flying. I think it was more real back then. It got pretty rough. They got into it and much of the blood was real. It was a different childhood for me considering how religious my grandfather was.

My grandfather used to get the Jewish newspaper along with the local paper which I guess at the time was *The Red Bank Register*. It came out every day. Once a week he'd get the *Sunday New York Times* or *The Daily News*. I would sit there on the weekends and watch him read the news. With the Jewish newspaper, you know, we read in Hebrew, starting from right to left. Well my grandfather used to pick up the newspaper and start with the obituaries. I said "Why, Grandpa? Why are you reading about the dead people?" And he said "If I'm not in there, it's going to be a good day." I never really knew what that meant until I got older. But to him, he was looking to see if any of his friends had died.

I have fond memories of the big family dinners even though there were some foods I didn't like. But I also remember the bad things. One of my earliest memories was from when I was about three years old. Being very little, I guess I was kind of wild. We always had a maid and her name was Fanny. She would be there watching over me from morning until my parents got home from running the jewelry store. Our kitchen had the old hard floor tiles. I had a little 78 RPM record player and my favorite record was "Woody Woodpecker." I played it until it was bald and blank and I used to dance to it in the kitchen. Well, my father had a 78 RPM record collection and I decided to dance with his records on my head. Not a smart idea with how fragile and breakable the old 78's were. I think that I got my first real beating when my father came home from the store and found I had danced and crashed about 25 or 30 of his prized original Enrico Caruso recordings. I was running every which way to avoid that belt. From there things got worse.

My father was very abusive to me and very abusive to my mother. Fortunately, my youngest sister wasn't born yet and my other sister was too young to understand what was happening. So my father would take his frustrations out on me. It didn't take much to set him off - a bad day in the store or a couple of wrong notes on the piano was all it took. With a normal childhood, even back then, you might get a smack on the ass. But my father used a razor strap and I was beaten with that thing. The razor strap from the barbershop, you know? It was brutal.

I mentioned the piano. I don't know if my incident with the records had anything to do with it but the Steinway piano arrived in our house soon after that. I guess my parents figured I was hyperactive and needed some guidance so they bought a Steinway and started me on lessons. Actually, they had an older Chickering piano but the minute I started playing, a Steinway appeared. I've now been on a Steinway since the age of three.

My mother's friend was a band conductor at Rumson High School and at the age of three they took me over there for my first lessons. I remember looking out of the window watching the kids playing in the field and there I was sitting there trying to reach the pedals on the piano. That's where it all started for me at such a young age. It was kind of crazy.

Of course, being so young, my hands were too small. My first couple of teachers, after the original one, used to sit me on the table and give me a plum or anything that was soft. They would ask me to just move my fingers in. They wanted my hand to be curved. In those days, it was a curved hand position. If I pushed too hard the plum squirted. I had to go wash my hands and wash the table where I squished the fruit all over. Then I could go to the piano and start practicing.

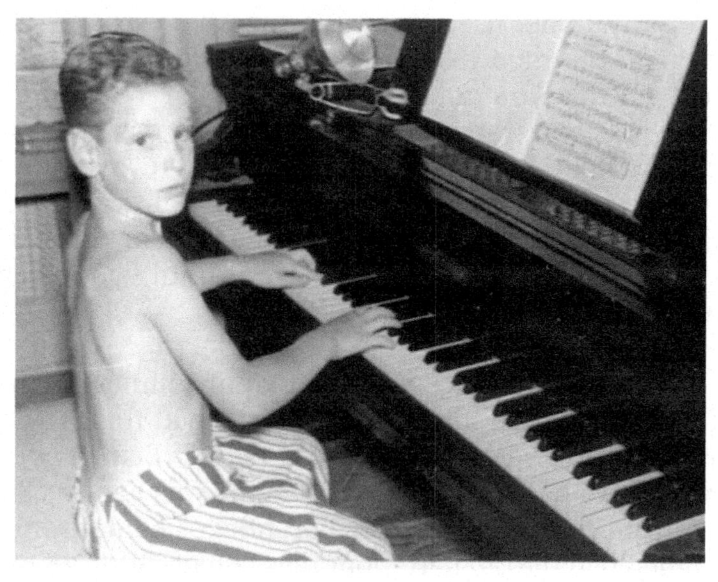

Norman at the piano at a young age.
Photo by Earl Stout

After that, my early teachers were friends of my father's from the symphony. They were Russian or Italian or German and a lot of them didn't speak any English. The only way they knew to tell me I hit a wrong note was to hit me with a knitting needle. They were metal in those days, and I had welts all over my fingers for the first couple of years. Nobody had to ask me how my lesson went. I had these welts all the way across my fingers. If I didn't have any, it was usually a pretty good lesson. It built me up to a point where I kept outgrowing the teachers, which was a little strange because they were really good. I had a Korean teacher who was phenomenal and used to do concerts at Red Bank's Carlton Theatre (now the Count Basie Theater). He moved me along greatly.

Meanwhile, the abuse from my father went off and on. I had to take it because I was only a kid and I had nothing to say. But he also was the same way to my mother, and I saw all that. It was pretty bad. I think that I buried myself in the piano so much that the hours went by. It was a time passer and I was a natural at it. My problem was my photographic memory that retains everything I experienced. I'm telling you now, I can repeat almost everything I've heard from the of age three on up.

By the time I reached school age, I'd become a machine. I would get up at 5:30 or 6:00 in the morning and get two hours in on the piano and then do another two or three hours when I got home from school. It was five to eight hours practice a day all the time. It got to the point where I was practicing at 5:00 in the morning on the big Steinway in the front room. And I'd get picked up by the collar by my father and thrown back in my bed. That was my father. He'd say, "I like your playing but I'd rather hear it from 7:30 on, thank you. I'd like to get some sleep!" He just picked me up, opened the door, and threw me on the bed. "Thank you. Now go to sleep."

So, it was a crazy childhood. My grandfather started me at Hebrew School at six years old, which was very, very young. It was with an Orthodox teacher in Long Branch, New Jersey, about a 15 minute drive from Red Bank. Everyday after public school, my mother would run me to Long Branch. I'd go to this house with maybe eight or ten other students and have Hebrew school. Then I'd go up to the corner in Long Branch and get a bus back to Red Bank. The minute I got back to Red Bank, my parents would hand me a broom to sweep the store. Then they'd take me home and feed me and I'd practice some more. In those days you didn't get a lot of homework. It was all practicing and then some. When we watched TV it was always "The Arthur Godfrey Show" or "The Liberace Show" in black and white, with Oreos and milk.

I think music was the direction my mother wanted me to go in. My Hebrew schoolteacher wanted me to be a cantor or a rabbi. My grandfather was paying for all the lessons. Jewish people have a thing called the haftarah that you do at a bar mitzvah. I was so young in starting that I didn't have to learn one haftarah, I had to learn six because they didn't know by the time I was 13, which one I would do. There were dozens of them.

Of course, that was a time when I wanted to play baseball like the other kids but they didn't want me to hurt my hands. That was the whole Jewish protection thing. My Hebrew name was Nocham. So my Hebrew schoolteacher would say, "Nocham, you can play baseball, but only with Jewish kids." I mean, there were like two Jewish kids in my whole town! So I played baseball whenever I could sneak it in with some of the kids in the neighborhood when my parents were at the jewelry store or something. I was very good at it but basically I had to hide anything to do with sports. And I was buying records and sheet music because my mother was giving me the money, but I had to hide them so my father would not see them.

Nocham - my Hebrew teacher was basically the only person to call me that. Well, he and the cantors. My Hebrew schoolteacher was a kosher slaughterer. When my parents dropped me off in Long Branch, they dropped me off at a slaughtering house which was two blocks from my teacher's house. You know, he was killing chickens, with a razor blade. He walked with his back hunched over, but I never said anything. I saw him washing his hands when he got home, and I noticed there was a tattoo on his wrist. I said "What is that?" And he said "You're never to have one. This is from the concentration camp and I walk this way because they broke my back on one of those torture racks." He walked hunched over like that for the whole time I knew him.

There were a lot of disturbing things for a kid like me to see during that time. My Hebrew teacher had a very good friend, a cantor named Shalom. He came by a couple of times to hear me just practicing. When I was ten or eleven he asked if I would be interested in him sponsoring me for, I believe, the Westminster Choir College. He said, "I think you should be a cantor." I didn't really think about it, but I said I wasn't interested because I was so into piano then. I really, really didn't exploit my voice except at a Hebrew school. I mean, I hadn't really even started to do any singing because we didn't even have a band yet. So it was kind of strange. I didn't find out until later that it was a high honor that he asked me. I knew at the time he was getting $5,000 as a cantor to do the Holy Days. That was a lot of money. I found out that he too had been in a concentration camp with his family. His voice was so nice that they used to bring a microphone out at nights so he could sing the German officers to sleep. Then they called him out one night at 10:30 and he got up to the microphone to sing. As he sang and he watched them machine gun his entire family into a ditch.

I had a lot of problems in my elementary school music class because I was learning music that was way ahead of the other students. It was probably even beyond that of the music teachers who were teaching the kids. One time my teacher made a mistake in the class and it was blatant. I stood up and up said, "Listen, that's wrong. That's not middle C, that's E." Well, the teacher got so mad that she sent me to the principal's office which prompted a phone call home to my parents. First my mother came in and then my father followed. The four letter words were flying because I remember them well.

The Jewish population in Fair Haven was small and not always accepted. It became a problem even in school because they didn't allow us time off for the Jewish holidays then. I was suspended for three days for taking the High Holy Days off when we went to the synagogue with my grandfather. That's when my parents had to come in again. There was a brutal, brutal argument. The school did not recognize Jewish holidays and there were not many Jews where I lived. At times it was almost like the prejudice African Americans were facing and it caused a lot of problems.

It was a strange childhood. I never got invited to the parties in town with the other kids. I later found out why from a long time friend. She too also wondered why I and kids from these two other families were never invited. She had asked her parents and they told her, "Well, they don't want Jews in their homes." That's when I realized the real prejudice. It got to the point where at recitals, I noticed some kids got up and left without playing. I wanted to know why. I finally heard the teacher tell my mother that they didn't want to be embarrassed by the curly headed kid in the back. I said, "Who is that?" And she said, "It's you." I was like eight or nine years old. These kids were 16 and 18. They didn't want me to play before them or even at the same recital.

Even at my elementary school graduation I was slighted. My father's jewelry store always did the music awards, giving out little charms. I was clearly the most musically talented in my class but when it came to that year's music awards, the music teacher stood on that stage in front of everybody and gave the music award to her own daughter instead of me. I was the little curly-headed kid who everybody wanted to hear play, but I wasn't deemed worthy of recognition.

Religious prejudice and racial prejudice are just different sides of the same coin. Now my grandfather's neighborhood over by Shrewsbury Avenue in Red Bank was all immigrants and black people. That's the environment my father grew up with. Our family doctors were the Parkers, two extraordinary African American physicians, father and son — Dr. James Parker Sr. and Dr. James Parker Jr. Dr. James Parker Sr. treated my father and mother and his son treated me. The Parkers' office was right across the street from my grandfather's store. There's now a Dr. James Parker Boulevard and a special medical center named after the father.

Sisters, Sarita and Rochelle,
Norman and mother, Helen Seldin.
Photo by Earl Stout

My parents were not prejudiced. In the jewelry store, my father had a black apprentice, Horner Williams, who started out sweeping floors, learned his craft and eventually became one of the first black jewelry store owners in Red Bank. My father taught him jewelry making. But one time my mother's mother came to visit and saw Horner Williams sitting next to my father. She walked right out of that store and didn't speak to my father for six months. How could he dare hire a black man to work in the store?

My youth became a rotation of schooling, work, more work, practice and more practice. My mother did all the runnings to New York for the jewelry for the store. But as soon as I was old enough to get on the bus, they handed me a briefcase and gave me instructions to go get this stuff. So it was pretty much work and work and work.

Meanwhile I was getting pretty skilled at piano. I played a wrong note one time at a pretty intense recital. And rather than stop, I transposed it to a key that had five sharps in it, which was brilliant. I didn't know any fear. I didn't know any better. When it was over, the teacher came up and said to other teachers, "I've never heard anything like that. He played a wrong note, transposed it to five sharps and never blinked."

Right before my bar mitzvah time, I guess I was just twelve-and-a-half, I finally was allowed to try out for the Little League baseball. My father was vehemently against it. I think that he played catch with me maybe twice in my whole life. He had gotten gloves, but he refused to really do anything. Ten minutes and he was done. That was a big deal for me then when the kids came over. In setting up the Little League teams, the coaches paid Monopoly money to draft which kids they wanted on their teams. And a kid came running up to me saying, "The elementary school said you're going to be in the Fair Haven Hawks." Now the Fair Haven Hawks were a really good kid's baseball team. I said, "I am?" He said, "Yeah, my father paid every bit of his money for you. I think it was a thousand dollars in Monopoly money." But I was the only one they added. My mother came out to see me play a few times, but my father refused. He came one time and when I was announced to come up to bat, I watched him get on a bicycle and ride away. That night that I hit two home runs. The hurt of watching him leave rather than see me play has never left me.

Of course all of my piano training was in classical music. There was nothing that my teachers ever gave me that resembled the chords, the things that I do now. But soon my musical interests began to expand. There was a gentleman, in my father's store who worked in the back because besides jewelry, we sold firearms. Firearms could be sold there because my parents were licensed retail firearms dealers. And people brought guns in for repair. We carried Brownings, Colts and Smith & Wessons. It seemed like there was almost always a member of the police force there. We sold most of their guns to them. In those days, we knew all the police officers and they knew all of us. They used to walk the beat, shake the door and come in. There was always coffee for them.

Now the fellow we had working in the back of the jewelry store, Earl Battersby, was a phenomenal gunsmith and marksman. He taught me how to shoot at the skeet range and usually broke 25 out of 25. I became a really good shooter but I never broke more than 20. Earlier, Earl had worked for Brunswick Pool Tables and was a remarkable pool player. He was a wonderful man and ultra smart, having previously worked on airplane engines and the first police radar machines. Well, Earl used to listen to a little AM radio and although he was white, he listened to all the black stations. Back then I had all these dirty jobs of polishing jewelry and anything my father would give me to make me learn the business. Whenever things would get really busy up front, this fellow would say, "Come back here, come listen to this. But don't let your father know. Don't let your father know I let you hear this." And the radio was playing Fats Domino's “The Fat Man,” Freddy King's “The Stumble” and “The Hide Away” and some really heavy Rhythm & Blues songs. And I listened.

Being young, I had a babysitter. She was a teenager and the police lieutenant's daughter, so of course they hired her. And she used to bring her records with her and would play them. I would stand there and she would use me as a dance partner. It was hysterical. But I remember she had the Mello Kings' “Tonight Tonight” and records by Frankie Lymon and the Teenagers. I was saying to myself, "This stuff is heavy." I started to like this stuff while I was very young. When I got about a year or two older, I started taking 50 cents out of the cash register and going around the corner to Anderson's Record Store to buy records by Little Richard and others. I started collecting records but I had to hide them from my father. I made a big mistake one time by bringing home some Elvis Presley sheet music and leaving it on the piano. My father went ballistic! My mother didn't mind. She'd lived down South and loved Rhythm & Blues. But for my father it was only classical music.

The Fire

A few days before Christmas, 1960, I was in school when someone said Seldin's Jewelry was on fire. The kid was cruel and started laughing about it. I ran to the store as fast as I could, but by the time I got there, there were fire trucks and smoke everywhere.

Apparently an electrical fire had started in the bootery next door. The bootery owner called my father to help put it out but by then it was already too late. By the time the fire trucks arrived both the boot store and my parents' jewelry store were just a mass of flames. The fire drew eight fire companies from surrounding municipalities and threatened to turn into a major disaster. The firemen were worried that the ammunition and two or three pounds of gunpowder that my father had stored in the back of the store might explode. Their concerns heightened with several small explosions which turned out just to be four oxygen cylinders that my father used in his work. The ammunition never did explode.

My mother (left) and father (right).
Ribbon cutting at the grand opening of Seldin's Jewelry after it moved to 43 Broad Street in 1961.
Courtesy of The Dorn-Severini Historic Photography Collection at the Monmouth University Murry & Leonie Guggenheim Memorial Library

When the fire started, my mother had tried to rescue some of the jewelry but was driven back by the thick smoke. Many pieces of jewelry were washed into the street by the water from the hoses. Some were washed down the drain and others were scarfed up by onlookers, never to be seen again.

The fire was eventually brought under control but not until after the roof collapsed leaving just the charred shells of the two buildings. A former fire chief suffered a fatal heart attack after leaving the scene and several firemen suffered minor injuries. Firemen removed all of the guns from ruins, most of which were damaged.

The fire made the front page of the local newspaper. It took a about seven months, but my parents opened a new jewelry store at 43 Broad Street in July, 1961.

Chapter Two
The Other Kid From Red Bank

A newspaper article once proclaimed me, "The Other Kid From Red Bank." Of course, the first Red Bank musician labeled "The Kid From Red Bank" was William Basie. I'm flattered that anyone would compare me to the world famous entertainer and I don't pretend to have had the impact on popular music that "The Count" did. However, he and I were both pianists from Red Bank and did share some common traits. As youngsters, we both had a passion and dedication for developing our music skills with an unparalleled work ethic that drove us to be the best that we could be.

The Naturals

Sometime around 1959 when I was twelve years old and still attending Knollwood School, I decided to form my first band. I'd gotten pretty well known in my own neighborhood. I used to walk home from school and on the way different neighbors who owned pianos would invite me in to play for them. I'd stop and play for my friends' parents or anyone who asked me and then proceed home to go about my business.

I tried to find people who were musicians like me. First I looked for people of my age who were playing instruments in the school. There really weren't any. Knollwood didn't have a school orchestra or anything, which was a great disappointment. Most of the young musicians that I found were in high school already while I was still in elementary school. As a consequence, my first bandmates were older than me. There weren't many bands around for them to join so they took a chance with me.

Dave Kenny, my first drummer, was from Fair Haven. He was in high school at the time and played drums in the school band. I knew him from the neighborhood. In fact, I used to walk past his house every day on my way to school. My first guitarist was Allen Butler. Allen was from Little Silver and went to Red Bank High School. He played rhythm guitar. Basically you had to have an electric guitar and amplifier just to get in the band. Then I got Jimmy Barr, who was an exceptional guitar player. Jimmy Barr was playing with a band called the Clique when I met him. The Clique was a very popular band in this area. Jimmy was a superb guitar player, I mean, way, way ahead of musicians that were five or six years older than he was. But we managed to

The Naturals, 1960. Left to right:
Dave Kenny, Allen Butler, Jimmy Barr, Norman Seldin
Photo by Earl Stout

get him in the group and that was it. We didn't have any bass players then. The first band was just drums, two guitars, and the piano.

We used pretty much any piano that I could get because at the time we didn't yet have the electric one. Whatever piano they had at the churches and the schools we played at, is what I got to play on. I just crossed my fingers and hoped the piano would be somewhat in tune. But we rehearsed and rehearsed in my parents' front room. There were often a few flats and sharps in there that didn't belong but that was to expected with a new band. We learned our first 18 or 20 songs. We had enough to do maybe a short dance. Or if we did one of those festivals, we'd only need six or seven songs because there were other bands.

Our repertoire was whatever was selling and being played on radio at the time. Of course, we also did older songs, whether it was a Ricky Nelson or Bobby Darin song, or whatever. We just played jitterbugs and whatever we could find.

Our first paying gig was at a church dance in Red Bank. I think the band members received three or four dollars each and we thought we were millionaires. Knowing what I know now, I don't think I would've dared go out to play for anybody, as bad as that band probably was. But it was something to do and it was the beginning of my work with bands.

At first we didn't have a name but we soon started calling ourselves the Naturals. One of our early performances was at an afternoon reception the day after my Bar Mitzvah. It was only after my Bar Mitzvah that I got an electric piano. Before that, my godfather, Nat Daniel, who owned Danelectro, kept giving me amplifiers that he was experimenting with. Then he made the first piano pickup ever made and he sent it over for me to try out. It had three clips on it and three microphones that hooked onto the inside of the piano. Then it had a dial to turn from one to ten and a plug. It worked, but it would give feedback. It also used to pick up radio stations. I would be playing and in the background all the sudden I'd hear Dandy Dan Daniels of the WMCA Good Guys announcing a song. It was coming through the PA system. I told my godfather, "This invention might need to be tweaked a little bit."

So we started playing teen dances. One of the dances we played was at the parish house of the Trinity Episcopal Church on West Front Street in Red Bank. At the time, my piano teacher was Charles Gottschalk, the choir director and organist at Trinity Episcopal.

My mother did the promoting for me at the start, because I was just a kid. I guess to the audiences it sounded pretty good because there weren't that many bands out there. There was certainly nobody as young as me out there. My mother wanted us to have a uniform look, so we all wore dark blue blazer jackets and matching pants. That's the way the country clubs and festivals were then. Everybody really dressed up. Everybody had a blue blazer and such outfits were common so we were pretty matched up. We looked a lot better than we sounded.

The Allenhurst Beach Club's Jazz Festival

In July 1960, we performed at the Allenhurst Beach Club's Jazz Festival. All told, there were fourteen local groups performing that evening, including the Criterions, El Dorados, Del Tones and Aztecs. At the time we had Thomas Ahern from the Atlantic Highlands filling on for Jimmy Barr on electric guitar. I believe the Rediker Brothers. local promoters who owned a chain of local jewelry stores, had something to do with that festival but I'm not sure.

Every band in the area played at that festival. I think there were as many musicians as there were people in the audience. Each band had only so much time. If you had a lead singer, you got a microphone. The rest of your band members brought up their amplifiers, plugged them in and tuned up. You played your three or four songs and got off the stage.

Everybody there was very good and I thought that we did a great job. Some of them were much older than me. The Aztecs from Red Bank High School had a record out called "Dreamy" (*Sultan* label) that they'd recorded in New York. It did fairly well locally and they were very popular. So was a group called The Del Tones. The Del Tones were all from Red Bank Catholic or Red Bank High School and they also had a

The Naturals, 1960. Left to right:
Dave Kenny, Allen Butler, Tom Ahern, Norman Seldin
Photo by Earl Stout

record out. The Criterions, a group that included future music celebs Tim Hauser (Manhattan Transfer) and Tommy Picardo (Tommy West), had a couple of records out, including "I Remain Truly Yours" (*Cecilia* label). It was on that show that I actually first noticed Billy Ryan, who was playing guitar with a group from Asbury Park. Billy was a standout guitarist and he'll fit into the story a little later.

The Monmouth Shopping Center

About this time in late August 1960, we, the Naturals, started playing the Monmouth Shopping Center. Now the huge Monmouth Mall on Route 35 in Eatontown, the Monmouth Shopping Center had just opened six months earlier as a 50-store shopping center with an open air center.

They had an actual music room called the Campus Center in the rear of Braddock's Shop For Men. They had a different music group there every week. It was a regular musical entertainment thing that they used to bring people into the new shopping center. This was the same place where a few years later, Sonny Kenn and a young Vini Lopez opened for Jerry Lee Lewis when they were playing there as part of Sonny & the Starfires.

My mother promoted me for this gig, as if I was 17 or 18 already which I wasn't. I don't recall being paid but it's possible we were. They had a piano there. We'd play and they'd draw a crowd of 100 to 150 people. That went on for quite a while, and it was okay, but I did have a few temper tantrums there. One time, somebody started saying that they wanted to hear this, they wanted to hear that. They really got quite annoying and I just didn't appreciate the comments being made. I think was the first time that any real arrogance came out in me. We had really lousy microphones then and the sound systems left a lot to be desired. I finally said, "Listen, if you want to hear that, why don't you go listen to somebody else?" Well, the harassment stopped as soon as I said that. I remember someone in the audience, and it might have been my mother, said, "You can't say that." I said, "Well, I just did."

At that young age, I was very cocky. I think that I was 13 when I did that. I felt that I knew what I was doing and I don't think I was quite ready for what was coming in my career as a musician. That's just the way I felt at the time.

Dances, Lessons and Songwriting

So, the band kind of came together loosely, but kids loved it because it was a band. It was somebody they knew and they hired us. There were big jobs too. You think you're famous when you're that young. I started getting more gigs, both with the Naturals and as a soloist. Many of the jobs with the Naturals were teenage dances. We did pretty well at dances, actually. It reached a point where we'd play an hour and a half's worth of, let me say, passable music. If I had to listen to it played back now, I'd probably want to take the tape and dissolve it acid. But at the time it was exciting. The kids saw their friends playing for their dance and they danced whether they liked it or not. In those days, most of the time the girls sat on one side of the room and the guys sat on the other. It was hardly couples. It was kind of like the dancing lessons which we took where you had to go ask somebody to dance. Elementary school was a very trying time for me.

The firehouse used to have dances led by the band directors from various schools. You know, you got the corsage for the girl you were going to take and your parents dropped you off there. There was soda refreshment and you danced a little bit. I remember that I went to a girl's house to pick her up for the dance and her father said that she'd had already left with her date. I was stood up. I was standing there with this corsage. I just went home, threw it in the sink and didn't go to the dance. I found out later that the girl's parents just didn't want her going to a dance with a Jew. It actually happened twice. So then I said to myself, "You know what? I think I'd rather play these dances than go to them."

The Naturals, 1961. Left to right:
Jimmy Barr, Bob Girardin, Norman Seldin, Stanley Johnson
Photo by Earl Stout

It was a very prejudiced community at the time and it was tough on someone my age. Between that and the brutality that was going on in my family, I just buried myself into the piano even more.

When I had solo engagements I'd use a fake book. For those not musically trained, a fake book is a collection of sheet music pieces where each is merely a "lead sheet" of just the melody and the chord progression. It is not a full arrangement with parts written out for each musician, so it allows the musician to improvise. I used to run to New York City when I was 13 years old and get fake books from a musician named Frank Rehak. Frank was a famous jazz trombonist who'd worked with Miles Davis, Dizzy Gellespie, Quincy Jones and many others. I used to buy them from him for two or three dollars, bring them back home and sell them for six or seven dollars to make a few bucks. I had shopping bags full of them.

Once, I got called to play a New Year's Eve job. My parents dropped me off at that job in the Highlands. Everybody there that was playing had to be in their late 20's or early 30's and I was 13, reading from one of these fake books. I didn't know what New Year's Eve was about, except that I was getting 35 dollars to play these standards. A woman came out in this costume and started passing a hat around. Then she came over and gave me 80 dollars of tip money just for myself. That was like making a million dollars to a kid like me. I came home and I told my mother and father that I made 80 dollars in tips plus 35 dollars for playing the gig. My father's gigs didn't even pay that much and he had a whole band!

From that point on, I started wanting to do more, including yacht clubs. I worked them either solo or with the band. I played the Red Bank Yacht Club a number of times with the Naturals. They loved the group. One time the air conditioning broke in the middle of the summer. Another time, they wanted us to play outside. We got all the expensive electronic equipment set up when a thunderstorm came in and blew the tent down. The equipment got soaked. I played a few weddings there along with some private affairs.

We played dances at the Monmouth Boat Club, the Fair Haven Yacht Club and the Ft. Monmouth Teen Canteen as well as many church dances. We also did some charity events like a 1960 Halloween dance for the Monmouth County Unit of the New Jersey Association for Mentally Retarded Children (now known as the New Jersey ARC). From that, they asked me if I would be willing to come over and spend a day or two with children who were intellectually and developmentally impaired. I was a child myself but I started to realize how lucky I was. No matter what misery I was going through, it wasn't anything close to what these kids and their parents had.

In February 1961, the Naturals played the Monmouth County Heart Association's Queen of Hearts Coronation Ball at Asbury Park's Convention Hall. What a thrill it was playing a huge venue. By then I had Robert Girardin on drums and Stanley Johnson on electric guitar. Jimmy Barr was still in the Naturals but couldn't make that gig so I had Bill Trainer fill in. Also on the show with us was the local band, Jimmy Quinn & the Del Tones who had record releases. Playing Convention Hall was the biggest show the Naturals had done up until then.

In the early years we were playing a lot of instrumentals. At best, my vocals were poor because my voice hadn't yet developed. We played a lot of songs by the Ventures and Duane Eddy because we had the electric guitars. But my favorite group, really when I was young, was the Bill Black Combo. There was a friend of my father's, a multimillionaire who owned Strongheart Dog Food in Long Branch. He always used to play their records for me and he'd say, "Norman, if you're going to have a band, the only band that I ever liked that sounded tight was Bill Black's Combo." And you know, he was right. That group was tight. I went out and bought their records and I listened. It was just meter, meter, and the saxophone came in. The organ wasn't a Hammond B3. It was a Farfisa combo organ. But listening to Bill Black Combo records set the tone for me about what a studio session should sound like.

I remember, we played the Rumson-Fair Haven Regional High School and Middletown High School freshmen dances in April 1961. Of course, I was still in eighth grade at Knollwood Elementary School at the time.

When it came time for me to graduate from Knollwood in June of 1961, I accompanied the graduation ceremonies. Then, my band the Naturals played the graduation dance. I wasn't yet into doing very many vocals, so I had Joe Clark, a senior at Rumson High as a featured vocalist. Besides me, the other Naturals at the time were Bob Peypon on guitar and bass, Bob Girardin on drums and Jimmy Quinn from the Del-Tones on sax.

I started Rumson-Fair Haven Regional High School in the fall of 1961. The Naturals were flying high throughout this time. And I was beginning to develop my skills at song writing. Some of my early songs had titles like "Harmecron," "Jazz Waltz," "Norm's Song" and "My Last Night With You." It was a long time ago and I don't remember a lot of them. I was writing what I felt was great stuff but it was always belittled and made fun of by everybody. I wasn't quite a composer yet. I didn't even know about joining ASCAP at that time. I didn't know about anything. I was self-taught. Back then, I just played but I also wrote some beautiful melodies.

One thing I did do was join the musicians union, Local 399. In those days, you had to be in the union. Everyone else was in it. They said that you had to be 18 years old to join but they wrote me an official permission thing. At the time, the musicians union was very powerful. They wrote to Chicago and they got permission for me to audition and join. The audition was a joke. I went to their office in Bradley Beach and played for four guys who weren't half as good as I was. I played "By the Light of the Silvery Moon" or some mediocre standard and I was approved. I paid them 25 dollars and they gave me a union card. That was about it. I was just 13, the youngest one to be accepted into the union at that time.

Then the union used to send me a letter every month about the nightclubs that were on the "Off List" because they didn't pay their bands. Of course, the "Off List" didn't tell you that in some cases the band wasn't paid because they showed up two hours late or anything like that. They just said you can't work for that club. I had people call me who wanted to hire me and I had to say, "You're on the 'I can't play for you' list." Later on, I played some of these clubs and I always got paid.

In the fall of 1962, one of the Shore area's best known organists, Bob Brittingham, retired from performing and opened a home teaching workshop in Asbury Park. I started taking lessons from him. Brittingham had graduated from New York University back in 1934, with a degree in Music Education, Piano and Organ. Long a fixture in the local music scene, he had once mentored 20-year-old Erroll Garner when the two were playing together at Paul's Edgewater Garden in Wanamassa in 1942. Bob Brittingham would often teach songs to young Garner who never learned to read music. Bob was also a talented composer and had written many songs.

Bob Brittingham was the one who turned my left hand electric instead of just playing what I was reading. He used to come to my home for my lessons and one time he was late. I didn't know it but he was sitting on the porch, quietly listening to what I was playing. I was playing Rock & Roll. He said, "Do you like that music?" I said, "Yeah." So he was teaching me classical music but he also started teaching me chords and chord changes. He told me, "If you want to play that music, your left hand is dead. You've got a white man's left hand. You got to change that." And he gave me exercises. Sometimes he'd just sit there and say, "I don't believe I'm doing this to somebody who has your goals." He said, "I'm ruining my pianist." He knew what I wanted to do.

Bob Brittingham
Publicity photo

Once Mr. Brittingham decided what I'd be doing, he said, "You need to have a Hammond B-3 organ." I said, "I don't think I can find one of those for what I can afford." He said, "Give me a day or two." Sure enough, he called me back and said, "Meet me at this house and he gave me an address.

I went to a fellow's house and was directed down the stairs to the cellar. There was a brand new B-3 with a Leslie combined amplifier and speaker with all the foot pedals. It was sitting there like it had just come from the showroom. The guy said, "I've gotten too old and I've never even played this thing. I should have never bought it." I remember the price on the ticket was around four or five thousand dollars.

Mr. Brittingham said to the owner, "Well give him a good deal." The fellow said, "If you can give me $700 you can take it." So I got a brand new B-3 and a Leslie for $700. It was complete with all the foot pedals that the organists played which of course I didn't.

I thought about doing some of my original songs and I visited Bob Brittingham's home in Asbury Park. Bob opened up a trunk of sheet music and I said, "What are those?" He said, "Oh, those are all originals of mine." He pulled one out. I said, "Which one is that?" He said, "Oh! This is just a reminder to make sure you copyright all your songs." The song had been a huge hit for Nat King Cole. It was one that Bob Brittingham had written for which others had gotten writer credits.

One other thing I credit Bob Brittingham with was getting me to start singing. He said, "You need to sing. You can sing." I said, "I don't know." He said, "Listen, the first time that Nat King Cole sang a man gave him $10 to sing a request. And after he sang, the man asked him for the $10 back. In the beginning, Nat Cole was a great jazz pianist but not a singer. Then look what happened. Persistence pays off." So, I listened to my teacher's advice and I started singing.

Meanwhile things were not going well for me at Rumson- Fair Haven High School. I got through my freshmen year there fine. I played my high school freshmen dance in April 1962, along with my group, the Naturals. But at the beginning of my sophomore year, I had a problem. They wanted me to try out for the school band. Now, the school band wasn't very good. In fact, calling it a band would have been an overstatement. And the teacher said, "Well, we already have a piano player, so why don't you change instruments and learn how to play bass because we could use a bass player." Well, having been playing piano for the past twelve years, suggesting I change instruments was an insult. Being the cocky kid that I was back then, I told the band instructor where he could go. And while I was at it, I told him what I thought of his band and the other piano player's musical skills, or lack of.

Of course, off to the principal's office I went. My parents were called and things went from bad to worse. Then the choir director told me that he wanted me to be a high tenor in the choir and I firmly told him no. With that he wanted to talk to me out in the hallway and he kind of shoved me, so I hit him. That was, of course a big mistake. Not my finest moment. I was off to the principal's office again. My father was tied up in the jewelry store, so my mother came in. There was a lot of yelling and finally my mother said, "Alright, I'll just take my son out of Rumson and put him in another school." I remember vividly the exact words from the superintendent and the vice principal. "If your son doesn't graduate from Rumson High School, he will become nothing, as he is right now. The best that your son will ever be will be a garbage collector or a bum."

So at that point, my mother took me to the Burton Hall School on East Front Street in Red Bank. The Burton Hall School was the oldest private school in Monmouth County, started in 1922 by Georgie B. Hazard. Miss Hazard had a doctorate from Brown University and ran this one room schoolhouse for all ages. Burton Hall was just this little house that was across from Riverview Hospital at the time. Everybody was taught individually, but at different subjects at one time. I ran through stuff there from eight in the morning until three when we got out. Miss Hazard had graduated hundreds of kids over the 40 years she was there. I just flew through, took whatever exams there were and got my diploma. Miss Hazard said, "There's nothing left for you to do but to pursue your music if that's what you want to do." So after a year and a quarter under her I graduated.

Of course my father being as nasty as he was, said, "Well, let's see what else you can pass. You need to go to regular college." I said, "No, I want to write music." "Well, you'll go to Manhattan School of Music. Let's see you fail out of there."

I attended the Manhattan School of Music for the summer, commuting back and forth every day. I took music theory, harmony and dictation. Everybody in the class was in their early twenties and I was only 16. I would go in some days early in the morning. The rehearsals were in what seemed like a cellar. I keyed in on some pretty brilliant players who were playing stuff that was so gorgeous it was unimaginable. But I watched the frustration every morning of young musicians crinkling up the paper, throwing it in the garbage. After about the third month, the guy who always practiced next to me, picked up his stack of music, maybe 50 pages high all written out. I asked, "Leaving early?" and he just said, "Leaving. I'm leaving." He took every page of what he written for those three months and threw them into the incinerator. I never saw him again.

That's when I came to realize that what I really wanted to do was be a part of the entertainment business. I wanted to perform. I wanted to produce shows. I had that instilled in me from the store with all the R&B stuff. I started thinking about having a real band. I decided on doing shows first before I had put the new band together. I was still very young but I wanted to make things happen.

Chapter Three
Soul, Doo Wop, Rock & Roll

After leaving Manhattan School of Music, I decided to start producing shows. For that, I needed a real band. I started talking to Alfred Wright. Alfred T. Wright was a musician with the Sun Ra Arkestra under the name of Alzo Wright. The famous jazz band had toured all over the world. Alfred and his family lived right across the street from where Count Basie's parents lived on Mechanic Street in Red Bank, only about two blocks from my home. At the time, Alfred was tired of traveling and was teaching grades five through eight at the elementary school. He always dressed impeccably with a tie and a jacket. He stopped me on the street one day and said, “Don't you play piano?" We started talking about jazz and he said, "You know, I think I need to drive you up to New York to hear Les McCann and Roland Kirk." It became a ritual. Al used to take me to the Metropole Cafe and other great jazz clubs. He opened my eyes to a lot of great jazz music.

Alzo Wright
Courtesy of Alfred Wright

Once I said, “I really could use a drummer.” Al said, "Well, I'm a drummer." But, of course, I needed other kinds of musicians and Al said, "Well, we can get the players." I didn't know anything about how to get more musicians. I said, "Where are we going to find these guys?"

Al said, "Well, you’ve got to have some horns." So we went over to the band room at Fort Monmouth and Al found an excellent trumpet player named Danny Brown. He found a sax player named Palmer Jenkins who was phenomenal. He got tenor sax player Lew Tabackin who later was with the Tonight Show Band. Al even found Herman Green, the Memphis sax player who’d played with Rufus Thomas and B. B. King before touring with Lionel Hampton. Herman had come in from the West Coast and was gigging around Asbury Park at the time. We became good friends and Herman ended up playing a lot of shows with my band. Later, he returned to Memphis and reached legendary status as a session sax player on so many of the great Stax and Hi Studio recording sessions.

All of these musicians Alfred found me were the heavyweights of jazz musicians. I could get an all-star horn section for just $20 a man. These guys were so far ahead of me, I was in the woods. But Alfred got them together for a horn section for me and we went out and played jobs. The only white player I had, besides me, was the guitarist Billy Ryan. Billy was going to Red Bank Catholic High School at the time. Billy used to sit in his room for two or three hours at a time just learning one Chuck Berry lick. He had to have it exactly how it was, whether it was the blues, rock and roll or whatever.

I started getting bookings at different places, big bookings at schools, at colleges, at fraternity houses. We played the Molly Pitcher Inn in Red Bank, the Rainbow Room in Asbury Park and the Rumson Hotel. I was still calling my band, the Naturals, but the personnel varied from gig to gig, depending on which musicians were available. I was getting pretty well known but what I really wanted to do was to produce shows. It was time to put out the word that I was looking for talent.

Selsom Productions

It was May of 1963. I ran into a young singer who was also from Red Bank by the name of Walter Summey. Summey said he'd just come back from touring the South with some pretty big names so we agreed to be partners in a new venture, Selsom Productions. We decided we'd manage groups, record them on our own record label and produce shows. The name came from SELdin and SOMmy. Well, OK, he spelled his name with a "U" but Selsom looked better as we thought we'd "sell some" records. Each of us was to put up $250 to start. We printed up promotional material and everything with the words "Selsom Productions." I paid for all of that.

Well, Walter's $250 never did show up and Walter would soon be out of the picture. I left the company name as it was, but then I had to figure out how to promote and produce a show. I knew could promote. I just had to figure out how to do it without a driver's license and without any money. My father didn't approve of my R&B and R&R music business plans but my mother offered to help me out.

I was at Thom McAn's shoe store where I met a guy named Lenny Cuozzo. Lenny was from Matawan and he loved the music. Being so young, I didn't even have a driver's licence yet. So, Lenny said, "I'll drive you around and help you put posters up and things."

But then, I had to start gathering talent. I started auditioning and boy, did I get a response. I had people from the churches. Singers and musicians from everywhere were interested in auditioning.

So I found acts for the next couple of shows. I found the Wathington Brothers, Otis, Charles and William Wathington. They were from Cliffwood Beach, near Matawan. If you want to know what they sounded like, listen to Shep & the Limelites. And they were all superb ballplayers. I had sponsored baseball teams and if your team was going up against a team with the three Wathington Brothers playing the infield, you might as well go home. Three power hitters. Charlie Wathington was one of the nicest people I'd ever met in my life. The brothers' harmony was ingrown from the ages of 5 or 6 years old. They were just terrific as human beings and as singers. And we still had Walter Summey at that time. So we started rehearsing all the acts.

I figured with the band, we'd try a teenage dance at McGuires Grove in Middletown. I went over there with my mother, of course, because I was too young to sign any checks. I remember them saying it would be a hundred dollars. And I said, "A hundred dollars just to rent a place?" Well, I decided to do it. We had to design posters by hand and then they made a plate and pressed them on the printing press.

So Lenny Cuozzo drove me around the area in his Oldsmobile and we put the posters up everywhere. Lenny was always busting my chops. He said that men's fragrances were where the money was going to be. I should have listened to him. Some years later he developed a fragrance called Paul Sebastian which he and his partner then sold for twenty million dollars. But back then, my mind was on producing shows. And it finally started to sink in. I said, "Oh my God. We're having a show."

The Naturals playing McGuires Grove, 1963.
From left to right: Pat Mash, Ronald Rubin, John Sagato, Norman Seldin
Photo by Earl Stout

We called the show "The Bee Bop Hop" and started promoting it like crazy. It was scheduled for Friday night, May 24, 1963. The Naturals (Pat Mash, saxophone; Al Wright, drums; John Salgato, bass; Bobby Brooks, saxophone and me, keyboards) backed all the singers. The master of ceremonies was John Hemleb from the Monmouth Players. We also had a dance contest that was judged by Middletown Mayor Earl Moody and local composer Dixie Wilson. Well, the show was a huge success. We had over 500 people attend, many from nearby Monmouth College (now Monmouth University). The venue kept the bar and I kept the door. My friend, Lenny Cuozzo and his date happened to win first prize in the dance contest. And I said, "Oh my God. This can really work."

The McGuires Grove show was so successful that I decided to hold another one there. I quickly scheduled the next concert dance there for Sunday night August 18. But now I started looking for more groups. Nineteen fifties doo wop music was big in the early sixties, only it wasn't called doo wop then. I decided my next show would be an "Oldies But Goodies" show.

I rounded up a few more singers. One guy told me he was with the Charts of "Deserie" fame so I added the Charts. I auditioned a female group from Keyport called the Velvetones. I liked them because the lead could sing "Just Two Kinds of People in the World" and do the high part like

Top photo: The Dubonaes, Left to right, top: Jack Olsh, Sonny Andrews. Bottom: Kathy Freeman, Margo Scarpino.
Bottom photo: Me rehearsing Margo Scarpino
Photos by Earl Stout

Little Anthony. When I heard that I said, "I don't care what else they sing if they only sing that one song." They did three or four songs on the concert. Of course I had the Wathington Brothers again doing Shep & the Limelites style harmony. One group that I found was the Dubonaes. The group consisted of two young women (Margo Scapino and Kathy Freeman) and two young men (Sonny Andrews and Jack Olsh). Both Sonny and Margo could sing lead. Finally I added a few more singers, the Adelphies and Ray Sharabba. Ray had just gotten out of the Navy and he was working at the printing press where I was getting my posters printed. I was dying for some more singers and I heard him singing "I Left My Heart in San Francisco." He sounded just like Tony Bennett. I asked him if he'd ever sung with a band and he hadn't. I called him "Radiant Ray Sharabba" and put him on the show. He drew probably a hundred people on his own and they loved it. Ray never sang at another show, but he became my security guard because he had formerly been quite a boxer. Well that second show was another big success.

Springwood Avenue and Asbury Park's West Side

By now I was trending more and more toward black music, both Rhythm & Blues and Jazz. It all went back to listening to those R&B songs that the fellow played for me in the back of my parents' store. I started amassing a sizable collection of records and most were by black artists. But when I wanted to hear black music either to discover talent for my shows, or to just enjoy listening to the hottest music around, I headed to Springwood Avenue on Asbury Park's West Side.

Asbury Park was only eleven miles from my home in Fair Haven. Since its beginning in 1871, Asbury Park had been a segregated city with most African Americans living west of the railroad tracks. The main thoroughfare was a ten-block stretch called Springwood Avenue. Springwood Avenue was awash with music venues, both big and small. There were places like Madonna's, the Orchid Lounge, the Turf Club, Cuba's and Big Bill's. I knew some white folk were nervous about strolling Springwood Avenue at night but as a teenage kid, all I ever thought about was wanting to hear the music. When I was as young as fourteen-and-a-half I started sneaking out of the house and making my way to Asbury Park's West Side to catch the music. I'd be back by ten o'clock but I'd caught the first hour of an organ and drum combo by Jack McDuff or whoever was playing that night.

Without a driver's license yet, I had people drop me off at night, right at the borderline to Asbury Park's West Side. I'd walk across the tracks and right up Springwood Avenue. People would say, "You can't go there. You just can't." I just said, "I can and I will." In all the times I walked Springwood Avenue I only had one negative incident and that was later on. Some guy started really giving me a bunch of crap. All of a sudden three or four people came out of nowhere said, "Don't lay one finger on that boy. Not one." I don't know if they came out of the stores or their houses. And the guy said, "He doesn't belong here." And the people said, "Oh, he belongs here. He's supporting half the groups on the street."

Asbury Park's Springwood Avenue, ca. 1960's. Al's House of Hits Record Store is on the right. Photo by Joseph A. Carter Sr. Courtesy of Madonna Carter Jackson.

I used to go to the Orchid Lounge first. That was right at the start of Springwood Avenue. Then I'd walk all the way down to Drummond Avenue to get to Big Bill's. I wanted to hear what Sammy Pugh, the great blind organist, was doing on a B3 organ. My friend Al Wright would sometimes sit in with Sammy on drums. They always let me in there even though I was under age. Often I was the only white guy in the whole place. Since I was only about 16, they would get me Coke with cherry juice.

And they invited me back. Sometime later on they had the Soul Sisters there, a female duo from Newark who recorded the song, "I Can't Stand It." Oh, God, they were great. It was the kind of show that you just read about. Big Bill's was clean and it was run so well. There were never any fights in that place.

I used to buy records at Al's House of Hits, a record store on Springwood Avenue. It was right across from Fisch's Department Store. A fellow named Alfred Cinter opened the store in August 1963, just as I was beginning to produce shows. House Of Hits had black records that I couldn't get in Red Bank. A short time later, when I started my record label, Al would carry my latest records.

I learned so much musically from the West Side and I just couldn't understand why none of that music was across the tracks on the white side. They told me that black musicians couldn't go to a lot of the clubs on the white side of Asbury Park. I didn't get that. I'd find out later for myself when I tried to book integrated or all black acts into certain venues.

The Uniques

The Uniques were a fine black vocal group playing around the Asbury Park area at places like Big Bill's and the Turf Club on Springwood Avenue. When I first became aware of the group the lead singer was Billy Brown, who later found fame with the Broadways, Moments and Ray Goodman & Brown. The others in the group were Leon Trent, Ron Coleman and Ray Morris. After I'd booked the Uniques a couple times, Billy Brown left the group for a short time and the Uniques got Nicky Addeo to fill in as lead.

Nicky Addeo was a talented young white singer who members of the Uniques knew from singing in the hallways of Boston Way, one of the housing projects in Asbury Park. Nicky's voice sounded black so he fit right in with the Uniques. With either Billy Brown or Nicky Addeo, the Uniques were a superb R&B vocal harmony group that I was thrilled to add to my group of talented artists.

At this point I was ready to branch out from the McGuires Grove shows and start producing shows elsewhere. I wanted to produce something much bigger. But to do that I needed to book big name headliners. That's when I went into New York to find a booking agent. I ended up visiting Arnold Klein who was in the 1650 Broadway Building. He had the typical Manhattan one desk, one room office. Arnold Klein was booking almost everybody at the time, including the Duprees and Randy & the Rainbows. And he offered me Johnny Thunder.

Johnny Thunder, ca, 1964
Publicity photo.

Earlier that year, Johnny Thunder had just had a monster hit with the song "Loop De Loop." Arnold told me that Johnny Thunder was just coming off a Dick Clark national tour with Bobby Vee, the Tymes, Jimmy Clanton, the Ronettes and several others. And I could have Johnny Thunder for $250. So Johnny Thunder looked like the headliner I wanted.

I scheduled Johnny Thunder for Val Ernie's Sea Girt Inn in Sea Girt, New Jersey, on Friday night, November 22. The concert and dance was to be called "The Cavalcade of Stars" and would also feature the Wathington Brothers, the Uniques, the Velvetones and Little Margo Scarpino from the Dubonaes. We would do the show with my 14-piece band including the black musicians. We sold 500 tickets in advance.

The afternoon of the show, I was watching TV and saw that President Kennedy was shot and killed. Every nickel I owned was tied up in that show. Johnny Thunder called me up and said, "I don't want to take your money. We'll redo the date." But by then we'd sold 500 tickets and I had to go through with it. People were calling me every name in the book, but we had to go through with the show. We ended up with 395 people on the night the president was assassinated.

Johnny Thunder pulled up in a great looking car. He looked at me and said, "How old are you? How did you even get here?" I said, "Well, my mother dropped me off." I had all his money for him so he didn't mind my age. Johnny Thunder did the show and he was phenomenal, just off the charts. We're still friends to this day.

Meanwhile, the list of local singers and musicians that I was managing and booking grew rapidly. I was signing acts that I knew of and auditioning acts that I didn't. Everybody saw that I had a black band and wanted me to manage them. People would call me or come to my parent's jewelry store. So I started listening to them and auditioning them in the front room of my parents' home. My parents came home once and saw twelve black guys sitting on their carpet singing the Students' "My Vow To You" and me pounding away on the piano. My mother loved it. But my father said, "What the hell is going on in this place?" And I said, "I'm going to manage them." He said, "Manage? You're not old enough to sign a check!" I said, "I'm going to manage."

Tony Maples
Photo by Earl Stout

The black groups were all clean-cut. With the younger groups I had to get their parents' permissions. But their parents were all very nice. My taste was now trending heavily toward black music.

One Asbury Park singer I started booking was Tony Maples. Tony had been singing for about ten years when I met him. I'm told he sang with an early version of the

Del Vikings when he was stationed in Pittsburgh while in the Air Force. Following that he'd recorded with a couple of Asbury Park groups - the Ray Dots and V-Eights. I was also booking singer Leroy Brown, who like Tony had been in the Ray Dots and V-Eights.

I started managing a girls group from East Shrewsbury, New Jersey, called the Shondelles. The Shondelles, Carol Hawkins (now Hagins), Rhonda Kirby, Cheryl Lynn Brown and Brenda Harris were attending Monmouth Regional High School in Tinton Falls, New Jersey at the time. One of my finest discoveries was Harry Ray and his group, the Valtairs.

The Shondelles. Left to right:
Carol Hawkins, Brenda Harris,
Cheryl Lynne Brown, Rhonda Kirby
Photo by Earl Stout

The Valtairs

This young man from nearby Long Branch called me up and said he had a group that he wanted me to audition. His name was Harry Ray. I asked around and found out that Harry's brother had an even better voice but the brother had a substance abuse problem. So I had Harry and the Valtairs over and everybody loved them. Besides Harry Ray there was Gregory Henson, Kenneth Short and Joe Gardner. They had a repertoire of "Dear Lord," "Oh What A Night" and "Tears On My Pillow" – mostly doo wop songs. I had to teach them choreography. Imagine me, a white kid, teaching the Valtairs steps, but I just learned dance moves from watching TV.

The Valtairs
Photo by Earl Stout

Then I said, "We'll all need outfits. All embroidered waist fitting jackets." I went out and bought them outfits. I remember the arguments in my house because I spent $125 on four jackets for these guys with Lamay collars. I had Earl Stout take publicity photos. Then I made sure the girls were all dressed nicely. Everybody on my shows had to look like they were something.

I started taking my shows to the Rainbow Room in the Albion Hotel in Asbury Park. My first show there, "The Rhythm & Blues Show & Dance," was held at the end of January 1964 and featured Tony Maples, the Valtairs, the Shondelles, Pearle & the Wathington Brothers, Harold Gilmore, Leroy Brown, Margo Scarpino and Charles Williams. And of course, the Naturals backed the singers and played sets for dancing.

Next, I decided to produce a "Leap Year Show" on February 28 back at the Sea Girt Inn. I went back to Arnold Klein and he suggested I book the vocal group, the Olympics as headliners. The Olympics were best known for their 1958 song, "Western Movies," but had followed that with popular songs like "Big Boy Pete," Shimmy Like Kate" and "Dance By The Light Of The Moon." They were coming off of a moderate hit called "The Bounce" and I thought they'd be a good act for kids to dance to.

Now, the Olympics were from the Compton area of Los Angeles and they planned to drive to New Jersey. Unfortunately, as the Olympic's car was leaving Los Angeles the Monday before the concert, they were struck by another car. The group's lead singer, Walter Ward was seriously injured. Ward's injuries were not life threatening, but the Olympics would be sidelined for the next month until he recovered. I was forced to make a quick replacement.

Vito & the Salutations
Publicity photo

Arnold Klein then suggested a white doo wop group from Brooklyn called Vito & the Salutations. I said, "Who are they?" Arnold said, "You know, they have that up tempo version of 'Unchained Melody' out." I said, "Oh yeah. It's a pretty good record and they sing great," So I decided to hire them. Dave Rick was their manager and he was in the taxi business. I signed the original contract in the taxi for which he held the Medallion.

I was worried about the last minute change in headliners and I didn't want anyone to be disappointed. So I also added the Shells to the line up. The Shells were another popular Brooklyn group known for songs like "Baby Oh Baby," "Happy Holidays" and "Angel Eyes." They had just released a new record called "On My Honor."

The Shells. Publicity photo

Besides Vito & the Salutations and the Shells, I had the Uniques, the Shondelles, Tony Maples, Harold Gilmore and Margo Scarpino. Of course, the band was my Naturals with Herman Green on tenor sax. I thought that we were all set until that day. We were buried with a foot of snow. Still, 200 people showed up and they got a great show for their $3 admission.

The Shells had an incredible act. Besides their great harmony they had a great dance act. They did splits, back flips and cart-wheels.

Vito & the Salutations did sing great. They sang "Unchained Melody" and "Your Way" and they sang the daylights out of those songs. The remainder of their set was kind of like a Temptations set. I must admit, I was a little concerned at first when they all climbed out of one car. It looked like the wreck of the Hesperus. I never saw a more disheveled, unruly bunch of guys in my life. But that was before they changed into their tuxedos.

The Salutations' music conductor and drummer, Barry Lynn, was calling out the chords to me. He would call out a C, or a G, or A minor. Barry was a stand up drummer. He didn't sit down. He ran that group and I just looked at everybody in the group and I thought, "That's a drummer I want. For some strange reason, that's who I'd want in my group." I kept thinking about it and thinking about it. Barry would later become one of my key musicians.

Meanwhile, I had my local acts performing at the Paddock Lounge in Long Branch on April 4. Harry Ray & the Valtairs headlined, as this was their home town. The show there also featured Tony Maples, the Shondelles, Harold Gilmore and of course my band, the Naturals.

Then we moved the shows to Keansburg. Keansburg is small beach town at the tip of Monmouth County at a point where the land pokes out into the Raritan Bay. At one point, Keansburg was home to at least forty bars, taverns and nightclubs, so it was a logical place to start doing shows. The first shows I produced there were in the Empress Room of the Empress Hotel. The idea was to start a regular "Empress Teen Nite Club," a show, dance and get-together for young people to be held each Friday night. Every week there was to be dance music by the Naturals and singing by headline groups and soloists. There'd be dance contests with pizza and soda on tap.

The Olympics
Publicity photo

I held the first show and dance in Keansburg on Friday night, April 24. Remembering the great reception they had in Sea Girt, I brought in Vito and the Salutations. Of course, I had the Valtairs and the Shondelles there. Margo Scarpino was my female soloist and Tony Maples was my male soloist. My plan was to have Tony Maples and Harold Gilmore take turns as soloists and emcees on alternating Fridays. The Naturals that first night included Herman Green on sax, Paul Grabow on flute and sax, Billy Ryan on guitar, Bob Lynch on bass, my friend Alzo Wright on drums and me on piano.

The following Friday in Keansburg, I brought in the Shells along with Harold Gilmore and a couple of new groups - the Exceptionals from Long Branch and the F-85's from Red Bank. I probably would have continued Friday nights at the Empress Hotel but I still had plans to go back to Sea Girt.

By then, Walter Ward had recovered from his auto accident and I was finally able to bring the Olympics to the Sea Girt Inn. They went on along with my local groups and did a superb job. A year later the Olympics would record the first version of "Good Lovin'." The song became a hit, not for the Olympics but for the Young Rascals who covered it. At about that time I heard that Charles Fizer of the Olympics was killed in the Watts riots. So sad.

The Party

It was May, 1964 and my parents were going to be gone for a weekend in Boston. I planned this big party for the backyard of my parents house without their knowledge. I think that we called it "The Horror Show." We printed tickets and charged $5 a piece. I had some very big friends who were going to be my bouncers. Another friend of mine got four kegs of beer which he put in my father's garage.

Well, I took in around $2,000 which at $5 a head was about 400 kids. And word must have gotten around because it took only about thirty minutes to have over 900 people flood the street. We were selling more tickets at the entrance to the yard. The police received several calls about a loud party and crowds were blocking the streets.

I think one of my bouncers threw the chief of police into the bushes. The chief showed up in a tee shirt and said, "I'm the chief of police." My bouncer said, "Yeah, and I'm Attila the Hun." With that the chief called for backup and police came from Little Silver, Rumson, Red Bank and Fair Haven.

My younger sisters were watching from inside the house. I'd hired a band but they only got to play about 15 minutes before the police broke up the party. Police used bullhorns to disperse the crowd which had now grown to over 1,000. It took fifteen police officers hours to disperse the traffic. The traffic backed up into Rumson and in Red Bank all the way up River Plaza. Everyone was trying to get to this party. The police had to stay on the scene another three hours to turn away hundreds more partiers.

So I got arrested as a minor and taken down to police station. They had a dictaphone machine and wanted me to tell my side of the story, but they couldn't even get it to work right. They had to call my uncle who lived not even a mile away to come and get me. My other friend was charged with purchasing beer and distributing it to underage kids. He was 19 at the time. We had to go to court. I had to get a lawyer and the lawyer, of course, was a Jewish neighbor. He was the mayor of Fair Haven. Two of my guys were charged $50. I was charged as a juvenile but the judge ruled that it was really my parents fault for allowing the party. They were still in Boston and could not attend my court appearance. The press made a big story out of this and it even made the Boston newspapers. I believe that my parents read about it in the paper. That's how they found out.

Chapter Four
In the Groove

Suddenly it was the summer of 1964. I was through with my legal issues resulting from the party and it was time to again concentrate on music. That meant going back to Keansburg.

Instead of going back to the Empress Hotel, this time I arranged to bring entertainment into a place called the Shamrock Bar. The Shamrock was partly owned by Arthur Stock. Art Stock would later gain the reputation as "King of New Jersey Nightclubs." He would come to own fourteen night spots, including one in Florida, but the Shamrock Bar was his first. Art Stock's other partners were a fellow named Eddie and his father who I called Pop. I never really met Art Stock until years later when I was involved in horse racing. More on that later.

Keansburg was an all white area and I'd heard that they didn't like black people. I had shows that at times were 90 percent black and now the audience was going to be 100 percent white. Somebody said to me, "You're bringing black groups to Keansburg? The last black guy that settled there, they burned him out," I said, "What?"

The one exception to this racial intolerance was 1950's music. It's what they now call doo wop but was just called oldies back then. Keansburg was a huge oldies town and I mean, huge. You couldn't really bring black entertainers there unless they were doo wop. At one point, if you didn't listen to the Heartbeats or Frankie Lymon or the Moonglows, you might as well leave town. I mean, it was a hotbed of just oldies lovers.

I was already running into a lot of clubs that wouldn't take my shows because I was using black musicians. But I could certainly produce oldies shows and the owners of the Shamrock Bar said, "Bring them in," so I did.

The Shamrock Bar was just across Beachway Avenue from the boardwalk and of course the ocean. Opposite us, on the boardwalk side was the Club Miami. Over the years, the Club Miami had big name entertainers like Cab Calloway and Jerry Lee Lewis. In fact, while we were playing the Shamrock Bar, the Club Miami had Little Anthony & the Imperials.

The first show I did at the Shamrock Bar was in June of 1964. I brought in Vito & the Salutations to headline plus a seventeen-year-old female vocalist Diane Pine. Pine was also managed by Vito & the Salutations manager Dave Rick. She had just recorded a single called "Lucky Girl." Under the stage name Maggie Thrett, Diane would later appear in movies and TV shows including an episode of "Star Trek." My emcee and male vocalist was Tony Maples and my band, the Naturals, included a black drummer and bass player.

Vito & the Salutations
Publicity photo

Appearing Tonight!
"VITO and the SALUTATIONS"
"TONY MAPLES"
"NORMAN SELDIN & his NATURALS"

SHAMROCK BAR
94 Beachway
Keansburg, N. J.

Dancing All Evening
No Cover
Shows At 10:30 and 12:30

Things went so well the first night that we were asked to do a show there every Thursday night for the rest of the year. I returned the next week with Harry Ray & the Valtairs, the F-85s (named after the Oldsmobile) from Red Bank and of course, the Naturals. I didn't know how a black group like the Valtairs would go over but the audience loved them! The following week, I brought in the Shells and after that, the Shondelles along with Don & Juan of "What's Your Name" fame.

I rotated the groups I managed, pairing them with bigger acts from out-of-town. The Uniques, with Nicky Addeo singing lead, were usually enough of a draw that I didn't need another vocal group. I wasn't doing that great financially then, but I was the one putting gas in the cars and bringing the groups together. And I was getting lots of great acts through Arnold Klein in New York.

At that point, I wanted to have a nationally known act so I brought back Johnny Thunder. He was phenomenal. Johnny Thunder is a top class guy. He showed up with arrangements and everything for our band. As I recall, my friend Al Wright didn't play that job. Buddy Lowell who was the house drummer at the Copacabana in New York filled in for a few weeks when Al couldn't make it. Buddy was also in the jewelry business.

I was working from contract to contract with agent Arnold Klein. We had no cell phones back then and I would call from the phone booth in my father's store. I remember Arnold saying, "Listen, there's an act that you could really use, but he's

Tony Orlando
Publicity photo

2 SHOWS & DANCING for no admission?
YES! PLUS MODERATE PRICES TOO.
TONIGHT July 23RD In Person
"TONY ORLANDO" "Bless Him"
Also — Tony Maples — The Naturals
NO COVER—SHOWS AT 10:30 & 12:45
Shamrock Bar
94 BEACHWAY, KEANSBURG, N.J.
— NOW APPEARING — Mon., Tues., Wed., Fri., Sat., Sun. The "Hi-Tempos"
JULY 30th "THE 4 EVERS"

young and there will be restrictions. He will be a thousand dollars a night and you'll only have him in a certain area." I said, "A thousand dollars?" Arnold said, "Yeah, his name is Little Stevie Wonder." A thousand dollars to me back then might have been a hundred thousand dollars. I said, "No thanks. I can't do that."

So, for the next act to play the Shamrock Bar in Keansburg I settled on Tony Orlando. Yes, the same Tony Orlando of "Tie A Yellow Ribbon" fame, but that would come later. Tony had recorded "Halfway to Paradise" and "Bless You" back in 1961, but was between hits when I hired him for $250. He did a great show. He played rhythm guitar with the band and did two 40-minute sets. Tony sang "Bless You" and "Halfway to Paradise" and we did "La Bamba" with him. We had a great crowd.

For July 30, I hired another white act, the Brooklyn-based Four Evers. They were great. They had just released the song, "Be My Girl" and they sounded just like The Four Seasons.

From there I brought in the Belmonts and then Vito & the Salutations again. Vito & the Salutations were so popular I think I had them at the Shamrock Bar four times in a five month span.

Keansburg, and especially the Shamrock Bar could be a rough place with plenty of hard drinkers. I never had any real trouble at the shows there but I did have to be watchful. Somebody told me to be careful around the end of every month. There was always a brawl between personnel from the military bases. That was when they got their paychecks and they'd get drunk and fight over who was tougher. They had fights there

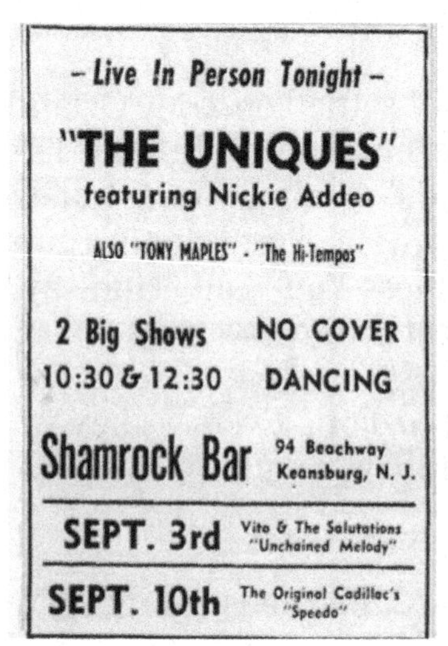

– Live In Person Tonight –

"THE UNIQUES"

featuring Nickie Addeo

ALSO "TONY MAPLES" - "The Hi-Tempos"

2 Big Shows 10:30 & 12:30

NO COVER DANCING

Shamrock Bar 94 Beachway Keansburg, N. J.

SEPT. 3rd Vito & The Salutations "Unchained Melody"

SEPT. 10th The Original Cadillac's "Speedo"

The Uniques performing at the Shamrock Bar, Keansburg, New Jersey, 1964. Top photo, left to right. Ron Coleman, Ray Morris, Leon Trent, Pat Millo on sax, Nicky Addeo, and Norman Seldin on keyboards. Bottom photo, left to right: Ron Coleman, Ray Morris, Leon Trent. The Naturals are in the background Photos courtesy of Ronald Coleman.

all of the time and it seemed like there were no bouncers. They just punched each other until they were pulled apart by groups of friends. The Shamrock had cigarette vending machines in those days with the glass fronts. And believe me, I don't think I ever got through a week or two where the front plate of one wasn't broken by somebody being thrown into it.

They had a near riot one night and I almost got killed. Someone requested "In the Still Of The Night" but instead of playing the Five Satins song, I started playing the old Cole Porter standard. The bartender yelled, "Duck!" and a Budweiser bottle went flying by my head and broke against the wall. I could have used chicken wire sometimes. It was an eye opener for a 17-year-old kid like me. Now that I think about it, I had to be out of my mind to do shows there. But you do things in life that you want to do.

I guess what bothered me most was the racism. On one August night a bus load of black people arrived in Keansburg to visit the amusement park and were harassed and attacked by a group of white youth. We were off that night but heard about the incident as it made the newspapers. Most of my groups were black like the Valtairs, Wathington Brothers and Shondelles or integrated like the Uniques with a white Nicky Addeo singing lead. People there told me to bring in more white groups and I did try to mix it up by bringing in Vito & the Salutations, the Four Evers and the Belmonts. But I was not afraid to bring in black groups like the Original Cadillacs and Bobbettes.

One of the groups that I became close to was Larry Chance & the Earls. I first booked them into the Shamrock Bar in September, 1964. The Earls had a monster East Coast hit with the song "Remember Then." But this show was the start of a long relationship I'd have with Larry Chance & the Earls. Larry is one of the great song stylists. I'd stand Larry Chance up against any R&B singer in the business. He's that good. I eventually ended up managing Larry Chance & the Earls for about a year, but more about that in a later chapter.

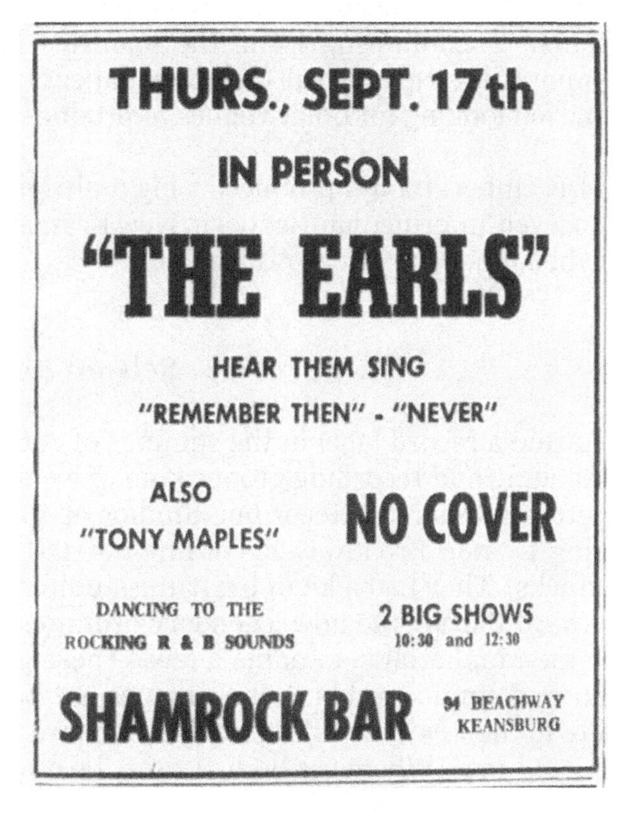
THURS., SEPT. 17th
IN PERSON
"THE EARLS"
HEAR THEM SING
"REMEMBER THEN" - "NEVER"
ALSO
"TONY MAPLES"
NO COVER
DANCING TO THE
ROCKING R & B SOUNDS
2 BIG SHOWS
10:30 and 12:30
SHAMROCK BAR
94 BEACHWAY
KEANSBURG

As the fall of 1964 rolled on, while continuing to book acts into the Shamrock Bar, I started using a band called the Marvels to back the singers instead of the Naturals. The Marvels were a great band that featured guitarist and vocalist Jimmy Eldridge. Jimmy was a beautiful man who always made the right choices musically and had that rare guitar technique heard in the stylings of Curtis Mayfield, Don Covey and others. That, of course, freed up my band the Naturals to play elsewhere.

GALA PRODUCTIONS . . .
PRESENTS IN COOPERATION WITH SELDOM & MELO-DEE RECORD CO.
THE 1965
MOTORCADE REVUE
2 SHOWS on FRI., DEC. 11 at 7:30 and 9:45 P.M.
AT ROOSEVELT INTERMEDIATE AUDITORIUM
LIVINGSTON AVENUE NEW BRUNSWICK, N. J.
ADMISSION $1.25
ON STAGE ★ ★ ★ IN PERSON
THE FABULOUS NICKY ADDEO | THE EXCEPTIONALS | SINGING SENSATION LITTLE CHUCKY
TWIST KINGS THE APOLLOS | THE DYNAMIC F-85's | THE FANTASTIC SYNARD
—PLUS—SPECIAL GUEST STARS . . .
"THE TICKS" ★ "B. BOP"

In July of 1964, I played the grand opening of Pat Brady's Inn in the Highlands. Pat Brady's was an upscale restaurant with music for dancing. I did that as a trio for the first couple weekends.

Back at the Shamrock Bar, I was still booking singers each Thursday night with the Marvels backing them and also doing sets themselves. I booked the Bobbettes ("Mr. Lee"), the Cookies ("Chains"), the Cadillacs ("Gloria"), The Salisbury Twins ("Am I In Love") and some new groups like the Emeralds, the Hi-Tempos, the Florals and a girl group called the Jaymatics. Of course, I kept bringing in my own acts, the Valtairs, Wathington Brothers, the Shondelles and Nicky Addeo. I still had Tony Maples emceeing and singing on just about every show. But the venue started adding exotic dancers to the entertainment and billing the shows as "Adult Fun For Adults." The following Spring the Shamrock Bar was raided and had its liquor license temporarily suspended as the exotic dancers performances were considered too lewd. I started looking for other venues to produce shows.

In December, 1964, I produced a big multi-group stage show in the auditorium of the Roosevelt Intermediate School in New Brunswick. Called the 1965 Motorcade Review, the headliner was Nicky Addeo.

Selsom Records

I started a record label in the summer of 1964 to record the groups I was managing. Managing and recording groups kind of went together. I went to see Pat Jaques who operated Broadway Recording Studios at 1697 Broadway in Manhattan. He took a liking to me. Broadway Recording did 12-track recording when everyone else had 2-tracks. They had a lot of big name studio musicians there. That's where I first met Bernard Purdie, the now legendary drummer and Richard Tee, the big time organist for the Manhattans, to name a few. These guys would each eventually have several hundred studio credits to their names but back in 1964 they were still young. Most were in their early or mid-twenties. Richard Tee didn't care for very many people but he liked me. Whenever he had time, he'd come in and show me something on the organ. It was at Broadway Recording Studios that I met Teacho Wiltshire. Teacho had literally arranged and/or led the orchestras backing hundreds of hit records during the 1950's and 1960's. In addition, he managed the Drifters. Teacho was doing all the arrangements at Broadway Recording Studios. I was around all these guys getting their input and I was just 16 or 17 years old. I learned from everybody and soon I was even doing mixing.

One day I brought the Naturals, Valtairs, Uniques, Shondelles and Tony Maples to Broadway Recording Studios. We recorded two sides by each act, all in one day. We started at ten in the morning and went until four in the afternoon.

Harry Ray and the Valtairs recorded a couple of my compositions - a soul harmony ballad called "Strangers Way" and a dance record, "Soul!" "Soul!" was a high energy song that kept building in excitement, much in the style of the Isley Brothers' "Shout." We added studio shouting so the song sounded as if it was recorded live.

The Uniques' songs including a doo wop infused "Over The Rainbow" and a medium tempo soul side called "Fool Number Two." These had originally been planned for Billy Brown's lead, but the Uniques' new lead, Nicky Addeo, handled them well. I asked Sam Siciliano of the Asbury Park group, the Darchaes, to arrange the Uniques' harmony on the two sides. Sam could coordinate harmony with three or fours voices that had never sung together before and after an hour, make them sound like they'd been rehearsing for days. No one was better at arranging vocal harmony than Sam. Sam also filled in on bass vocals on the Uniques record. He was really a high baritone but whatever he needed to do, he did.

The Shondelles recorded a female group cover of the Teenagers' "Why Do Fools Fall In Love" and an original, "Upsetter Of Her Heart." The Shondelles also sang background to Tony Maples two sides. Tony recorded the Eugene Church song, "Pretty Girls Everywhere" and another of my compositions, "I'm Your Lover Man." I released the Valtairs and Uniques records first, followed by the Shondelles and Tony Maples records shortly after. I also released an instrumental version of "One Mint Julep" by the Naturals on *Selsom*. It didn't sell and I didn't press very many. It remains the most obscure of my recordings. That was the start of *Selsom Records*. As a songwriter and publisher, I was now a member of ASCAP.

Top left photo, The Shondelles. Left to right, top: Brenda Harris, Lynne Brown, Bottom, left to right: Carol Hawkins, Rhonda Kirby. Photo by Earl Stout. Bottom right photo: Nicky Addeo, courtesy of Nicky Addeo

The Valtairs, Left to right: Joe Gardner, Harry Ray, Ken Short, Greg Henson
Photo by Earl Stout

Soul! Takes Off

Releasing a record means little unless you have promotion and distribution. My contact in the record business was a popular radio disc jockey named Harold Ladell.

Harold Ladell was a real pioneer in R&B radio who is rarely given the credit he deserves. Back in 1949, Ladell went to work for Essex Record Distributors in Newark, New Jersey, as their chief salesperson. Essex was a family owned company run by the Cohens who, like Ladell, were descendents of Russian Jewish immigrants. Essex purchased airtime on radio station WNJR-AM out of Newark and gave Ladell his own nightly radio program. Ladell started playing Rhythm & Blues records that were distributed and sold by Essex Records. His "Mr. Blues Show" was soon number one in the ratings, with the signal reaching into Manhattan as well as most of Northern New Jersey. As R&B was just breaking big in 1949, Harold "Mr. Blues" Ladell became one of the first to play R&B music in the New York area and Essex soon became the largest record distributor in New Jersey.

Harold Ladell helped me get things going. I had played piano at his daughter's party at a very young age and he'd taken a liking to me. Harold only wanted to play black music on the air and he liked my Valtairs record. As a matter of fact, he played everything on my label. Of course, it didn't hurt that I was Jewish. But I was getting lots of free airplay and Essex Record Distributors began distributing my records in New Jersey. I had Beta Distributors for New York, David Rosen for Philadelphia and Schwartz Brothers for distribution in the Washington - Baltimore area.

"Soul!" by the Valtairs got an outstanding review and rating from *Cashbox*, the music trade magazine. In fact, it was listed as "Best Bet" for the week of September 26, 1964, the highest rating they could give a record. The reviewer wrote, "The Valtairs lash out with a driving uptempo multi-dancer affair that should put plenty of teen coin in circulation. It's a rapid-fire affair the deejays should be on early."

Douglas "Jocko" Henderson
From the Paul Ressler Archives

Howard Ladell said to me, "Call this number and ask for Douglas. Tell him I told you to call." So I called the number and introduced myself. I still didn't know who it was but I asked Douglas his last name. He said, "I'm Doug Henderson, but you can call me Jocko!" I could hardly believe, I was speaking to the legendary radio personality and one of the most powerful figures in black music.

Jocko invited me to his home in the Wissahickon neighborhood of Philadelphia. He opened the door and said, "Can I help you?" I said, "I'm Norman." Jocko looked surprised and said, "You're white!"

Jocko was very nice. He asked if I'd brought any of my records with me and if so, how many did I bring. I told him I'd brought a twenty-five count box of each and he said, "Let me have five of each." He was taping a USO radio broadcast from his home and he had a big tape recorder, microphone and turntable. Jocko picked up my Valtairs record and said, "Is this what I've been hearing Harold play?" I said, "Yeah." He said, "How are both sides?" And I said, "Good."

Jocko looked at me and asked, "How old are you?" I replied, "Seventeen." He again asked, "They're good, huh?" And I again said, "Yeah."

With that, Jocko went right on the air and said, "This is Jocko on the radio for our military base. We have a new record coming out of New Jersey. This is the Valtairs!" He played it four times.

So we had lunch and Jocko said, "Do you know how to get back to New Jersey?" When I told him I did, he asked if I could come to New York the following week. He wanted me to meet him at *Tangerine Records,* the company founded by Ray Charles and run by famous tenor saxophonist and bandleader Al Sears. Jocko gave me the address and

I put on a suit and tie for the meeting. Per Jocko's instructions, I brought with me five 25-count boxes of the Valtairs record.

WWIN's Larry Dean
Publicity photo

When I got to *Tangerine Records*, I sat at this huge table and there were all these black men and women who I later found represented the East Coast's most prominent black radio people. There were all there getting their records for the month. Jocko said, "This is Norman," and everybody looked at me. Jocko said, "Norman has all black groups. So I'd like each of you to start playing his records tomorrow."

Then Jocko said to me, "This is Fat Daddy. He owns Baltimore." Paul "Fat Daddy" Johnson weighed about 340 pounds. And Fat Daddy said, "What's in it for me?" Jocko said, "Here's 25 records. Plenty more where those came from. Put it on the charts this week." Fat Daddy said, "But I haven't heard it yet." Jocko just repeated, "Put it on the charts this week."

"Chatty Hattie" Leeper from Charlotte was there. She was the first female black radio broadcaster in North Carolina. She said, "I don't need 25 copies but if it's any good, I'll play it for you." These were people I'd read about in *Billboard Magazine* but never thought I'd meet. And around the table it went. At the time, I was pressing the record for about 35 or 40 cents apiece and I gave away about 125 at that meeting. But I trusted Jocko's advice.

Al Jefferson, also from Baltimore, said to me, "When you come to Baltimore, come to station WWIN and ask for Larry Dean. You'll stay at his house." Now, Larry Dean was another prominent black deejay in Baltimore but I didn't know him from Adam. Larry called me before I went down there. Apparently Jocko had told him about my father's jewelry store because he said, "Jocko told me you pierce ears?" I replied that I did and he said, "My daughter wants her ears pierced. Can you...?" And I said, Yes." So Larry said, "Good. When you come down you will stay at my home."

Before I went down South, my mother went and got eight or nine Longines watches from the jewelry store and said, "Take these with you and give them to every program director you meet at the radio stations."

So, I went down to Baltimore and stayed with Larry Dean. He took me to Lenny Moore's Steakhouse, owned by the star halfback for the Baltimore Colts. There were all these professional football and baseball players there. Larry bought me a big steak dinner. The next day he took me to his radio station. WWIN was a beautiful radio station in a run-down section of Baltimore. We walked in and some guy took one look at me and said, "What's he doing here?" Larry said, "He has this new record and I want it on the air now!" The fellow said, "Well, Al Jefferson's on the air now." Larry knocked on the window and they took the next record off the turntable and cued up "Soul!" by the Valtairs. And Al Jefferson announced, "We have a brand new record by the Valtairs. One of the singers is here now and we're going to interview him." Now, I didn't have any of the Valtairs with me, so I went on the air to be interviewed as Harry Ray. The record was put on WWIN's song rotation as "Pick of the Week."

Lenny then said, "When we leave here, I'm going to call Bill Justice at WSR in DC and tell him I'm sending you down there to see him. Can you get there today? The building will look like a garage in the middle of nowhere, but Bill Justice controls D.C. He'll put your record on. Take him five or ten copies."

So I went down to Washington to see Bill Justice. I went in and said, "I'm Norman." Bill Justice looked at me and said, "You're white! Are we playing a white record?" I said, "I don't handle white groups" and he said, "OK."

We went into the control room and Justice locked the door behind me. He took the microphone and said, "Hot off of the presses. We have Harry Ray of the Valtairs with us in the studio and according to Jocko, this is the hottest record going." And Bill Justice put on "Soul!" And when the needle got to the end he said, "Oh! Sorry you missed that!" And he put the needle back to the beginning and played it again. Eight times in a row. They called from the front office and wanted to talk to him but he kept the door locked. And he said, "Take this record to the *Washington Post* and tell them it's our "Pick of the Week."

Valtairs' Harry Ray
High school yearbook photo

Within four weeks "Soul!" by the Valtairs had charted in the Top 20 in eight different East Coast R&B markets.

They knew "Big Daddy Jack" Holmes, the popular deejay on WRAP in Virginia Beach, Virginia. So I drove down there and visited his station. Jack said, "You know, I have a friend on a white station. Would you also be interested in having it played there?" Of course I did, so I drove over to meet him and he agreed to play it. He called a competitor on another white station who agreed to play it. The song started charting on white stations in Virginia.

Early in 1965, Jocko called me and said, "I want you to bring the Valtairs to a show at the Audubon Ballroom in Washington Heights, Harlem. I'm telling you in advance, the only two white people there will be you and the owner and he'll be behind a steel grate taking money. You'll be two Jews in a strange place. But we've got a great stage and it'll be a fabulous show."

Me with Jocko and the Valtairs at the Audubon Ballroom, 1965

I'd just recently gotten my drivers license and so I drove the Valtairs up to Harlem. Meanwhile, since I had talked to Jocko, Malcolm X had just been assassinated on stage at the very same Audubon Ballroom. The piano was right there over the silhouette drawn on the floor where Malcolm X fell. But we went there and did the show.

It was a monster show. It had Jackie Wilson, Billy Stewart, Joe Tex, King Curtis and of course, Harry Ray and the Valtairs. Jocko was the emcee. I told Jocko, "We don't belong on this show." But Jocko said, "Sure you belong on it. I'm putting Billy Stewart on first." Billy had just charted with the sing, "I Do Love You." I thought, "Oh my God! This guy's got a monster record out and Jocko's putting the Valtairs in the middle of the line up." But Harry Ray smoked the place.

And Jocko said, "My advice to you now is to go back to your car and leave." I went to the men's room and the guy next to me opened his coat and he had a sawed off shotgun. He had been in the audience. Jocko got someone to escort me and the Valtairs to my car. I didn't know where the hell I was. Jocko said, "Just go straight to the light, make a left, keep the doors locked and go home."

All told, "Soul!" by the Valtairs sold a few thousand records. To me that was like a million seller back then.

Chapter Five
Acappella, Blue-Eyed Soul & the Birth of Jersey Shore Rock

As 1965 began, I was still booking 1950s doo wop groups into local venues. As the year progressed, I booked Bobby Lewis ("Tossin' & Turnin'") and Billy Bland ("Let The Little Girl Dance") into the Shamrock Bar and I put Shep & the Limelites ("Daddy's Home") into Mrs. Jay's in Asbury Park. Mrs. Jay's would become the Stone Pony but that was years later. I booked the Valtairs into Major's Lounge in Keyport, New Jersey.

Major's Lounge was a black club that had major acts like James Brown, so the Valtairs were really moving up in the world after the Audubon Ballroom show. In fact, in May of 1965, I released a second record by the Valtairs on *Selsom Records*, "Moonlight In Vermont" and "The Ko Ko Mo." Both sides were arranged by me and my sax player, Paul Grabow. I was still performing with the Naturals, but I was looking for new challenges.

Acappella

Around New Jersey a new genre of music was taking hold. It was mostly a niche underground thing promoted by several small independent record labels, like *Times Square* and *Catamount Records*. The new sound was called "acappella," a take on the

Barbaroso & the Historians. Left to right: Nicky Addeo, Ray Dahrouge.
Dennis Testa, Louis Scalpati, Sam Siciliano.
Photo courtesy of Nicky Addeo

Italian phrase, "a cappella," meaning "in chapel or choir style." In other words, vocals without instrumentation. The word acappella came to mean pure fifties style R&B vocal quartet or quintet harmony without musical instruments. While many R&B vocal groups in the fifties began singing acappella on the street corners, major record companies recorded these groups with a band to make them more commercially acceptable. But in the early 1960's, for the first time, a growing number of independent record companies were recording just the pure vocals.

Many of the fans of acappella were white youth who loved fifties-style R&B vocal harmony and were alarmed by the new music of the Beatles and the British Invasion that was sweeping the music scene. So I decided to record some acappella sides.

When I told you about the Uniques record, I mentioned that Sam Siciliano had been singing with the Darchaes. Nicky Addeo had also been in and out of the Darchaes for a time singing lead when the Darchaes' original lead, Ray Dahrouge, was away at college. Ray Dahrouge would later become one of the country's great songwriters and producers of soul music. But this was 1965 and I asked the Darchaes - Nicky Addeo, Ray Dahrouge, Sam Siciliano, Denny Testa, Sal Capalongo and Lou Scalpati - to record some acappella songs for me. At the time I was reserving the *Selsom* label for black music so I created a subsidiary label called *Jade*. I didn't want it to be associated with the earlier Darchaes records so I renamed the group, Barbaroso & the Historians.

While the Darchaes had recorded earlier, I wanted to give the acappella sound real clarity so I took them to Broadway Recording Studios and recorded each of the six voices separately on their 12-track machine. By alternating leads between Ray and Nicky, I recorded a number of acappella sides by the group. They did the Cadillacs' song,"Gloria" in both a fast and slow version with Nicky doing leads. Nicky also led on "Zoom," "When I Fall In Love" and "My Love For You Will Never Die." Ray Dahrouge sang lead on the Bopchords' song "When I Woke Up This Morning" and a couple of original songs that Ray had written, including "I Don't Care."

I listened to the tape playback and decided the two strongest songs were "Zoom" and "When I Fall In Love." Those I issued as a single on *Jade Records*. I remember Pat Jaques saying to me, "They're good but you're not going to sell a lot of that record." He was right, of course, but I just wanted to do something different. That record is now one of the rarest and most sought after records by collectors of the acappella genre. I did put both sides of the single and three other cuts including the fast version of "Gloria" on my 2008 CD, "Asbury Park Then And Now."

The Motifs and the Beginnings of Jersey Shore Rock

The Beatles and the British Invasion ushered in a seismic change in popular music. I was still managing the Valtairs, Shondelles, Uniques and Tony Maples, all black Rhythm & Blues acts. But the white teenagers were now getting into the Rolling Stones, Eric Burdon & the Animals and the Kinks. As a promoter of teenage dances, I was mindful that I needed to stay current. That's when I met the Motifs.

The Motifs were a teenage garage band out of Howell, in western Monmouth County, New Jersey. They called my parents' jewelry store and asked if I would manage them. I invited them to come and audition in my parents' home. I told them to bring their amps and I'll never forget the look on my parents faces when the Motifs walked in. The black groups were one thing. When my father and mother saw these guys with their hair down to the middle of their backs, that was it. They said, "What in the hell is that?" They both thought I lost my mind. I'd always been taught that musicians wore suits and ties when they performed. The Motifs showed up in street clothes looking somewhat disheveled and unkempt. They came and set up their amps in our living room. The first song they played for me was the Kinks' "You Really Got Me." I didn't initially know what to think of them. Their music was loud, raucous and raw. They didn't sound anything like the R&B groups I was managing, nor anyone else I'd ever heard. They had a unique sound.

The Motifs were made up of 18-year-old lead singer Walter Cichon, his brother and the group's lead guitarist Raymond Cichon, drummer John Lewandowski, guitarist Murray Bauer and bass player Vinnie Roslin. In listening to them, something told me back then that this was going to be a very hot group. I just heard something that was viciously raw. I heard hints of Eric Burdon, Mick Jagger and the Kinks in lead singer Walter Cichon's voice. Walter was lean and muscular with a chiseled face. I just heard this rawness of a voice and the look of the muscles and just the sweat, everything about him. But he was a sweet guy, just very, very smart. His brother, Raymond was a great guitar player.

The Motifs, 1965. Top, from left to right: Walter Cichon, John Lewandowski, Ray Cichon, Murray Bauer. Seated, Vinnie Roslin.
Photo by Earl Stout

By the end of the audition, I'd decided to manage the Motifs. Even my mother thought I should give them a chance. I'm glad I did. The Motifs were my first all-white band and they turned out to be one of the best bands that I managed, booked and eventually recorded. They molded and created a sound all their own.

One of the first things I did was have Earl Stout take and print promotional photos of the Motifs. The classic photo of the Motifs, seen here with the water in the background was taken by the pond off of Newman Springs Road in Red Bank.

The first gig I booked for the Motifs was at a place called The Oaks on Highway 35 in Middletown, New Jersey. Initially I had the Motifs in a "Battle of the Bands" with another local rock band, the Mods. But I quickly found out the Motifs could hold their own, so I had just them at The Oaks every Thursday night during the month of July. From there I moved my shows to the West End Casino.

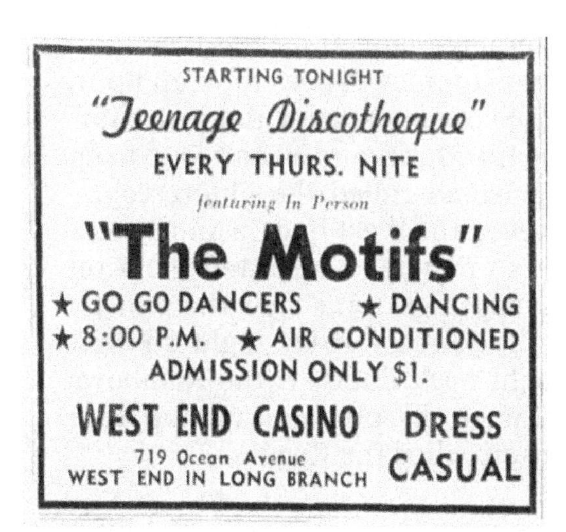

The West End Casino

The West End Casino was located on the beach at 717 Ocean Avenue in Long Branch. Beginning in August of 1965, I started having a "Teenage Discotheque" every Thursday night. The place was air conditioned and huge, holding almost a thousand people with still space enough for dancing. I had the Motifs there and Go Go Dancers and only charged one dollar to get in. As word got around, the crowds of teenagers started growing.

To advertise the location change to the West End Casino, I had the Motifs perform a couple of sets outside Seldin's Jewelry on Broad Street during Red Bank's Sidewalk Sale Day. Anyone coming into the store could also get a free autographed photo of the Motifs.

Then I got the idea to also run oldies shows on Wednesday nights with the Motifs opening for the bigger name groups I was booking through Arnold Klein in New York. So I brought in Vito & the Salutations and I had a capacity crowd of 1,000 people.

I followed that the next Wednesday night with the Motifs opening for Randy & the Rainbows, who'd just had the hit record, "Denise." Meanwhile, the Motifs were becoming so popular, I also booked them into the Rainbow Room in Asbury Park.

The Motifs performing outside Seldin's Jewelers during Red Bank's Sidewalk Sale Day
Photo by Earl Stout

I'd initially planned for the West End Casino summer dances to wrap up in early September, with the last show being the Motifs and and a group from Long Island called the Fluorescents. However, the West End Casino dances were so popular I restarted them on Saturday nights through the winter. For the first Saturday night show, I brought back Randy & the Rainbows and the Motifs, plus a rock group from Rumson called the Rogues.

The Motifs at the West End Casino
Photo by Earl Stout

In the meantime, I also started up a new series of winter dances, every Friday night at the I. B. Club on Bergerville Road in Adelphia, Howell Township, New Jersey. I regularly featured the Motifs on both the West End Casino and I.B. Clubs dances. Other acts that I brought into the I.B. Club included the Kingsmen of "Louie Louie" fame and Johnny Thunder.

At this point I decided to record the Motifs. Instead of taking the Motifs to Broadway Recording Studios, I took them to Bell Sound. It was the first time I used a studio other than Broadway Recording, but I didn't want a black sound. It did feel a little strange, not working with Pat Jaques. But I recorded "Molly" and backed it with "If I Gave You Love." Both sides were written by the Cichon brothers and were songs they were singing in their live shows. In fact, we made "Molly" sound as if it was done live. The song "Molly" had an unusual introduction with Walter Cichon reciting a short poem he'd written. That's the way he wrote and performed the song. "I wrote a poem," Walter began. "Molly, my baby and I fell out. And what do you think it was all about. Cause she liked coffee and I liked tea. And that's the reason we couldn't agree." From there he launched into the song and with the live atmosphere, record buyers could just picture Walter Cichon on stage pounding a tambourine or banging a cowbell as he sang.

I bought some advertising time on radio station WMCA in New York City. In doing so, I asked Joe O'Brien, one of the "WMCA Good Guys" radio personalities to write a short blurb about the group for the reverse side of the 45's picture sleeve. O'Brien was the #1 morning man in New York City radio at that time and I hoped having Joe O'Brien's photo and endorsement on the sleeve would sell some records. At that time, the WMCA disc jockeys would meet periodically to pick the records the station should be playing. Well, the Motifs record never made the WMCA weekly rotation. Whether or not Joe ever slipped in a spin or two, I don't know. I do know that when the record came out, WMCA requested I remove Joe O'Brien's photo and name from the record

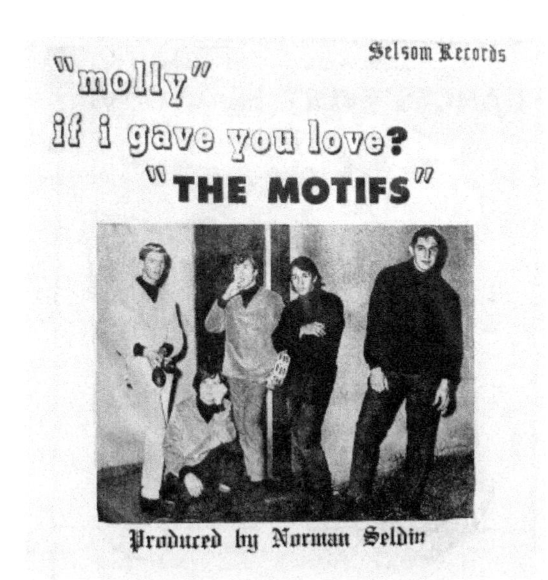

sleeve. By then, of course, we'd already printed a thousand copies, so there was nothing I could do. We just sold them.

WMCA GOOD GUY "JOE O'BRIEN" SAYS:

In today's rough and tumble music world, there's a new group born every minute! And here's a brand new group with a different sound.

Meet "The Motifs" - five swingers from New Jersey: John, Murray, Vinnie and brothers Walt and Ray.

This is their first record and they have been together for only six months. But in a world of tough competition, these boys have succeeded in putting together a new, original sound that's strictly their own.

Swing with "The Motifs"!

WMCA DOES!

Best wishes to all my friends.

JOE O'BRIEN

WMCA RADIO — NEW YORK, N. Y.

Well, all of the sudden, the record started to take off. I put the Motifs' photo up at Anderson's Record Store in Red Bank and had the Motifs play a set there and sign autographs. Anderson's had a downstairs area where they used to have little promotional events like that. So instead of having the Motifs at the West End Casino one night they played at the record store. There must have been four or five hundred people show up for that.

"Molly" by the Motifs became a regional hit, selling a couple thousand records. Record sales were primarily driven by the excitement created from their live performances. I think at the Motif's first performance after the record came out we must have sold 200 copies at the dance.

The Motifs were great and everybody loved them. When Walter Cichon got on stage he would instantly start to sweat. His hair would be drenched and it would hang down. You just couldn't duplicate what he had. He was just dynamic. He was special.

Whatever impact the Motifs had on their legion of followers, it was nothing compared to the influence they had on other young and up coming musicians. Two musicians who particularly took note of the Motifs were Bruce Springsteen and George Theiss of a new group called the Castiles. Springsteen has called Walter Cichon "the greatest rock-and-roll front man on the Jersey Shore in the bar-band '60s."

In his recent musical, "Springsteen On Broadway," Bruce Springsteen reminisced about about the impact the Motifs had on him. "They were Gods... On stage, Walter was deadly, and he was aloof and raw and sexual and dangerous... Raymond was my guitar hero." Bruce added, "The hours I spent standing in front of their band, studying, studying, studying, class in session, night after night, taking it all in, watching Ray's fingers fly over the fret board. These nights were essential to my development as a young musician. I loved them. I loved these men."

I heard later that Bruce would sometime attend the Motifs' practice sessions and that Raymond Cichon would show him some guitar riffs. I wouldn't have known about that, but I do know that I put the Castiles on the next I.B. Club show. I think that October 8, 1965 concert and dance may have been the first commercially advertised concert that Bruce and the Castiles ever did. I had them open up for the Long Island group, the Fluorescents. Bruce had earlier played briefly with the Rogues, but I don't recall him being with them when I had the Rogues at the West End Casino two weeks earlier. By that time he'd already joined the Castiles.

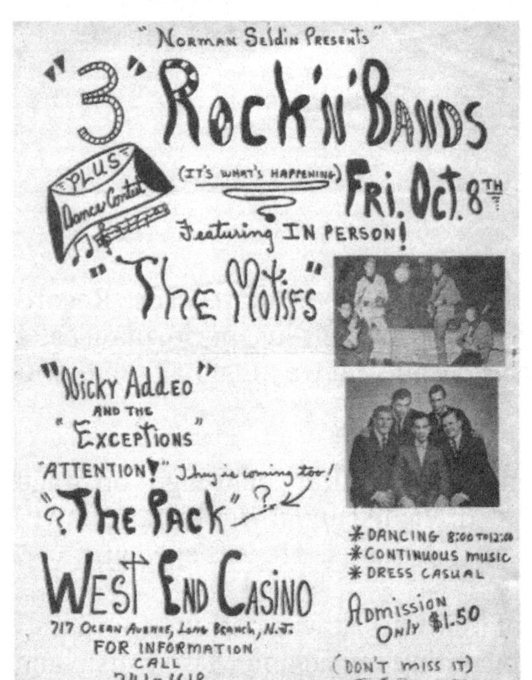

One of my hand made flyers.

At the time, The Castiles were just getting started and the Motifs were better known. The Motifs could earn $125 or more for gigs, at a time when the Castiles took home $75 a show.

Actually, the October 8 dance that the Castiles played at the I.B. Club had competition. There must have been a scheduling problem with that Saturday's West End Casino dance and I ended up having the Motifs, the Pack and Nicky Addeo with his new group, the Exceptions, in Long Branch the same night.

I kept running these dances and concerts at both the West End Casino and the I.B. Club throughout the fall and winter. And while I did hire the Castiles, the Motifs were my main rock group. They were huge. I thought, "My

God, what have I got here? I just kept promoting the Motifs and for two or three years they absolutely reigned the area. Everybody wanted them. I mean, I even brought them out to Dickinson University in Carlisle, Pennsylvania.

The Motifs
Photo by Earl Stout

The Lost Souls

I began booking another group called the Lost Souls. I bumped into the group's manager, Joseph Shafsky, in the Brill Building in Manhattan. He told me that the Lost Souls had been performing under the name of the Townzmen at a discotheque on East 154th Street called Arthur. Arthur, a club owned by Richard Burton's ex-wife, Sybil, was one of the hottest clubs in Manhattan. So I figured that the group must be pretty good. On top of that, Joseph Shafsky told me the Lost Souls had signed with Bert Berns' *Bang* record label. In fact, they'd just released their first record, a Bert Berns composition called "The Girl I Love" that *Cashbox* had named "Sleeper of the Week." With the British Invasion in music, they were being promoted as an English group but I think they were actually from Brooklyn and Queens. Shafsky told me one of the guys was from England and they had the look and sound of a British group so who was I to question the hype.

The Lost Souls. Left to right:
John Cannon, Thom Caccetta,
Mike Matino, Bob Hefernan
Courtesy of John Cannon Music

I had never really seen the group perform, but I had them them sign autographs at Seldin Jewelers and then booked them at the West End Casino on October 16. Besides the Lost Souls, I had the Motifs and two other groups, the Pack and the Berries. I think that show almost broke every attendance record there was. We drew 1,200 attendees.

The Lost Souls' lead singer, Michael Marino, was a paraplegic as a result of polio. He was unable to walk and came in a wheel chair. They had him seated in the center of the stage and they ripped the place apart. I used them again and every time I had them, they just tore the place up. The Lost Souls were a more musical version of The Motifs. The Motifs were raw and unorthodox. Nice kids, but raw. Whereas, the Lost Souls were organized. They had some money behind them.

Me congratulating Joseph Shafsky.
The Lost Souls are in the background.
Photo by Earl Stout

The next couple of Saturdays I brought the Fluorescents back with a rock group called Links 'N' Chains and then the Motifs and the Four Pages. I brought back the Lost Souls for a West End Casino dance in November, pairing them with the Motifs, the Pack and Nicky Addeo and his group, the Exceptions. Again, we had a great turnout and the Lost Souls tore the place up.

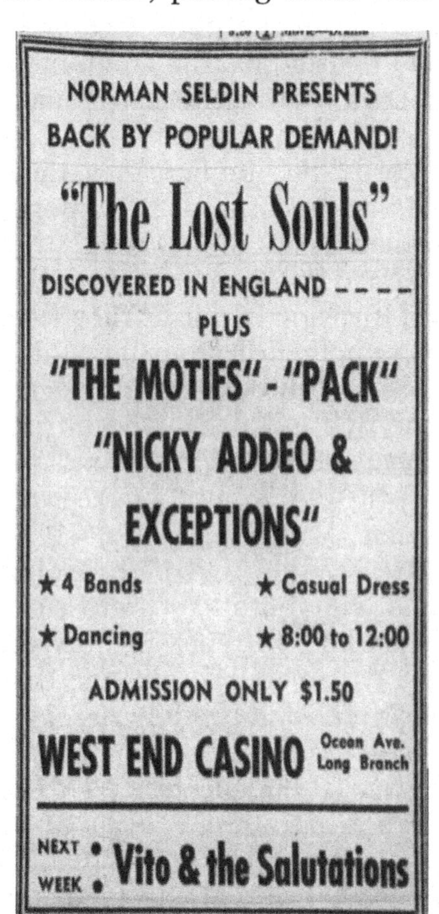

NORMAN SELDIN PRESENTS
BACK BY POPULAR DEMAND!
"The Lost Souls"
DISCOVERED IN ENGLAND ----
PLUS
"THE MOTIFS" - "PACK"
"NICKY ADDEO &
EXCEPTIONS"
★ 4 Bands ★ Casual Dress
★ Dancing ★ 8:00 to 12:00
ADMISSION ONLY $1.50
WEST END CASINO Ocean Ave. Long Branch
NEXT WEEK: Vito & the Salutations

Meanwhile, I brought Vito & the Salutations back to the West End Casino and Johnny Thunder into the I. B. Club in November. A couple of days prior to that I had him drop by Seldin's Jewelers to sign autographs. But I continued to rotate the local groups (the Motifs, Marvels, Berries, Nicky & the Exceptions, Rogues, 5 Illusions) through the two venues.

Folk, Jazz & Blues: The Tom Rush Concert

By the end of November, 1965, I wanted to expand into other areas. So in the middle of the West End Casino things, I decided to have a folk show. Don't ask me why. I guess that I just wanted to try something different.

I wanted to try it to see what it was like, because I do like folk music a lot. So I scheduled a two-hour concert for a Saturday afternoon at the West End Casino. It was a mix of Folk, Jazz and Blues. I put together a little progressive jazz trio with me on piano, Al Wright on drums and another fill-in musician on bass. I had Ruth Johnson, a vocalist from Middletown and a vocal duo named Frederick and Sherri Ann. And I hired Tom Rush.

Tom Rush
Publicity photo

Folk and blues singer and songwriter Tom Rush's name is legendary now but in 1965 he was just beginning to help shape the folk revival of the 1960's. While an undergraduate at Harvard University, his distinctive guitar style, wry humor and warm, expressive voice made him a local favorite in Boston area folk clubs. When I hired him, Tom Rush had recently been signed to *Electra Records* who had just released the album, "Tom Rush" including the song, "Long John."

I sold tickets at local record shops, including Anderson's in Red Bank, CJ's in Asbury Park and Harmony House in Eatontown. Tom gave a great performance and at one point said, "I've got a friend of mine here." He welcomed Ramblin' Jack Elliott who came up on stage and did thirty minutes for free. As good as the concert was, it was not well attended. Maybe it had 150 people at the most. I was used to having five to six hundred people in attendance. I enjoyed the concert but the low attendance discouraged me from doing any more folk concerts at that time.

So I went back to my regular dances and concerts. In December I had two new groups at the West End Casino, the Monks and DuCanes. The DuCanes contained future music producer Doc Holiday. More about Doc in the next chapter.

I followed that with the Motifs, Nicky Addeo & the Exceptions and a new group, the Justice League. I produced a big Christmas Eve concert at the West End Casino starring the Duprees along with the Motifs and the Jaywalkers.

The Duprees were one of the best doo wop groups around, especially when it came to ballads. They had scored big in the early 1960's with "You Belong To Me," "My Own

NORMAN SELDIN PRESENTS
CHRISTMAS DANCE
SAT., DEC. 25th
STARRING
"THE DUPREE'S"
Hitmakers of "You Belong to Me"
'JAYWALKERS' 'THE MOTIFS'
★ Dance Contest ★ 8:00 to 12:00
★ Casual Dress ★ Two Bands
Admission Only $2.00
WEST END CASINO
717 OCEAN AVE., LONG BRANCH, N. J.

The Duprees. Publicity photo.

True Love" and "Have You Heard." By this time Michael Kelly had assumed the role of lead singer and the group had just signed with *Columbia Records.* Their latest release, "Around The Corner" was just beginning to chart.

The Jaywalkers

The Jaywalkers were an established and popular rock and blue-eyed soul band that had been performing around the Jersey Shore since the late 1950's. They'd actually made a couple recordings back in 1962 and had played the Peppermint Lounge in New York City in 1964. By 1965, the Jaywalkers were mainstays at Mrs. Jay's Disc Au Go Go, the first of several Asbury Park night spots to have Go Go dancers that summer. As the Jaywalkers rocked, twelve Go Go girls in fringed glow-in-the-dark bikinis gyrated on top of the bar and the bandstand. And Mrs. Jay's club was packed every night.

Over the years that they played, numerous notable shore musicians and singers were either members of or made guest appearances with the Jaywalkers. But in 1965, the Jaywalkers consisted of co-founder and original drummer John Shaw; saxophonist Billy Lucia; organ, bass player and vocalist Mickey Holiday; and guitarist and former member of my Naturals band, Billy Ryan.

The Jaywalkers' leader John Shaw was a terrific businessman and always had his group booked. John was known for using a really clear, excellent PA system. He used Electro Voice cone speakers and a Binson Echorec echo machine. The group sang mostly cover songs but if you heard Mickey Holiday sing, it was like hearing the Righteous Brothers

Left: The Jaywalkers Selsom record. Right: The Jaywalkers, left to right:
Billy Lucia, Billy Ryan, Mickey Holiday, John Shaw
Courtesy of www.MickeyHoliday.com

or Gary Puckett from the Union Gap. And if you heard Billy “Cherry Bomb” Lucia, it was like listening to Little Anthony.

I used to sit in with the Jaywalkers sometimes. Mickey Holiday was their organ player. Mickey played keyboard bass like I ended up doing. And whenever Mickey was missing, I would be a fill-in because I was one of the only guys proficient enough to play that kind of thing.

I remember doing songs like Lee Dorsey’s “Working In A Coal Mine” and Rufus Thomas’ “Walkin’ The Dog” and some of those classic hits with the Jaywalkers. And Billy Ryan’s guitar parts on Chuck Berry songs were so precise that it was scary.

As I said earlier, Billy Ryan was in and out of my bands. When I first walked into a place and I heard Billy Ryan play, Hendrix and Clapton were in their heyday. This guy, Billy Ryan, would stand up there as a guitar player and do whatever they did. I mean, it was magical at the time. He had every bit the ability to be them with no problem. Springsteen looked at Billy Ryan as an idol. Billy was it. People came to hear him play. He was a sensational blues player. But every time I tried to get Billy for my band, he was with the Jaywalkers. When he had a falling out with them, he'd come and play with my band. Then all of a sudden when things began to roll right, he’d go back to the Jaywalkers. It was just hard to get Bill in the studio at the time. When the session came up, he wasn’t available. It prompted me to go to other guitar players. But Billy Ryan was a major player.

And the Jaywalkers always worked. They were in that Asbury Park circuit. They drew crowds. They were R&B enough to actually go down to Big Bill's, the black club on Springwood Avenue. They were one of the only white bands to play there.

You wouldn't think I could mix fifties doo wop groups and sixties rock groups on the same stage, but it actually worked out quite well. The crowd loved it, because you had one group that loved doo-wop and you had another group that loved modern rock. As long as each group got what they wanted, there were no problems. I had the Jaywalkers with the Duprees and another night the Crests with the Motifs and yet another night the Del Satins with Monty Rock III. These were some of the strangest combinations in the world but they worked. At these shows, people would start saying, "When are you bringing your band up?" The Naturals would come up and people loved the band too. They loved whatever I put up there.

So, the Jaywalkers became another of my "go to" groups. I never did really much managing with them. I booked them a few times. I decided to record and release a record by the Jaywalkers on my *Selsom* record label. The "A" side was an uptempo soul rock thing called "I Got My Own Thing Goin'." It was written by Bobby Darin and Rudy Clark and the Jaywalkers did it in a style that is now referred to by record collectors in the UK as "Northern Soul." The same song was also recorded by the New York City black group Little Charles & the Sidewinders around that time but theirs was a funk-soul style rendition. The flip side of the Jaywalkers record was a Mickey Holiday composition called "I Do" and Mickey sang lead on both sides.

1966

The new year, 1966, began as a continuation of the previous year. On New Years Night I featured the Motifs, Nicky Addeo & the Exceptions and the Jaywalkers at the West End Casino. The following Saturday night I had Don & Juan of the song "What's Your Name" fame along with the Motifs and a group called Russ & the Vibrations,

The dances got so big that just the two cops I had couldn't handle things. I had to have two or three security guards. I mean, if one kid was a clean-cut "surfer" and the other one was a tough leather pants wearing "greaser," they would fight. I'd have to separate the fighters. But I had 500 to 700 kids, two nights a week, for a long time. I promoted what I thought would sell. And it sold.

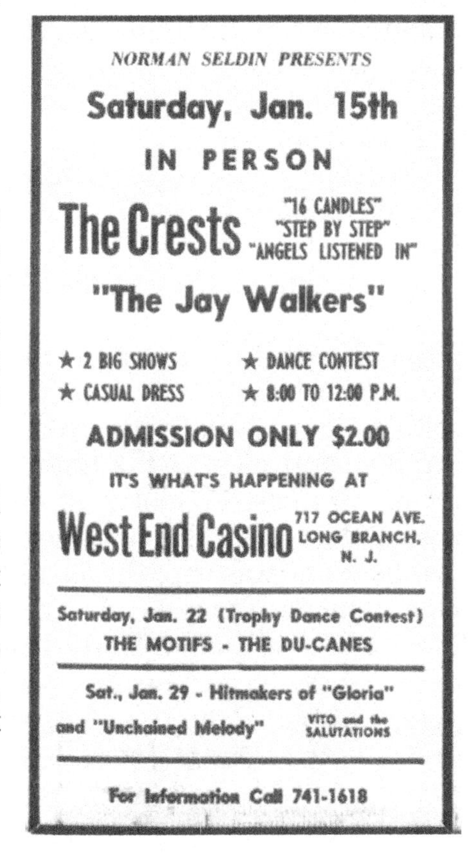

Santo & Johnny performing at the West End Casino with Norman, upper left.
Photo by Earl Stout

In the weeks that followed in January, February and March, I booked Johnny Maestro & the Crests ("16 Candles"), Vito & the Salutations {"Unchained Melody"), the Bobbettes ("Mr Lee), the Del Satins ("Teardrops Follow Me") and the Duprees ("You Belong To Me") into the West End Casino. I paired them with the local groups, the Motifs, Jaywalkers, Justice League, DuCanes, Emeralds, Shondelles and Rogues. I even brought back the Lost Souls. By then, Billy Brown had rejoined the Uniques and they'd resurfaced as the soul group, the Broadways. Harry Ray had been drafted into the service marking the end of the Valtairs. I didn't know it then but Billy Brown and Harry Ray would eventually team up in the Moments and Ray, Goodman & Brown.

One of the notable acts that I brought into the West End Casino in February was Santo & Johnny. The Brooklyn-born brothers, Santo and Johnny Farina, had scored a #1 hit back in 1959 the the instrumental guitar duo, "Sleep Walk." I had the Motifs open up for Santo and Johnny along with the Emeralds from Long Island. Instead of using two guitars, Santo and Johnny used a steel guitar and keyboard. It was beautifully done.

Chapter Six
The Soul Set

The Soul Set

The Soul Set
Photo by Earl Stout

I mentioned earlier that I'd been booking a group called the DuCanes on my shows. The leader of the DuCanes was a fellow named Eddie Wohanka from Keyport, New Jersey. Eddie would later become a highly recognized music producer in Nashville under the name Doc Holiday, but in 1966 he was just Eddie the guitarist with the DuCanes. The DuCanes used to play the Candy Cane Lounge and all the clubs in Long Branch.

I'd met Eddie for the first time when he came into my father's store to purchase some jewelry. He said, "You play music?" And I said,"Yes and I'm also producing shows." Eddie said, "But you're like 16 or 17 years old. What do you mean you're producing shows?" He became really, really interested and said, "Why don't we start a band together? I'll pull my drummer, Donald Scascia, from the DuCanes and we'll perform as a trio. I'll do the lead singing."

We called the new group the Soul Set. I really needed a name change from the Naturals. My mother kept reminding me of the importance of promotion. She'd say, "The Natural... what?" It sounded like something should follow the name Natural. At the same time we were into a more soulful Rhythm & Blues sound. We were doing songs by James Brown and Joe Tex. So I thought the name Soul Set fit better. The Soul Set became Eddie on guitar, Donald Scascia on drums and me on keys. As a singer, Eddie had this deep the Righteous Brothers kind of real rich voice. I would also do some singing. We started playing and the Soul Set went over really big. The Naturals continued performing for a short while. But I liked the scaled-down feel of a trio so the Soul Set became my new musical vehicle.

The Jagged Edge

In March 1966, I booked a group called the Jagged Edge into the West End Casino, pairing them with the Motifs. The Jagged Edge was a New York City band that had been playing the Greenwich Village club, the Night Owl Cafe, with groups like the Lovin' Spoonful. Many of the rock groups I hired, though often talented, were "garage bands" whose music careers came and went. On the other hand, the Jagged Edge (Shelly Leder, lead vocals and rhythm guitar; Don Brown, lead guitar and vocals; Joel Brigante, bass; Peter Goetch, drums; Leni Matlin, organ) were a step above most. In fact, they had just recorded the song, "How Many Times" for a New York label. I booked the Jagged Edge four or five times and considered recording them myself but it never happened.

Photo on the right, the Jagged Edge. Left to right: Peter Goetsch, Joel Brigante, Don Brown, Shelly Leder, Leni Matlin. Publicity photo.

The Matawan-Keyport
Roller Drome

The Matawan-Keyport Roller Drome had formerly been a bowling alley on Lower Main Street in Matawan, New Jersey. It was directly across the street from St. Joseph's Catholic Church and School. In late 1965, it was purchased and converted into a roller skating rink. The sizable brick building was also used for boxing matches and training.

Opened in December 1965, the Matawan-Keyport Roller Drome featured skating to recorded Rock & Roll music when there wasn't a boxing match. WNJR Radio deejay Danny Stiles began presenting live music shows and dances there, as the rink also served as a dance floor. Through March of 1966, Stiles held several live shows there with major recording stars the Dubs, Jive Five, Vito & the Salutations and Connie McGill & the Visions. Stiles also had local groups like the Five Old Men, Berries, Rogues, Wathington Brothers and Darcels as opening acts. In fact, on January 29, Danny Stiles' dance had Bruce Springsteen's Castiles opening for Don & Juan.

By April, I guess the WNJR shows had fizzled out. I was looking to wrap up the I. B. Club shows and needed a new venue. I recall first walking into the Matawan-Keyport Roller Drome and seeing a boxer there named Rocky. Rocky asked me if this was a dangerous neighborhood and I said I didn't think so, as there was a Catholic church across the street. Rocky offered to give me a few pointers on boxing to defend myself. Even though fights would occasionally break out at my dances, I didn't think I needed his self-defense techniques. I usually had a large bodyguard or two with me. However, I politely listened to Rocky as he demonstrated how I could tightly roll up a newspaper to use as a defensive weapon.

Well, the Matawan-Keyport Roller Drome looked perfect, so I started holding shows and dances there. My first show there was on Friday night, April 8, with the Duprees, Motifs and the Soul Set.

Then on April 15, I had the Soul Set and a New York City band, Curtis Knight & the Squires at the Roller Drome. At that time, the Squires had a relatively unknown 23-year-old guitarist named Jimi Hemdrix. Looking back, I can't swear that Hendrix played that dance but I believe he did. If so, it might have been Hendrix's last gig with Curtis Knight's Squires as he quit the group on May 20.

By May, I had decided to stop doing shows at the West End Casino I replaced that venue with Saturday night dances at the Old Village Firehouse on Route 35 in Middletown. As the Firehouse was smaller, I used local groups like the Motifs or the Dekes from Middletown plus the Soul Set. I also had the Jagged Edge there. I kept the bigger Friday night dances going at the Matawan-Keyport Roller Drome. .

The Battle of the Bands

Next, I booked Vito & the Salutations along with the Soul Set into the Matawan-Keyport Roller Drome . When that worked out well, I decided to kick off the weekly shows with a huge "Battle of the Bands" contest. I got the word out that any bands except my own groups could sign up to compete. The response I received was phenomenal. I had bands signing up from Neptune, Perth Amboy, Englishtown and everywhere in between. I limited the entrees to the first 25 that signed up and I had to turn away a number of bands that applied late.

Among the bands that signed up were the Castiles, Rogues, Syndicate, Bronzmen, Dekes, Breed, Beau Monds, Silencers, Henchmen, Roffes, Blue Denims, Prisums,

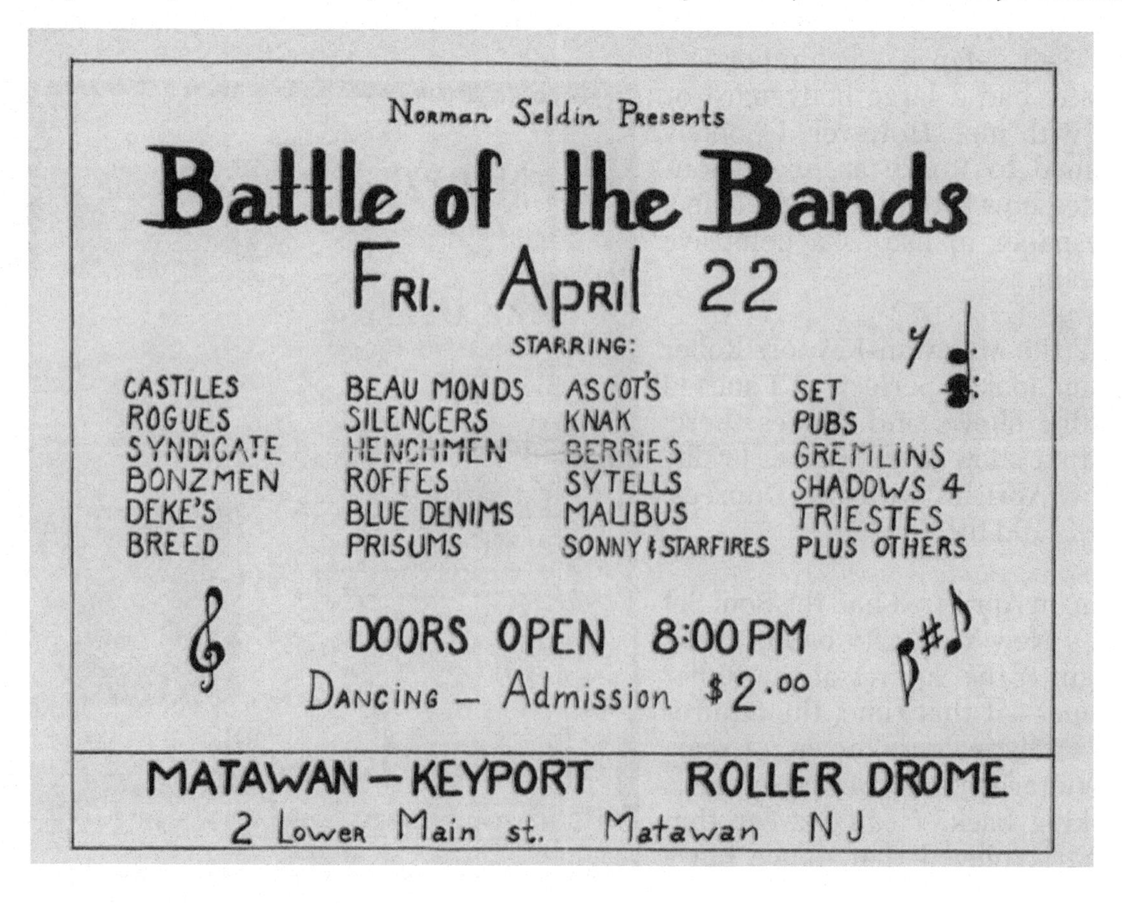

Ascots, Knak, Berries, Syrells. Malibus, Sonny & the Starfires, Set, Pubs, Gremlins, Shadows 4, Triestes, Mags and Brew Masters.

The Rogues of Middletown, New Jersey
Publicity photo

That night, April 22, 1966, each group appeared together in a circle around the perimeter of the skating rink. Bands played three songs each in rotation. I headed a panel of four judges who scored each group on musical sound, appearance, originality and audience reaction. I offered prizes of $100, $50 and $25 to the top three groups. The winners plus any others that were particularly popular with the crowd would be invited back the following week for the big "Show Of The Year."

Future E Street Band member Vini Lopez has said that was where he first met Bruce Springsteen. Vini was playing drums with Sonny & the Starfires and Bruce's group the Castiles were set up next to them. As a matter of fact, it was at my Battle of the Bands that Bruce Springsteen and Vini Lopez first met future Steel Mill band member Vinnie Roslin. As a member of the Motifs, I had Vinnie Roslin as a competition judge.

The Battle of the Bands went well. It drew 1,500 teenagers and is still talked about today. Of course, every band thought they deserved to win. But when it was all over, the judges selected the Rogues (from Middletown), Sonny & the Starfires and the Brew Masters, in that order.

As I promised, the following week I featured three national acts along with eight local bands. Headlining were the Dovells from Philadelphia, known for their song, "Bristol Stomp." I also had the Crystals ("Uptown," "Then He Kissed Me") and the Ad Libs who were just coming off of their Top Ten hit, "The Boy From New York City." My group, the Soul Set, backed the main attractions while the local bands played for dancing.

I also had the previous week's contest winners, the Rogues and Brew Masters and several of the better local groups, including the Dekes, Mods, Breed,

Roffes and the Knak. The multi-group event also served as a birthday celebration for me. That week I turned nineteen.

During the month of May, I continued running dances at the Matawan Keyport Roller Drome. On successive weeks, I booked the Motifs and Jagged Edge; Sonny & the Starfires and the Breed; and Vito & the Salutations and Soul Set.

For my next major concert, I was looking for a really big act. My agent said, "Hey, listen. I've got a shot to get you a really hot group." I asked, "Who do you have for me?" He replied, "I've been booking the Orlons and Len Barry and all those groups for the Roller Drome. Well, there's that group that just opened for the Beatles at Shea Stadium called the Young Rascals."

The Young Rascals Concert

By this time, everyone had heard about the Young Rascals. In 1965, when promoter Sid Bernstein brought the Beatles to America he also happened to be managing the Young Rascals. The August 15 Shea Stadium concert, drew 55,000 screaming fans, the largest crowd in the world to witness a concert at that time. Not only did Bernstein slip the Young Rascals into the concert, he had the electric scoreboard keep flashing "The Rascals Are Coming" throughout the event. By the time I had a chance to have the Rascals at the Matawan Keyport Roller Drome, the blue-eyed soul group's record, "Good Lovin'" was #1 on the music charts.

Well, the Young Rascals were available to me for only $1,000. I said," I'll take it." I booked the Young Rascals for the Roller Drome for Friday, June 3. I would open the concert with the Soul Set. Also on the bill would be the Motifs, Michael, Breed, the Jagged Edge and the Five Old Men, a teenage Red Bank group that put white powder in their hair to make them look old. Bruce Springsteen, Stevie Van Zandt and so many of the future Jersey Shore rock stars were in the audience that night. Of course, they were relatively unknown at that time.

As it turned out, I did not get along with Young Rascals manager, Sid Bernstein, whatsoever. I guess I wasn't used to the demands their manager kept making. Sid and the Rascals showed up and said, "We're going to have to rent an organ." I said,

"You can use mine." Sid said, "My guy needs two Leslie speakers." I said, "I have two up there." He aggravated me so much.

Now, my band was opening that show along with the Motifs and the other groups. The other guys in the Soul Set came to me and asked what song we'd be opening with. I said, "We're opening with 'Good Lovin'." They just looked at me in disbelief and exclaimed, "What?" I said, "I don't like these guys." My guys pleaded, "You can't do that." I said, "Yeah, I can." And I did. We opened with "Good Lovin," in the front of the Young Rascals with the song they were known for. I don't know if the audience loved it or they just clapped for me because they were in shock.

Their manager went crazy. When I came off the stage he called me every name he could think of. Now, one of the guys in my band had given me a little Dr. John cane that I used to carry around like the nightstick. I took the damn stick, broken in half and threw the two pieces at him. I said, "I'm the one paying the bills." He yelled back, "I need to see your boss." I said, "Your looking at the boss." I had just turned nineteen, but opening up a Young Rascals show with their hit record just wasn't something groups did.

After that I started searching out other new venues. In July, I held a dance at the Clearwater Pool along Highway 36 in Highlands, New Jersey, that featured the Soul Set, the Mods, the Dekes, the Exceptions, the Simple Noize and the Vick-ters, a vocal harmony and instrumental group from the Red Bank area that had been appearing regularly at the Pin-Up Lounge in Highlands.

From there, I moved back to the West End Casino Playroom in Long Branch. The Playroom had reopened under the new management of Rennie Jessel. In August, I did a show there with the Broadways. The Broadways had evolved from my old group, the Uniques. Since I'd last booked them, Billy Brown, Ron Coleman, Leon Trent and Ray Morris had signed with *MGM Records* and had a local hit record with a song called "Going Going Gone." For the next two years, the Broadways would be one of the hottest groups around. Billy Brown would eventually become lead of the soul vocal group, the Moments aka Ray, Goodman & Brown.

After that I brought Vito & the Salutations and the Duprees into the West End Casino

Publicity photo of the Broadways. Left to right:
Billy Brown, Leon Trent, Ronald Coleman, Raymond Morris

on different weekends. They shared the stage with the Soul Set. In October the Soul Set participated in a big West End Casino show emceed by WMCA Good Guy, Jack Spector. Besides us, the concert included former Asbury Park resident, and by then international star, Lenny Welch. Also on the bill were the Jive Five, Monty Rock III and the Demitrons

Our group, the Soul Set, was getting lots of work but underwent some personnel changes. Gone was Eddie Wohanka. Eddie would join several local groups including the Jaywalkers before taking the stage name Doc Holiday and moving to Nashville.

There he became a major music producer. I still had Donald Scascia but brought in Jimmy Eldridge from the Marvels to play guitar. We had a good sound so I thought about recording again.

Johnson Records

For some time, I'd been circulating around, finding places to learn more about the music business. I used to visit the Brill Building where *Brunswick Records, Laurie Records* and dozens more companies were located. On one of the floors, I saw a sign on the door proclaiming, *Johnson Records, Jim McCarthy, Publicity*. By chance, my knocking on the door was met by a tall, bald guy. After introducing myself, I asked him his involvement in the music business. Jim McCarthy said, "Well, I'm the publicity agent for the Peter Duchin and Lester Lanin Orchestra." Well, that was high society stuff. I asked him about *Johnson Records* and he explained, "That's my record label." He pointed to a shelf and I saw stacks of records - "Baby Oh Baby" by the Shells and records by the Dubs." Jim McCarthy said, "I'm their manager."

I got to know Jim McCarthy pretty well. Jim at one time had been the publicist for bandleader Buddy Johnson, whose brother Hiram Johnson had started *Johnson Records* back in the 1950's. Jim had bought out Hiram and now owned the label outright. Jim McCarthy was the one who introduced me to the Shells, whom I'd booked extensively. In fact, Jim had let me reissue a couple of his Shells recordings, "Can't Take It" backed with "A Toast To Your Birthday" on my own *Selsom* label. In addition to the great Shells vocals, the sides had King Curtis on sax.

That got me thinking. Here I was releasing all these records by other artists but none by my group, the Soul Set. I mentioned it to Jim McCarthy and he said, "Well, go cut your songs and I'll put them out on the *Johnson* label for you."

So I took the Soul Set to see Pat Jaques at Broadway Recording Studios and we cut two original songs that I had written, "Love, Love, Love" and "Surfin' Boogaloo."

That was an interesting recording session because the bass player, whom we'd hired through Broadway Studios, actually canceled out. I ended up playing keyboard bass. So the intro, the first four or six bars of "Love Love Love," was the bass bringing it to them. And the engineer, Pat Jaques, said," I can get this on there if you want to carry the bass through the whole song." I said, "Yeah, I do." So I did that. I sang lead on both sides. Jimmy Eldridge played guitar and sang backup on the record. And we had a couple horns, of course.

Jim McCarthy even let me redesign the record labels. The old *Johnson* records were orange with "Johnson" written in shadow print across the top. The new labels featured a catchier orange and black checker pattern.

While we were pressing up the record, the Soul Set underwent another reorganization. I brought Dave Brewer into the group to play drums, replacing Donald Scascia. Dave Brewer was a drum teacher. He was originally from Ohio but had moved to Red Bank where he opened a little drum studio. I used to go in there and we'd talk music. So I decided to continue the Soul Set band, at first with just Dave and myself. Then I thought about expanding the Soul Set. I brought in Tony Maples as vocalist and I got back Billy Ryan on guitar, replacing Ernie. The Soul Set was playing places like the Dew Drop Inn in Spring Lake Heights and the Pin-Up Lounge in Highlands, New Jersey. It became the "Soul Set Review."

The Soul Set Review. From left: Norman Seldin, Billy Ryan, Tony Maples, Dave Brewer. Photo by Earl Stout

The Soul Set record. "Love, Love, Love," was officially released the first week of December, 1966. We send out promotional copies to radio stations in those little cardboard mailers. I had to address them by hand or typewriter and put a postcard in with the record.

So one day I got a call from Jim McCarthy and he said, "You're on the charts." I asked "What do you mean I'm on the charts?" He said, "You're on a charts in Virginia Beach and rising."

The first Soul Set single. "Love, Love, Love"

I got in touch with Tom Scott who was the program director and deejay on a white station, WNOR in Norfolk. In those days, all the radio stations published their own printed hit charts that came out weekly. WNOR had listed the record as their "Discovery of the Week" two weeks earlier and now it was up to #30. I drove down there to see Tom Scott who was expecting to see a black guy, but he was very welcoming. So far, WNOR was driving all the excitement about the record. Now, the number one radio station in the Hampton Roads area that included all of Norfolk, Virginia Beach, Newport News, Portsmouth and Chesapeake was not WNOR but a station called WGH. And the most popular show on WGH was hosted by a deejay named Gene Loving. So I asked Tom how I could get the record played on WGH. He said, "Let's do a radio interview and give it a few extra spins and see what happens." Tom was right. Soon different area radio stations were playing "Love, Love, Love" including WGH. My Soul Set record went to the Top 10 on several stations and stayed there for 14 weeks. It was battling it out with songs like "Kind of a Drag" by the Buckinghams.

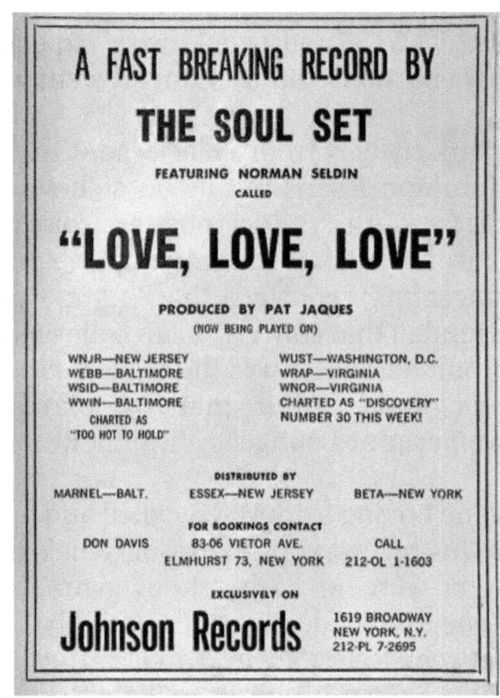

Cashbox ad for "Love, Love, Love"
January 14, 1967

We started getting a lot of ink in the music trade magazine, *Cashbox*, that even ran a photo of the group. By mid January, 1967, "Love, Love, Love" was "breaking fast" (a music term) on stations in New Jersey, Washington, DC, North Carolina, Georgia and Virginia. WWIN in Baltimore labeled the record "Too Hot To Handle" (another good music term).

Then radio station personnel started telling me their audiences wanted to hear me live. So I said, "I'll come down. I'll do the shows." They paid for me to bring the Soul Set down to Virginia Beach. I had to find a substitute guitar player who would go down there and play because my guitar player didn't want to go to Virginia. Actually, I ended up playing those Virginia shows with a substitute drummer, a substitute guitar player and myself on organ. I also did a TV show down there. It was hard lip-syncing to records in those days because I was always afraid the record would skip.

The most popular music along the ocean beaches from Virginia Beach to northern Florida was at that time, and still is, "Beach Music." Beach Music is a genre of rhythm & blues and soul music with a particular beat that audiences could dance 'The Shag" to. In early 1967, when I reached Virginia Beach, the hottest group was a Portsmouth, Virginia-based group called Bill Deal & the Rhondels. Bill Deal & the Rhondels had been playing area clubs, particularly a Virginia Beach oceanfront venue called the Peppermint Lounge. There, the Rhondels' rendition of the Zodiacs' song "May I" was making such a splash, Deal pressed up a few hundred copies on his own *Beach* label to sell to his audience when he played.

We did a show with Bill Deal & the Rhondels at the Virginia Beach Convention Center. The venue was called "The Dome" because of its geodesic dome auditorium. I don't know the capacity of The Dome but it was large enough that at various times it housed concerts by Louis Armstrong, Jimi Hendrix, the Rolling Stones and Ray Charles. Anyway, there was a huge crowd to see us and Bill Deal & the Rhondels. I was nervous because we were up there as just the trio and I was afraid people were expecting a horn section. But the concert went well.

"(Baby) You'll Get It"

Then a deejay from a black radio station in Hampton Roads put us on a show at the Portsmouth Armory not far from where Clarence Clemons grew up. *Cashbox* magazine reported that 1,500 people attended that concert. I can believe it. The promoter said it was the biggest crowd he ever had. After that we played the Peppermint Lounge in Virginia Beach.

Gene Loving from WGH called and had me do his record hops. Most of Gene's record hops were in high school gymnasiums. Gene used to do half court basketball shots between sets and he'd make 9 out of 10 shots from mid court. So, I got to know both Gene Loving and Tom Scott. These guys really pushed that record. I think we sold about 1,500 copies in that area, which is like having a million seller.

Returning to New Jersey the Soul Set continued playing local dances. Guitarist, Billy Ryan, left the group and I replaced him with Ernie Kara from Elizabeth, New Jersey. Tony Maples was off singing with another group and there was really no vocalist in the Soul Set except for me. I think Ernie Kara sang one Lou Christie song. He really wasn't a singer but he could play guitar and he was dependable.

By late spring we had released our second Soul Set record on the *Johnson* label. It was an R&B song called "(Baby) You'll Get It" backed with my rendition of the Ed Townsend ballad, "For Your Love." It didn't do what the first record did but I kept going.

The Purple Onion

In May, 1967, I went up to the Purple Onion in New York. The night club was right there at 135 West 3rd. Street, in the heart of the Greenwich Village. The Village back then was really the birthplace of the folk movement, but I didn't have much sense of folk music. I just walked in off of the street looking for a place my band could play. I don't remember what the financial arrangements were but the Village was jumping. The Blues Magoos , the Lovin Spoonful and even the doo wop groups like the Del Satins were working the same places in the Village. I think maybe Larry Chance might have worked there at one time. But the Purple Onion was a night club with a regular bouncer at the door. If you arrived without a jacket they'd put one on you. They had a stage

NORMAN SELDIN (ORGAN & VOCALS) DAVE BREWER (DRUMS) ERNIE KARA (GUITAR)

and go-go dancers in cages. That was the rage back then. The Purple Union was run by the two Ronga brothers, Joe and Jerry Ronga.

Well, Joe Ronga said he had an opening for a band and we started playing there. I had to make a lot of changes with the band because my guitar player's wife was never keen on him being out more than one or two nights a week. This was a six-nights-a-week gig, so I had to arrange for other guitarists to fill in when he wasn't there. We started playing there and we did pretty well. But it wasn't really soulful. It was just music. We did some songs by Wilson Pickett and Joe Tex and then James Brown. We did a few ballads, but I still hadn't really established my voice yet. Our sets were more just a mixed bag of whatever people would listen and dance to. We're doing a big business there, but it didn't feel right.

We were hired for what was supposed to be a four-week engagement. Well, we ended up playing the Purple Onion every night of the week except Mondays, for eight more weeks, twelve in all - no nights off, no Sundays off nothing. And we played from 9:00 p.m. until quarter of four in the morning. I would commute from Red Bank to the Village every night. I had a guy in the garage across the street park my car. It was $30 a month to park my car in an indoor garage. So we just kept working like that. People were coming from all over to see us.

During our run at the Purple Onion, we decided to cut an album. Actually, "The Soul Set featuring Norman Seldin: Live from the Village Purple Onion," was neither live nor recorded at the Purple Onion. It was about as live as a rubber ball. I think we dubbed in the soundtrack from Shea Stadium or something to get the the crowd noise. The album was cut at Broadway Recording Studios. In retrospect, it might have been better to have left out the crowd noise. But it does give you an idea of the kinds of songs we were playing at the Purple Onion. It was a mix of pop tunes like "If I Were A Carpenter" and soul songs like Joe Tex' "Show Me" and Eddie Floyd's "Knock On Wood." Of course, the music industry was moving away from singles and into albums and at least we could say we had an album released.

The album came out in August 1967. At that time we were booked for an appearance on Joe Franklin's TV show. Joe Franklin hosted a long-running TV show out of New York City where he interviewed entertainers. Franklin's show spotlighted what was going on in entertainment in New York City. The Purple Onion owner, Joe Ronga, heard that the owner of Trude Hellers' club was going to be on Franklin's show and they were also in The Village. So Joe Ronga suggested, "Norman, why don't you go on Joe Franklin's Show to represent the Purple Onion?" What a mistake!

I felt like a little kid in a suit. At best, the Joe Franklin Show was pretty historic in its day, but he had all these strange people on his show with me. It was like the Arthur Godfrey Show with some accordion players. I didn't know what the hell I was getting into. Joe Franklin started asking me to explain the New York entertainment scene. I mean, I hadn't been on the New York scene, but two months.

The show was done live so there would be no second takes. During the interview Joe decided to play a cut from my new album. As soon as he put the thing on, the record skipped for the first five seconds. Then it played a little and skipped the next four or five bars. So Joe stopped the record and started it over again. I was just sitting there horrified. It was like a bad dream. I couldn't wait to get off the air.

Afterwards, everybody told me, "You were great on the Joe Franklin Show." Either they were just being kind or they were just thrilled too see somebody they knew on TV. But it was horrible.

While we were still at the Purple Onion, I started having trouble with my drummer. Dave couldn't do some of the gigs so I called Barry Lynn. You may recall, Barry had been the musical director for Vito & the Salutations who had impressed me so much as a drummer. I asked, "Barry, would you consider coming over and playing a night or two to fill in?" Well, Barry came to play and everything changed that night. Needless to say, Barry Lynn became my new drummer.

After the Purple Onion I started picking up more local jobs. One was the NCO Club (non-commissioned officers club) at Fort Monmouth. The NCO Club asked me to put together a show there. I asked what kind of entertainment they wanted. They said well, R&B and all kinds of music. I asked if they'd be interested in a black comedian. They said, "We don't mind as long as he's entertaining." Jocko was the one who suggested I use Timmie Rogers.

Timmie Rogers

I didn't know a whole lot about Timmie Rogers at that time, so I started reading up about him. Having been in show business since the 1940's, Rogers broke racial barriers as one of the first black stand-up comedians to perform solo in front of white audiences without playing a character. He was a frequent guest on television shows like *The Jackie Gleason Show.* Timmie was known for the phrase, "Oh Yeah!" He played a tipple and told jokes and we knew we could play songs with him. At the time, Timmie was living in nearby Philadelphia. So, I booked him for the show at The NCO Club.

When we met him at Fort Monmouth, he looked at us and said, "Y'all are an all-white band!" I said, "Yeah, but don't worry about it." We rehearsed a couple songs and he said, "This is the craziest thing I've ever seen." Timmie told us that he thought we were one of the blackest sounding white bands he ever worked with. He was telling us about working the Apollo and he asked me if I had any records by comedians who played there. I said, "Yeah, I've got the first two albums by Pigmeat Markham and Moms Mabley. He almost fell over. He said, "You mean there's a white person that knows about them?" I said, "Yeah. Their material is a little off color, though." He said, "Off color? Redd Foxx was Red Buttons compared to them."

At the Fort Monmouth NCO Club.
From left: Timmie Rogers, Norman Seldin, Barry Lynn, Ernie Kara
Photo by Earl Stout

I told Timmie, "Just go out there and make them laugh" and he said he would. And he did. The audience laughed so hard they cried. My drummer fell off of the back of the stage he was laughing so hard. He'd been about a foot from the riser and he just went over on his ass. He took the snare drum with him. I said, "Where'd you go?" He said, "This man's killing me." He crawled back up and we finished the show.

Eventually, Ernie, my guitar player, quit the Soul Set to spend more evenings with his wife. We picked up a new guy, Freddy Billand. Freddy sang harmony okay and played guitar. He looked good on stage and was a fun kind of guy. He used to sound like Jimmy Clanton when he sang "Just a Dream." Of course he would hold his nose to get a nasally kind of sound. It was just that kind of thing, but it worked. There were three of us and we kept working. We didn't really pick up a lot of jobs. We played the Boom Boom Room in Paterson, New Jersey and the Hoffman House in Point Pleasant.

Then I got a call from Jimmy Lamare, who years before had run the big entertainment agency General Artists Corporation (GAC). Jimmy had opened his own booking agency and he said, "Well, when you get ready give me a call."

At the time I didn't know who he was. I later found out Jimmy had been the baritone sax player with the Charlie Barnet Orchestra back in the 1940s. During that time he'd made a lot of contacts.

Massena, New York

Jimmy Lamare called me and asked, "Do you want some work?" I replied, "Yeah, where's the job?" He said, "Massena. New York." I'd never heard of the place so I asked, "Where in the hell is Massena, New York?" He said, "It's a long, long, long ride. It's on the border of Cornwall, Ontario, and the Saint Lawrence Seaway." I thought that must be the end of the world but I took the job anyway.

My drummer and guitar player, of course, were all excited as the job paid well. But Jimmy told me that I had to make sure I was paid in American money because it was on the Canadian border. A lot of times clubs up there gave bands Canadian money as it was not worth as much as American dollars at the time.

So we drove up there. I was asked to take a go-go dancer with me because there were none up there. They'd supply rooms and all but it was my job to bring a good looking dancer up to there. They would pay the dancer and I'd bring her back home again. So I went in New York and picked up the dancer, who was gorgeous. It would made my couple of weeks up there a little bit nicer.

At the time, I had just purchased a brand new Jaguar XKE and I didn't realize how cold it was in Massena in late November. I found out that sometimes they'd get upwards of 24 to 30 inches of snow and the temperature could be 8 to 10 degrees below

From the left: Norman Seldin, Barry Lynn, Freddy Billand.
My new Jaguar XKE. Photo by Earl Stout.

zero. So, we got there, and of course, getting the Hammond organ inside the place was always a chore, because we carried our own instruments then.

We met the owner who said, "I'm glad you guys could make it. You can come in this door here." He opened up this big metal door. While we're carrying in the Hammond organ he let the door go and smashed into me and the guys carrying the organ. It was going to be that kind of gig. I said, "Oh my God. I signed up for two weeks of this?"

We got all the equipment up on the stage and I noticed that there was nobody really in Massena to speak of. It wasn't a big town but we were in a nice motel and I had my Jaguar. Before I left New Jersey, a friend told me, "You're going to Massena? Just remember, with the cold temperatures up there, you'll have to change the oil in your car so it won't will freeze up." I had the XKE and I didn't think any more about it.

I think they extended our stay by three or four weeks once we were up there. The owner really liked us. But I woke up one morning and went to open the door to the outside. I couldn't open the door. The snow had drifted about three and a half feet high. The entire parking lot was covered. I mean, I couldn't even see my car.

Well, I called the office and said, "This is Norman." The owner said, "Oh, you're experiencing our first snowfall of the season." I said, "Snowfall? How the hell do I get my car out?" He was a lot calmer than I was. He just said, "Your Jaguar? You'll probably have to let it sit for three or four days until the weather gets a little warmer.

You're not going to be able to start it." I asked, "How am I supposed to get work?" He said, "Well, they'll plow through and we'll get you to the club tonight." Because all our gear was already there.

So we went and we played. All the club's business came from across the border because the drinking age in New York was 18 then. Across the border, in Cornwall, Ontario, it was 21. So we played to about 400 people on a night when there was three foot of snow. By the end of the night they had the road cleared, but I could not start my car for almost four days. And it was a new Jaguar.

I actually started dating some of the girls from Canada and would give them a ride home. You had to cross a bridge to go over the Saint Lawrence River to Cornwall, Ontario, from New York. The toll was 50 cents or $1.

Well, one night, one of the girls had stayed until the club closed. Around 4:30 in the morning, I was taking her back over to Canada. When I came to the border there was a guy there with all these gold medals on his uniform. I figured he must have been the head of security for the Canadian border. He was looking at the Jersey plates and the Jaguar. He asked, "And your purpose for coming to Canada is?" I answered, "Well, I'm dropping off a guest, a Canadian resident, from the Massena club."

I had the window rolled down and the girl crawled across and she said, "Good morning, daddy." It was her father. Visions of going directly to Canadian prison immediately flashed before my eyes. The guy asked, "A little late, isn't it?" The girl said, "Well, the weather was a little rough." He said, "Yeah, yeah, yeah." So I continued across the bridge and all the toll lights on six different lanes started blinking when I went through. The girl said, "Oh, my dad's just saying hello." I saw 20 lights blinking on and off at one time. I guess he was just happy to see his daughter had made it home.

While I was in Massena, I got to go into Canada when I wasn't working. I went to see Ike & Tina Turner perform and got to meet and talk to Redd Foxx. He was sitting at the back of the concert stage talking to people. I also drove two hours to Montreal to hear Oscar Peterson and Andre Previn play. They threw a piano clinic together. That kind of cinched it for me that I'd never be a great jazz player. I heard those two and I said, "This is more than I can handle." I was 20 years old. Listening to them, my mouth just dropped open. I thought, "If I practiced an additional ten hours a day, I'd still be so far behind them I'd never catch up." So much was going on it all just became just a blur.

It was a unique experience and I spent a lot of time playing up there. From there, we hooked up with all the college towns. I mean, we were loaded with work. I don't think I got back to my apartment in Sea Bright very often over that six months period. Each time, before I left, I gave the landlord a check for three or four months and said, "I'll see you when I get back."

We just kept playing. We ended up at Endicott, New York, Middletown, New York, The State University of New York College at Oneonta, New York and Colgate University in Hamilton, New York. In fact, I played that show with Larry Chance & the Earls and the Chambers Brothers who sang, "The Time Has Come Today." The Chambers Brothers were the featured act, Larry Chance was the middle act, and we were the opening band. We had a huge crowd.

Then it was back to New Jersey at the Dew Drop Inn in Spring Lake Heights and a dance at Ocean County College with Philadelphia radio disc jockey, Hy Lit. We did a weekend at the College Inn in the Catskills.

In March of 1968, we were back at the Purple Onion in New York City. This time we'd added a 5,000 watt light show. The light show included strobes, kaleidoscopes, mirror balls, fog and color spotlights. The lights would blink in nine colors to the beat of the music. We kept adding to the act. I had a magician friend who had a pretty good act himself. He fixed up this thing, the original light show, in which we just basically put stuff on a mirror and amplified it through a projector to the stage. He also taught me how to eat fire on stage with these torches. He made me torches. It was pretty cool for the time. I had the first area band to bring a light show out, but it wasn't all that complicated. It was effective and it worked. We also added a singer, Tony Sal, and we packed the club every night.

And it was time for our third single on the *Johnson* label. "With My Baby Behind Me" and "I Don't Want Her But I Need Her" were both written by Ray Dahrouge. You may recall, I recorded Ray when he was with the Darchaes although I called them Barbaroso & the Historians. Ray was well on his way to becoming an extraordinary songwriter and arranger.

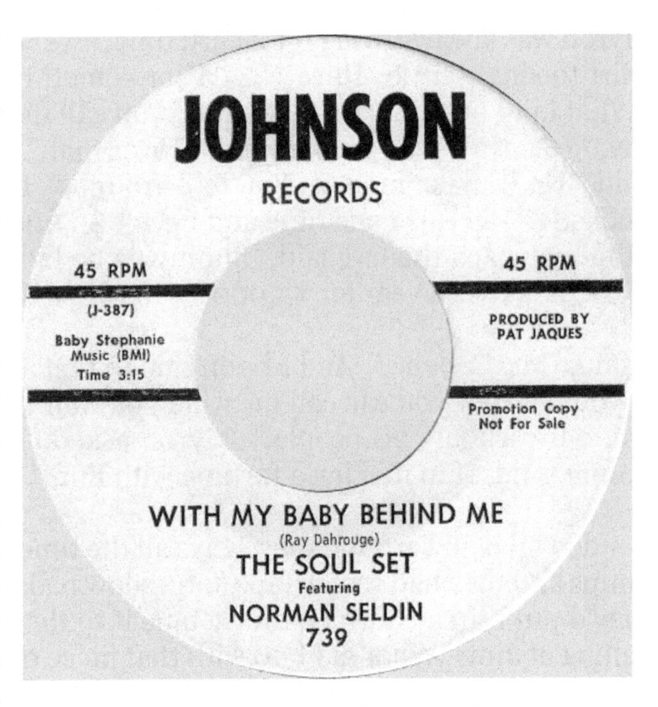

"With My Baby Behind Me"
Written by Ray Dahrouge

In April and May we moved our music and light show to the Down Sea Lounge in Sea Bright. We were doing this novelty song called "Here Comes The Judge." The TV show, *Laugh In* was big then and the record was based on some of the silly things from the show. It was basically an instrumental with Barry Lynn playing the drums. He'd cut in with *Laugh In* sayings like Artie Johnson's "very interesting." We issued it as a record on the *Johnson* label. It was a goof record and it wasn't very saleable. But we wanted a follow-up record, so we put it out. The flip side was "I'm Gonna Love You," another of my compositions.

Myron Cohen
Publicity photo

We just fell into a lot of stuff because of Jimmy Lamare. He booked all the big acts in Seaside Heights. He booked Jackie Wilson on the boardwalk. Jimmy was the one who really taught me how to book acts. And I was booking the Duprees, Larry Chance and the Earls, Johnny Thunder and others.

At that time I had my afro hair style, which was out of control. Jimmy had moved to a different scaled down office. I walked in one time and saw an old man sitting next to him. It was Myron Cohen, the comedian famous for his Yiddish-based dialect humor. Jimmy had a sense of humor as well and said, "Myron, I want you to meet my Jewish friend." Myron turned around, looked at me with my big afro and said, "He's a schwarzes. What do you mean he's a Jew?"

Myron was always giving me a hard time. Every time I walked into the office, he would start to sing a little "Hava Nagila" or something, just to make fun of me. He'd say, "What kind of hair is that? What do you call that?" I said, "It's an afro." Myron would say, "You can't even wear a yamaka over that." I said, "Well, I'm making money." He said, "No, I make money. You fool around." I overheard Myron talking about being booked for a cruise one time and he got $5,000 for the weekend. Now that was a lot of money back then. I said, "Jimmy, is he kidding?" Jimmy said, "Norman, he can work 52 weeks a year for $5,000 - $10,000 a week. Everybody wants him."

I said, "Mr. Cohen..." And Myron said in that Jewish accent, "You can call me Myron. If you're a Jew you can call me what you want." Jimmy said, "Listen, this kid Norman can outwork any 20 people." Myron asked, "Do you make money with him?" And Jimmy said, "I'm making a fortune with him."

I ended up being around those guys all the time. They had one of those old green desk lamps and they had scotch tape and yellow pads. Whenever they got a booking, before they'd put it in a contract, they'd tape it to the damn lamp. I can still picture Myron yelling at Jim, "What did I do with that piece of paper from yesterday?"

Then Jimmy came to me one day and asked, "Do you want to go back to Massena?" I said, "No, not right away." So, Jimmy asked, "Then, how would you feel about doing an audition?" Now, I didn't do auditions. I never did. I was a cocky kid. But Jimmy was persuasive. "Just for 20 minutes." I asked, "Where?" And he said, "Right in Manhattan. Just take a keyboard and set it up. Bring your drummer. There are drums already over there. Just do me a favor and play two or three songs for my friend."

Sam Donahue
Publicity photo

So we went to the Playboy Club on East 59th Street between 5th Avenue and Madison Avenue. The Manhattan establishment was one of Hugh Hefner's exclusive night clubs accessible only to those members holding a Playboy Club key. Inside were plush, dimly lit Playmate bars, dining rooms, cabarets, and club rooms all serviced by the Playboy bunny waitresses.

I don't know if anybody even listened to us that day. Jimmy Lamare told me the music director at the Playboy Club was Sam Donahue. Sam had been a sax player with a number of big bands including those of Tommy Dorsey, Benny Goodman, Woody Herman, and Stan Kenton. Jimmy had known Sam since the 1940's. So Jimmy said, "You need to go upstairs and see Sam." I said, "Okay."

"THE SOUL SET"

Featuring **Norman Seldin**
In Person—Mon. thru Sat.

AT

PLAYBOY CLUB

NEW YORK CITY

Exclusively Booked By
JIMMY LAMARE AGENCY
1697 Broadway
New York, N. Y.
212-JU2-1364

I walked upstairs and there was a guy sitting there with a saxophone. He was writing an arrangement for a 12 piece band, He looked up and said, "You must be Jimmy's friend." I said, "Yeah, I'm Norman, I came here to audition." He replied, "Oh yeah, by the way, you're hired." I asked, "I'm hired?" He said, "Yeah, you can start this week. And by the way, please don't take the Playboy Bunnies home with you."

I remember coming in there with Barry that first night. For members of the band, every drink was only $1. I didn't drink, but Barry was a Southern Comfort guy. We were getting set up and somebody was in the dressing room. Sam said, "Do me a favor. Go in there and tell that guy that we don't need him anymore." I said, "Who is he?" Sam replied, "He's the former drummer. Just go tell him we don't need him anymore."

So, I walked into the dressing room and said, "I'm Norman and I was told to deliver you a message. You're not working here anymore. I'm very sorry, I don't know your name but they just told me to deliver that message." He said, "I'm Gene Krupa." I was just standing there in disbelief. I walked outside and said to my drummer, "I just fired Gene Krupa." Barry said, "What? Did you get his autograph?" I replied, "No, I didn't." He said, "We're taking his trio's place?" I answered, "You got it." Now, the first band that Sam Donahue ever played with was Krupa's band, so I don't know what went down between those two. But, you never forget things like that.

The job at the Playboy Club featured my new guitarist, Freddy Billand, a.k.a. Freddy London. The shows were doing well and we were working steady. The fact that I could afford to buy a Jaguar gives you an idea of how well I was doing financially. Once we had a job up in Middletown, New York. On my trip there, a drunk driver ran a red light and ran right over the hood of my Jaguar. The steering wheels were wood in the Jags and I remember having about 50 splinters in my hands because I had such a tight hold on the steering wheel. The woman basically rolled up onto it with her '57 Buick - the model with those big bumpers. She destroyed my car. It took six months to get it fixed because there was a dock strike. But the shows went well and I kept going back and forth.

LIVE – IN PERSON
Direct from N.Y.'s
PLAYBOY CLUB!
Every
WED., THURS., FRI.
SAT. & SUN. NITE
"THE SOUL SET"
Featuring NORMAN SELDIN
5 SEASON'S BELMAR RT. #71
Coming! The Earls – Johnny Thunder
Call Now for Reservations!
681-9605

Rehearsing Larry Chance & the Earls at Broadway Recording Studios in New York

In December, 1968, we moved into Tom Breslin's 5 Seasons on Route 71 in Belmar, New Jersey. We ended up playing there five nights a week. In addition, I was given the job of producing shows there with big name groups. Naturally, I started bringing in acts like Johnny Thunder, Vito & the Salutations and a soul group from Brooklyn called the Invitations, who had been recording for *MGM Records* and had recently returned from a tour of Europe. I also brought in Larry Chance & the Earls who I was managing at the time. I think I had

When Broadway Recording Studios moved to a new location
Jimmy Lamare and I took out an ad in Billboard magazine congratulating them
and listing some of the groups I was managing.

Larry Chance and the Earls were at the 5 Season's four times over the winter months.

From there it was back up to the Willow Grove Restaurant in Massena, New York. Meanwhile, while performing with the Soul Set, I was also managing a number of groups including the Earls, the Vibrators, the Lil Giants and a blue-eyed soul group called Bread & Water. I did this through Selsom Productions - Management in cooperation with the Jimmy Lamare Agency.

Throughout the summer of 1969, the Soul Set played the 24 Karat Room of the new Castaway Motel in Long Branch. We played there four-nights-a-week and sometimes brought in other acts like Larry Chance and the Earls.

Horse Racing

It was about this time that I developed an interest in thoroughbred horse racing. Not just betting on the ponies but owning and racing them. Actually, my initial exposure to horse racing was a betting story.

I remember the first time I ever went to the racetrack. It was the Rumson Handicap. I was with a number of people and they had a big table up top and of course, they were betting on a certain horse. I got very nervous when they sent me down to bet on that horse. I had a hundred dollars of my own money, which was a fortune then. And they gave me 600 bucks and said, "Put it all to win on number eight." I got down to the window. I had the program and I was shaking. I looked down at the program and automatically said, "Give me $600 to show on number three." Now once they punch the tickets, you own them. When I realized what I'd done I said, "Oh my God, I bet on the wrong horse." It was my friend's horse but it didn't even belong in the race. The horse was called Do Sparkle. I was thinking, "How do I explain this to these guys up top? What am I going to tell them?

24 KARAT ROOM

TWO SHOWS TONIGHT....

Norman Seldin's

"THE SOUL SET"

Directly from N. Y. C. "Playboy Club and Living Room"

For Reservations Phone 229-1000

New Castaways Motel

BATH AND OCEAN AVENUES LONG BRANCH, N. J.

I actually stayed downstairs and was watching the race on TV while I figured out what I'm going to tell these guys when this race is over. Well, the bell went off and there was Do Sparkle and he was fifth but he was trapped. And I said, "Oh, shit." Well, all of a sudden, coming around the turn, one of the horses kind of broke down and knocked three of the horses about 20 feet wide. And there was a hole big enough to drive a Cadillac through. Here came the Do Sparkle through the hole. He finished third and I had him to show which paid $68. And I had it 300 times.

So I went back upstairs and I pulled my first joke of the racetrack. I said, "Guys." They said, "Man, I cannot believe we bet on that horse." The horse they bet on finished sixth. I said, "Well, I made a mistake and I didn't bet on the right horse." And the one fellow said, "Oh, that's wonderful. Great, good start." So I laid all this money down on the table. I said, "But I did bet on the horse that finished third." So they made thousands and thousands of dollars.

That was the start of another partial career. I got more involved with horses when the Soul Set was playing at the Castaways. The club was only a five minute drive from Monmouth Park Race Track. Freddy was good friends with Barry Pearl, one of the jockeys. They call them bug riders or apprentice riders. These kids were young, maybe 18 or 19 years old and they only weighed about 100 pounds. And Barry liked to sing. He came out to see us at the Castaways and said, "Can I sing a song with the band? I

One of my horses, Two Batons, winning at Monmouth Racetrack.

can do Wilson Picket's 'Midnight Hour.'" Well Freddy looked at me and said, "Well, I told everybody at the racetrack that he was going to sing." And they showed up in droves, every jockey, whether they were 21 or 45, just to hear him sing. And where the jockeys went, the girls went. I said, "This is crazy. I need a horse."

Norman Seldin, Stormin' Norman (the horse)
and trainer, Benny Williams
Photo by Earl Stout

For those not familiar with horse racing, most common thorough-bred races are what are called claiming races. A claiming race is a type of horse race in which the horses running in the race are all for sale at a set claming price. Before the race begins, any licensed horse owner can put in a secret claim to buy any one of the horses once the race begins. Win or lose, the new owner purchases the horse for the claim price. If the horse wins, the old owner keeps the purse, but has to sell the horse.

Horses are evaluated based on the amount of money they have the potential to win. When a horse wins a race, its value increases and you can race it again in a claiming race with a higher purse. The ideal situation is to have your horse win and not be claimed, so you can race it again at a higher price claiming race. Of course, there's considerable risk in claiming a horse that you know little about. It could race poorly or get injured, in which case, it's value would decrease from what you just paid.

In the racing business, claiming a horse requires preparation. First you need to get a license. But you still have to own a horse that you've run at that racetrack before you're able to claim somebody else's horse. Fortunately, a trainer from Red Bank that my family knew said, "Well, I've got one that I can sell you." It was a Connecticut-bred horse and I renamed it. At that time all the jockeys called me Stormin' Norman because I was always so busy and on the go. So I named the horse "Stormin Norman." I had to file papers that said, "You officially own the name of 'Stormin' Norman' internationally." So if the horse did well and went to race in France, the name was still Stormin' Norman. Other people have since used the name Stormin' Norman but I was the first to register it everywhere.

Now, Stormin' Norman, the horse, couldn't outrun you or me. But he did win a race at Penn National. I wasn't there that night but they put a strange rider on him and if he won by a nose, he won by a lot. But he did win and it enabled me to start claiming other horses.

One night. I claimed a horse called Northern Arrival in Monmouth Park and the owner was so mad that he chased me. This was an older trainer and he wanted to kill me. I claimed this horse for $3,500 and he won the race. All of a sudden one of the jockeys said, "You need to leave now. The owner was hoping nobody would claim his horse and he wants to flat out kill you." My Jaguar was parked very close so I headed for it. One of my friends said, "Where are you going?" I said, "As far away as I can get today." So I left and came back the next day. My trainer, Benny Williams, said, "Man, that man wanted to kill you yesterday. It was all that I could do to just get the reins back from the horse that you own." So I said, "What are we going to do with him, Benny?" Benny said,"We're going to run him." I said, "We'll run him for at least $6,000." Everybody started laughing." But we ran him for $6,000, he won again by two lengths. So I got the purse and all the money that I had claimed him for, and nobody claimed him.

One of the jockeys, Kevin Whitley, was actually my roommate for a while. Kevin wasn't doing so well at Monmouth Park. so we sent him up to a very small track called Lake Canandaigua up in the Finger Lakes region in New York. He just couldn't win down here, but up there we figured he'd be the king of the place. So when it came time for Northern Arrival to run again, I brought Kevin back from the Finger Lakes to ride. Everybody ridiculed me. I was in the stall and they were saying, "You bought this little jockey who couldn't even win at Monmouth Park, all the way from Finger Lakes to ride this piece of crap." They said, "How could you run this horse in the $15,000 Jersey-bred Stakes Race at the Meadowlands?" Art Stock, who owned all of the Art Stock night clubs was also running two horses in that race.

Well, the bell rang and I didn't even look because of all the crap I'd been getting. Then I heard my trainer say, "Hit him again" and I looked up at the TV. My horse was three lengths out front. I looked up at the board and my horse was 38 to 1 odds. He brought him across the finish line first. The daily double paid $1,900 and he paid $78 to win. So I just kept claiming horses from then on for a while, and I played music at the same time.

Incidentally, I played a kind of cupid role with Kevin Whitley and his girlfriend. Before leaving for the Finger Lakes race track, Kevin was dating a lovely young lady named Nancy Pierce from West Long Branch. I told him he would be crazy not to marry this wonderful girl. She is now Mrs. Kevin Whitley. The Whitley's have been happily married for more than 30 years. They are living in Tampa, Florida, and have a wonderful son.

Jockey Baseball

When not racing, jockeys from different racetracks entertained themselves with other competitive sports like playing baseball. The Monmouth Park jockeys had arranged to play jockeys from a New York track. Now the New York jockeys were good enough to play in the major leagues. Unfortunately. the jockeys from Monmouth Park, in spite

Northern Arrival ridden by Kevin Whitley wins the
$15,000 Jersey-bred Stakes Race at the Meadowlands by three lengths.

of being among the fittest athletes in the world, were the worst baseball players I'd ever seen in my life. I'd never seen anything so uncoordinated anywhere. But they had this game coming up so they asked, "Norman, will you be our coach?" I said, "I'm a musician." They pleaded, "Come on, Stormin', be our coach." So I finally said, "All right."

Now, they did have a few good players. Future Hall of Fame jockey Craig Perrett, who even then was one of the leading riders in the world, was a superb shortstop. And Kevin Whitley was great at third base. Beyond that, one other kid could pitch a little. But most of the others didn't even know if they batted right- or left-handed. I handed one kid the bat and he actually went up to bat holding the top of the bat instead of the handle. I asked, "What are you doing?" And he said, "Well, I'm going to hit it." I said, "Are you right-handed or the left-handed?" He looked puzzled and said, "I don't know, I can use a whip with both hands."

Well, I coached them and I coached them. So we went to this game and there were people from New York beating these conga drums. It was enough to drive you crazy. I stood there watching this New York team warm up by whipping the ball around the infield at 70 miles an hour. It was as if they've been playing since they were two years-old. Our shortstop Craig Perrett said, "Norman, this doesn't look good. "We might get ourselves an ass-whooping tonight." I just said, "I don't know. Let's just see how we play this."

We actually hung in there going into the last inning. There was so much noise, I couldn't hear myself think. Amazingly, we were only down by two runs and we had guys on first and second with two out. Our next scheduled batter had been hurt. Craig said, "What are you going to do? You have no pinch hitter." I looked around and the kid who didn't know which end of the bat to hold was the only one I had left on the bench. I reminded Craig, "We've got one. We've got Jimmy." Craig said, "Oh, Lord, Norman. Why don't we just give up and go home?"

I said, "Jimmy, you're up to bat." "What?" I said, "You're going to bat." I gave him a bat and I said, "Just listen to me. Do what I've been telling you. Just watch the ball. This is slow pitch so the ball will arc high in the air. When it gets about two feet in front of you just keep your eye on the ball and swing."

Well, Jimmy missed the first pitch by about six feet. The guys on our bench said, "Pack it up and let New York take it home." Well, the second pitch came and I heard this loud crack. The ball must have gone 300 feet. This kid hit a walk off home run that won the game. It's one of those thrills you don't ever forget. I had millionaire jockeys swarming around me, hugging me like I was something special. And this poor kid, I don't think he even realized he'd hit a home run. I yelled, "Please just touch all the bases."

The Soul Set, 1969.
From left: Harry Ray, Norman Seldin, Barry Lynn, Freddy Billand
Photo by Earl Stout

The Return of Harry Ray

Then finally, when we were doing the gigs on the Jersey Shore, Harry Ray joined the band. He had left the Valtairs a couple years earlier and gone into the Army. When he came out of the Army, he gave me a phone call. He said, "It's Harry. You wouldn't possibly give me an audition to join the Soul Set, would you?"

I said, "An audition? You start Wednesday night." I put him in there and put him up front. That, again, created another sensation with him just being so good. It didn't take him long to get the stage presence back that he had with the Valtairs.

Afterwards, I tried to promote him to everybody from Motown on down., I said, "This kid is untouchable, he's sensational." And they said, "Yeah, well, there are plenty of sensational black singers." I said, "No, no, no. Not when the guy sings the first four bars and you're ready to cry. No, there are not many like Harry." I would say, "Harry, can you do some Smokey Robinson?" And Harry would say, "Oh yeah." He'd start to sing and it was just like when he was back with the Valtairs.

So, then I had him, Barry the guitar player, Freddy London and me. We had a band that could do everything from Sly and the Family Stone to "The Book of Love" by the Monotones. It didn't make any difference to us. I remember one time a fellow came walking in and caused a big stir. He took all the attention away from the band. And Harry said, "That's Walt Frazier of the New York Knicks." And it was. Walt was in the middle of leading the Knicks to an NBA Championship that year.

We finished out the summer of 1969 playing the Castaways, sometimes sharing the bill with the Chris Lowell Trio, containing drummer Buddy Lowell and his wife Chris as vocalist. From there we moved to Luciano's in Lodi, New Jersey where we shared the bill with the Spiral Staircase who had just scored with the million selling record, "More Today Than Yesterday."

On Prejudice

Throughout my career, I never thought much about the race or religion of my band members. To me, a good musician was a good musician. On more occasions that I can count, though, I've had prejudice thrust on me. I thought nothing of booking all black and integrated bands into traditionally white clubs. In many cases I guess I broke the color barrier, for which I'm glad. This was, of course, the late 1960's and the Civil Rights Movement was in full swing. But I can't tell you how many gigs I lost by insisting on using black musicians. More than once, I came out of a club after a job with an integrated band to find the words "N***** LOVING JEW BASTARD" scratched onto the hood of my Jaguar. I'd take the car to my body shop and the owner would say, "Not you again."

End Of An Era

As the sun came up on the morning of January 1, 1970, I began to realize how much my world had changed in just the past couple of years..

Gone was the Matawan-Keyport Roller Drome. In August of 1968 it was consumed by a huge fire. When the smoke cleared only the brick walls were left.

Mickey Holiday abruptly left the Jaywalkers before a 1967 concert in Grand Rapids, Michigan to dedicate his life to God. I don't know if he had a premonition, but he was replaced by organist David Heth who happened to be at that Grand Rapids concert. Heth then joined the Jaywalkers full-time but a a few months later in February 1968 was killed in an automobile accident after playing the Upstage Club in Asbury Park. After that, the Jaywalkers called it quits.

In 1969, Billy Brown left the Broadways to gain fame as the lead singer of the soul group, the Moments. That spelled the end of the Broadways, though Leon Trent continues performing to this day. Eventually, the Moments would also claim my Soul Set vocalist, Harry Ray, but that was still in the future.

Walter Cichon

The Motifs had been going strong until Walter Cichon was drafted and sent to Viet Nam in the fall of 1968. On March 30, 1968, in Kantom, his platoon members said he emerged from a trench with a hand grenade and was shot in the head. Walter's body was never recovered and he was listed missing in action and presumed dead. I kept thinking Walter was a survivor and he'd return. But it was not to be. Walter was only 21. The Motifs continued on for awhile but it was not the same. Vinnie Roslin would leave the remaining Motifs and by 1970 joined Bruce Springsteen, Vini Lopez and Danny Federici in the group Child, that became Steel Mill. Years later, Bruce would write the song "The Wall" about a man visiting the Vietnam Veterans Memorial in Washington, D.C., searching for his deceased friend's name on the black wall. It was written in honor of Walter Cichon.

Within six months, racial tensions in Asbury Park would explode, leaving Springwood Avenue in flames. Asbury Park would take decades to recover. And the West Side, the area that gave me such an education in black music, would never be the same.

My band would continue on. But with a new era came a knew name and a new start. From then on, Soul Set would be the Joyful Noyze.

Chapter Seven
A Joyful Noyze

With a new decade my band received a new name, the Joyful Noyze. Psalm 100 says, "Make a joyful noise unto the Lord, all ye lands. Serve the Lord with gladness: come before his presence with singing." I guess it was my childhood religious upbringing but the name Joyful Noyze just seemed to fit.

Initially, the personnel stayed the same as the Soul Set: Barry Lynn on drums; Freddy London on guitar; Harry Ray handling much of the vocals; and me on keyboards. Freddy London's real name was Freddy Billand. He just used London as a stage name.

The Joyful Noyze, 1970. Left to right: Harry Ray, Barry Lynn, Fred London, Norman Seldin. Photo by Earl Stout.

The Wigwam: Waldorf, Maryland

While we were working the Castaways, some of the racetrack jockeys told me about the nightlife in Waldorf, Maryland. They were familiar with the area because there were so many racetracks down in Maryland. They kept telling me, "You've got to get the band down here." I'd never heard of the place but a few of my horses had run there. The jockeys said, "Oh, you've got to meet Ted. He owns a place there called the Wigwam Restaurant." So, I took the Joyful Noyze there with Barry, Freddy and Harry.

The Wigwam Restaurant, Waldorf, Maryland (postcard)

The Wigwam was located on Route 31, between Waldorf and LaPlata, Maryland. At one time this two mile strip of highway housed about a dozen eating, drinking and slot machine emporiums, of which the Wigwam was one. In its heyday, thousands of people used to come from afar to play the slots every weekend. There were nine or ten motels there, all in a row, each containing around 200 rooms.

The year before we went to Waldorf, the state of Maryland banned gambling and all the slot machine emporiums were forced to find other ways to draw in people. Several had turned to bringing in major name entertainers.

As our trailer loaded with the B3 organ and all of our music equipment was pulling in, we saw these huge advertising signs. It was like a miniature version of the Las Vegas Strip. The next thing we noticed was a big glass wigwam. As I soon found out, the tepee-shaped structure housed a supper club. I looked up at one of the nearby signs and it read, "Appearing this weekend - Fats Domino." I thought, "Oh, geez God. What have I gotten into?" I remembered the owner had told me, "Don't worry. You're going to do great. They're going to love you here."

Next door was an even bigger place called the Stardust Inn. The Stardust was a horseshoe shaped motel surrounding a pool and anchored by a nightclub containing 80 bowling lanes. It was the biggest bowling alley I'd ever seen in my life. The club was in the front and they had Fats Domino there. Before that they'd had Jerry Lee Lewis. Those were some pretty heavy heads to be bucking up against and this was my first time really, with a whole band, down south. They had us staying in the motel. All the truckers stayed there because they had a good restaurant up front.

When I first got to Waldorf, they tried to be accommodating and asked, "Would you like to come to church with us on Sunday?" They were quite religious in southern Maryland. I politely said, "Well, to be truthful, I appreciate it, but I'm Jewish." The fellow said, "A Jew? What the hell is that? There was a guy sitting at the bar who overheard the conversation and remarked, "Oh, hell, we got one of those across the railroad tracks. Damn Jew owns everything." I sat there saying to myself, "Oh my God." That's when I realized I wasn't in Kansas anymore.

The fellow at the bar kept talking. "Yeah, my neighbor, he shot a black kid for being on his property." I just listened and thought, "What the hell goes on down here?" He added, "Well, I warned him not to but he shot him on his own property so they never charged the guy." I thought, "Oh, shit!" I'd never heard anything like that. I didn't know whether to crap or run. The club owner remarked, "Don't mind him, He's lived here all his life." "Yeah, but I've seen it all," the guy at the bar noted, "The black people are taking over the world."

Well, the Joyful Noyze - Barry Lynn, Freddy London, Harry Ray and I - started playing the Wigwam Restaurant in Waldorf. Almost immediately we picked up an insane following. On "Ladies Night," our emcee introduced himself as Ray Vernon. While the name Ray Vernon seemed familiar, I didn't realize who he was until all the sudden I saw that Link Wray and his Ray Men were coming to perform next door. Link Wray, famous for the 1958 guitar instrumental, "Rumble," lived with his two brothers fewer than ten miles away in Accokeek, Maryland. Ray Vernon, whose real name was Vernon Wray, was Link Wray's brother.

I said, "Who else am I going to run into?" The locals told me, "Well, the Kalin Twins are from Maryland too and they are always popping in. And Ronnie Dove lives in Waldorf so he comes here." All those pretty classic acts were right down there.

Having heard us play, Ray Vernon said, "Oh, my brother's guitar player is going to be over here with you in a heartbeat." I said, "Well, I'd gone next door to listen, but I only caught ten minutes of their set. They went on break and I had to get back here to play."

Roy Buchanan

We were on break and a guy came over with a Telecaster guitar and a rope on it for a strap. He said, "Hey, man. I'd love to sit in with your band. They're really good." I knew a little bit about guitar players and I said, "What's your name?" He replied, "Oh, I'm Roy Buchanan." Roy Buchanan was pioneer of the Fender Telecaster guitar sound. While he may not have gained national fame, he was regarded as one of the country's greatest guitarists.

"I said, "What in God's name are you doing here?" Roy said, "Oh, I'm playing lead guitar for Link Wray. But, truthfully, if I have to listen to those same six or eight songs again, I'm going to kill myself." I said, "Shit, you sure can sit in."

Roy Buchanan, Publicity photo.

My guitarist, Freddy London said, "Well, how good is this guy? What does he need to use?" I said, "Just plug him in." Roy started to play I said, "God almighty." This guy was playing rhythm and lead guitar for Link Wray and Link Wray couldn't shine the guy's left shoe.

Now, Roy Buchanan was into pot. He was blasted all the time. But as far as playing a Telecaster, I've never heard anyone better. I'd put him up there with the guy who played Telecaster with Elvis Presley and Ricky Nelson. And such a nice guy. Roy was pleasant to talk with and so easy to play with onstage. It was as of you'd rehearsed with him for six months on songs and he knew everything. Playing with our band, he'd just say, "Let me know when you want me to play." With me it's always the thumbs up or a nod and away they go. I strongly considered trying to make a play to get him in the Joyful Noyze, but Link Wray and the Ray Men had a pretty big name then. I heard that several years later he committed suicide while in jail for public drunkenness. What a tragedy.

So, that was the start of us in Maryland. We were drawing people and I was getting in more and more trouble with women, because for some reason, the skinny Jewish kid was suddenly very attractive to women in the audience. I didn't think I looked one tenth as good as some of the other entertainers around there but I had a nice hotel room. And it seemed like I was always with someone else's girlfriend. It presented some horrible situations. I literally went on a sexual rampage. I don't think I've ever been on one that bad in my life, maybe not until I got to Florida, which we'll cover later. It was distracting me, but I was having fun with it. So, did I mind staying longer at the Maryland club scene? Of course not. I had a built-in job, playing four or five nights a week. And the money was really good.

I was in my hotel room with a young lady one night and suddenly there's a loud banging on the door. I said, "Oh, God." The first thing I thought was that it was somebody's husband or boyfriend. And the voice said, “It's the state police!” I opened the door and the officer said, "You need to come down to the Wigwam right away. There's been a robbery," I said, "A robbery?"

The state police barracks were only two miles from the club. I got dressed and went down to the club. Someone had broken in and stolen all the amplifiers, the entire PA system and the guitar player's guitars. They couldn't take the Hammond organ as it was too big to carry off. The whole building was made of glass walls that you could see through, right along a main thoroughfare. For somebody to get in there and have enough time to steal all that stuff without being seen was unbelievable. That happened the last night of the week so we had the next day, Monday, off. Now, I was one of the few musicians around who had actually purchased musical theft insurance. Everybody had laughed at me at the time because we were working.

Jimmy Clanton, Publicity photo

I said, "Oh my God." I had to call all the way back to Red Bank Music and I said, "I need a Gibson guitar, a Fender guitar. I need this part of the drum set. I need an entire PA system..." I started ringing up about $4,000 or $5,000 worth of stuff, which at that time was a lot. My next thought was how could they get it to me immediately. They actually ended up having somebody drive some of it and the rest shipped by airplane. It came in in two different shipments.

Our first stay at the Wigwam in Waldorf, Maryland, lasted almost six months. Then one day, the club owner said, "Norman, maybe you should put together a whole show." So I had to call back up north for some big name talent. I ended up producing two shows, one at the Wigwam and one at a military base right across the border in Virginia.

I got Jimmy Clanton, and Gary U.S. Bonds. So all of the sudden I was right back into booking acts again. Jimmy Clanton showed up driving this little sports car. He was young and really good looking. He played a guitar and sang. I remember all the girls saying, "Oh my God, how can I get a date with this guy?"

I mentioned earlier that my guitar player, Freddy London worshiped Jimmy Clanton. So when Jimmy Clanton sang "Just a Dream," Freddy got down on his knees and was praising him. I said, "Freddy, get up!" My drummer wanted to kill him. It was just one of the funniest things I ever saw in my life. But Jimmy Clanton did such a great show. He closed the show at the military base with "Go Johnny Go" and really tore the place up. God, he was good. Jimmy was just so friendly and such a wonderful person. We still exchange emails back and forth. That was a long time ago. Now he's older and grayer but I understand he still sings just as well, really.

Back to New Jersey

By May of 1970, things were changing. I was getting much heavier into the racehorses but still wanted to keep playing. I decided to come back to New Jersey, which I did. We, the Joyful Noyze, started playing the Banjo Palace at Second and West End

Avenues in Long Branch, every Wednesday through Sunday until 3 A.M.

WED., THURS., FRI., SAT., SUN., 'til 3 A.M.

"NORMAN SELDIN"
AND
THE JOYFUL NOYZE

EVERY THURSDAY
"SPECIAL ENTERTAINMENT"

The BANJO PALACE

2ND AND WEST END AVE. LONG BRANCH 229-9809

After coming back from Maryland, Harry Ray left the group. He'd been toying with starting his own Long Branch vocal group, the Establishment, and planned to take them to California. In the meantime, Billy Brown had left the Broadways to join the group, the Moments, and was hitting big with the song, "Love On A Two Way Street." With a number of bookings, the Moments' management had fired one of the group members for missing a gig. The remaining members, Billy Brown and Al Goodman suddenly were in need of another tenor and Harry Ray was persuaded to join the Moments. This group would become the world famous soul trio of Ray, Goodman & Brown.

We had one other change in the Joyful Noyze after coming back to New Jersey. Freddy London left the group and was replaced briefly by a bass guitar player named Russell Warmoltz. Russell was from Ramsey, New Jersey and had previously been with a group called the Band Box as well as doing some studio session work for Les Paul and Aretha Franklin. Russell didn't stay with the Joyful Noyze for very long. He left to tour the college circuit with the rock band, Free Flowing Salt that became J.F. Murphy and Salt. Russell was soon replaced by guitarist Harold Hollander.

In addition to playing five nights a week at the Banjo Palace, I also started bringing in big name entertainers there. I brought in Johnny Thunder several times. And I brought in Larry Chance & the Earls. That was a time when Larry Chance had the band with the horn section in it. Besides the oldies, he was doing stuff like the Ides of March song, "Vehicle" and things like that. He was tremendous. Oh, my God. It was off the charts when he had his guys plus all those horns and Jimmy Fracasse playing guitar. I don't know if Larry was experimenting, but it was a full sound and it was really good. I brought Larry & the Earls into the Banjo Palace and it blew me away. I'd known Larry forever, but that was pretty crazy. I loved him with a big band. Loved him with the vocals. Having two or three

Larry Chance & the Earls

horns made a huge difference. Larry had such a variety of music.

On the Fourth of July weekend of 1970, racial tensions boiled over in Asbury Park's primarily African American West Side. Most of the night clubs on Springwood Avenue went up in flames and members of the National Guard were brought in to patrol the ashes. Many black musicians who made their living playing the West Side had to find work elsewhere. Though I frequented Springwood Avenue clubs as a kid, I didn't play there, so my livelihood wasn't affected. But I felt bad for the musicians who did play there.

I moved the Joyful Noyze to the Windjammer on Ocean Avenue in Sea Bright, New Jersey. There we played indoors on Tuesday and Wednesday nights and poolside on Sunday afternoons. At the same time, I was playing solo on the baby grand piano every Friday and Saturday at George Webb's Cedar Inn in Highlands, New Jersey.

We played the Windjammer until September. At times, we had Eddie Dougherty filling in for Barry on drums. Eddie would be part of my band at different times throughout my career and in fact is with me today. We played the Windjammer through the whole summer with either a three or a four piece band. We had a bass player or two thrown in. We mixed people in and out of the band at that time.

In September we began playing the Pin-Up Lounge in Highlands, New Jersey, and stayed there for six weeks. The Pin-Up Lounge was a bowling alley and we played songs while people were bowling. The stage was off to the left and they were bowling two lanes over. The bar was up in the front, so it was crazy.

For a short time while we were there, we called our band the Storm. The name Storm was to be used for an album we were going to cut for *Buddah Records* but the album never happened and we soon returned to calling ourselves the Joyful Noyze. At the Pin Up Lounge, Dave Brewer returned to fill in. His stay was very brief, as Barry Lynn was the drummer 99% of the time. While at the Pin-Up Lounge, I brought in Larry Chance & the Earls again with their seven piece band. I also brought in the Duprees.

We played a week at Luciano's on Route 46 in Lodi. That was a place where Lou Caddy & the Panics and the Duprees played quite often. The place held 600 or 700 people. It was a Mob joint. I think it was owned by Lucky Luciano's grandchildren. While there, I was taught to play this gambling game, Spoof, with pennies concealed underneath in your hands. You put them out on the bar and the closest count keeps the money. I probably lost my first two nights' pay doing that, even at 25 cents and 50 cents.

We played Luciano's with Tiny Tim. Tiny Tim was the latest sensation then, playing his ukulele and singing "Tip Toe Through The Tulips" in falsetto voice. Tiny Tim was there with his wife, "Miss Vicki," whom he'd married on "The Tonight Show" the year before.

Miss Vicki Tiny Tim and Norman Seldin at Luciano's

In January 1971, the Joyful Noyze - Barry Lynn, Harold Hollander and me - moved back into performing at the Windjammer before a two-week return to the Wigwam in Waldorf, Maryland. When we returned home we went into the Royal Manor in Belmar and then the Bamboo Bar in Seaside Heights.

We were at the original Bamboo Bar, not the big one that's there today. The original Bamboo Bar was at one time a church. It was a small bar right in the middle of Seaside Heights. All of the police used to go there.

Besides Hal Hollander, Barry Lynn and myself, I added a female singer, Karen Cassidy, to the group. Karen added a Janis Joplin sound to the Joyful Noyze. That was when Janis Joplin was big. If anybody could do Joplin, it was Karen Cassidy. Over the years I've had so many lead singers. Karen was excellent.

I was making money playing and promoting. I could also write songs. I could always write songs but playing made money, Plus, I liked being in the spotlight.

In addition to music, while in New Jersey I was also managing my parents' jewelry store in Red Bank. One of my jobs was piercing peoples' ears for earrings or studs. I did my first ear piercing when I was thirteen-years-old, right after my Bar Mitzvah. People used to line up at the store to get their ears pierced. Most piercings were done for women but I also pierced men's ears. Back then, you got your right ear pierced if you were gay. But I had a lot of sailors come in because if you crossed the Equator, you'd get your left ear pierced. Later, ear piercing became fashionable for a lot of men. The local newspaper wanted to do a story on men getting their ears pierced so Barry Lynn had his picture in the paper with me piercing his ear.

In the spring of 1971, I was the exclusive booking agent for a group called Moses. Moses was formed from former members of the Jaywalkers. As you'll recall, the Jaywalkers broke up after the untimely death of organist David Heth. The group was organized by Jaywalkers founder John Shaw along with Mike Moses. Other members included Billy Ryan and future E Street Band member Garry Tallent, all Jaywalkers alumni. Also in Moses were Richard Berardi and Michael Berardi. At the time, Moses had just recorded a record called "Take This Load Off My Back" for a little New York City label called *Murbo*. The record actually got enough attention to get picked by Gamble & Huff's early *Gamble* label but didn't go much further. I booked Moses into a club in Wanamassa called John Barleycorn. Recently opened under new management John Barleycorn had previously been the club Pandemonium in the Shore Motel.

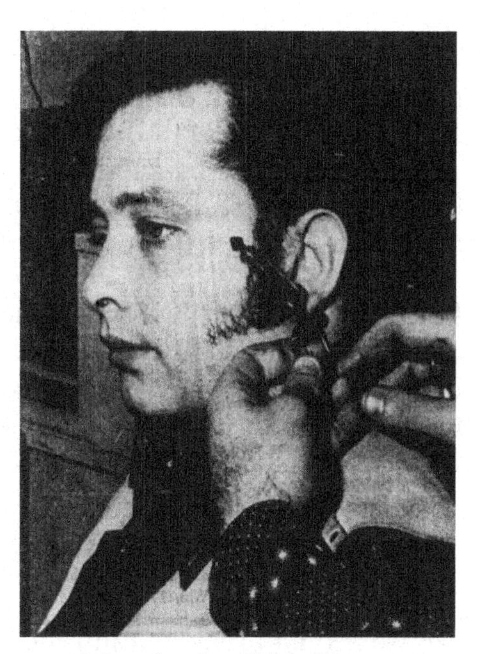

Me, piercing Barry's ear.

After that, I brought the Joyful Noyze into John Barleycorn for the summer. We played there four nights a week. In addition to playing music there, I reactivated my fire-eating act. As I alluded to in an earlier chapter, I had a friend, Arnie Peterson, who was a legit magician. I was looking for something different and he suggested I eat fire on stage. Arnie made up some sticks with the handles wrapped with asbestos and soaked them in lighter fluid. He lit one and explained everything to me. He said, "You do this and you're going to turn everybody's head even if the band doesn't."

The first time I'd done this trick was in Middletown, New York. It was a big club that held five or six hundred people. I turned down the lights and I went back and doused these sticks with lighter fluid. And I had flash paper, which Arnie had told me to just breath on it and it will go woof (ignite). He warned me not to get it too close to my eyebrows because that wouldn't be good. He said to just throw it out into the audience and it will just disperse in the air and go out in two seconds.

For eating fire, Arnie let me in on the secret to it. I'm not going to disclose a magicians' secret as I don't want any readers to try it at home. I will say what you shouldn't do is breathe in, or you will poison yourself. So I made sure I had plenty of breath to come out and I basically lit up my tongue and from there lit my hand on fire. I would have all five of my fingers lit up at one time for five, six seconds and then I would just close my fist and throw a piece of flash paper out. The fire was gone from my hand. It was quite a visual effect. The people in the audience went berserk. People said, "He eats fire! Nobody eats fire!" They knew some musicians set their instruments on fire but they never saw anything like what I did.

I do remember getting my mustache singed once when I breathed in a little bit. One time I was underneath an air conditioner blower and almost set myself on fire for about five seconds until I moved about six feet away from it. They had turned the air on and torches were lit. I told my guitar player, "Get out of the way and move to the left!" He did get out of the way in time.

Clarence Clemons

We were on a break at John Barleycorn when this guy walked in the front door and said, "Is there a telephone booth anywhere?" I said, "Yeah, right there." He looked over and I said, "Anything I can help you with?" He said, "Yeah, I've got a flat tire. I've got to call somebody to come fix it." Then he said, "Oh. You've got a band here?" I said, "Yeah. It's my band. I'm Norman." "He said, I'm Clarence. I play sax. Do you ever let people sit in?" I said, "Sure. What would you like to play?"

So Clarence Clemons asked, "Do you know any King Curtis songs like "Soul Serenade?" I told him, "Sure." He looked somewhat surprised and said, "What?" I replied, "'Soul Serenade,' 'Soul Twist,' 'Honky Tonk,' whatever you want to play." Clarence looked even more astounded. "This band plays that?" he asked. I said, "Oh, yeah. In a heartbeat," So he went out to his car and came back with his saxophone. He started going through a couple of songs and ended up playing the last two and a half hours with the Joyful Noyze.

People in the audience seemed shocked. I didn't know whether they were shocked over the sound or shocked that I put a black guy up on the stage. I had no idea. Barry Lynn looked over at me and exclaimed, "Oh, shit! I see this coming." And I said, "What's up?" He said, "You're going to put this guy in the band, aren't you?" I said, "Yep. I am." He said, "Two Jews and a black man. That's a great combination," I said, "I'll handle it."

In his autobiography, "Big Man," Clarence Clemons recalled asking me, "Are you sure about this? You have noticed that I'm not exactly white, haven't you?" To that I answered, "No I haven't."

Clarence knew that there were white bands and black bands and if you mixed the two, you found fewer places to play. What he didn't know was that I'd been through this

Clarence Clemons, Norman Seldin, Hal Hollander and Barry Lynn
on front of the Joyful Noyze van. Photo by Earl Stout.

racist crap before with Harry Ray and I didn't care. What was important to me was how the band sounded.

Clarence started playing with us and I finally had the band that I wanted. In addition to playing the Hammond organ, I think I was the first on the Jersey Shore to use a Moog synthesizer. I had a talented guitarist and drummer. I had a great female vocalist. And Clarence's saxophone added so much to our sound. We had a lot of bookings lined up at various venues.

But then I started getting calls canceling our gigs because they heard I had a black guy in the group. I wasn't deterred but it did disgust me.

I brought Clarence with the Joyful Noyze into the Wonder Bar in Asbury Park. That was when we broke the color barrier along the Jersey Shore. The Wonder Bar was one of the oldest clubs in the area, older even than Steve Brody's and Mrs. Jay's. At that time it had one of the longest bars in the country. But that was the first time in their history they saw a black guy with a white band. While we were there I got a call from a Seaside Heights venue that we'd played before. I won't shame them by naming them, but I was told, "When you come back don't bring 'that black bastard' with you."

The Joyful Noyze at the Wonder Bar, 1971.
From left: Hal Hollander, Norman Seldin, Barry Lynn,
Karen Cassidy and Clarence Clemons. Photo by Earl Stout.

I went through all of that shit. It was everywhere. As soon as they got word that I had a black musician in the band, most club owners flat out rescinded the bookings. They'd say, "You can come, but not with him." And the language used on me was not very nice. I was called a "N***** lover" so many times. And when you walk out to your car and it's carved into your hood, it gets to you. But I wasn't going to give in to such pressure. I was in my early twenties and I was arrogant. I stayed arrogant the whole time.

At first, the only people that didn't cancel me were schools where I was playing proms. Then things gradually started opening up. If I helped break racial barriers, I'm glad. Would the public have accepted black musicians like David Sancious, Ernest "Boom" Carter and, of course, Clarence Clemons in Bruce Springsteen's bands a couple years later had it not been for me. I hope so, but one never knows. I just wanted to concentrate on the music.

The Joyful Noyze. From left: Barry, Clarence, Hal, Norman, Karen
Photo by Earl Stout.

Freddie King

We were playing the Wonder Bar in August 1971, when Leon Russell and Freddie King were playing to 3,000 people in Convention Hall across the street. It was the dead of summer and while we were setting up, I said to George, the owner, "Damn, it's hot in here. Do you have air conditioning or anything?" And George said, "Yeah, I'll fix you right up." Now I was playing all the sudden I hears this whirling sound. George had put two of those commercial 90-inch fans right on the side of the stage and nearly blew everything off the stage. That was the air conditioning he gave us. But he moved it back and we continued. We were drawing people, lots of people, that night. Between sets I was standing out in front of the Wonder Bar because they sold the hot dogs in the front and everybody could come in and have a beer.

I saw this black guy just standing there just smiling. He said, "You're Norman, aren't you?" I nodded and he continued, "My name's Freddie. I'm done with my show across the street. Would you mind if I sat in with your band?" I said, "What do you play?" And he said, "Guitar, do you know any blues?" I answered, "I think we can handle that. How should I announce you?" He said, "It doesn't make any difference. My name is Freddie King."

Freddie King
Publicity photo

Blues guitar legend, Freddie King, had opened for Leon Russell that night at Asbury Park's Convention Hall. He'd left his guitar across the street but my guitar player had a Les Paul guitar and on most of Freddie's records, he used a Les Paul.

I had just about all of Freddie King's records and was a big fan. So I said to my guitar player, "Hal, we have a new guitar player here would like to sit in. You don't mind if our guest uses your guitar, do you?" Not that it would've made any difference because I would've made him do it. Hal asked, "How good is this guy?" I said, "Uh, he's pretty good,"

I asked, "Is there anything else you need, Freddie?" Somebody offered him a bottleneck to play slide guitar but he said, "No. I don't need a bottleneck for slide guitar." He reached into his pocket where he had an extra E string. It was not that well lit. He said, "Listen if I have to blow this string, it's going to take me about 35 seconds to change it. I can change one in 35 to 50 seconds so if I blow that string in the middle of a solo, just pick it up and I'll be right back with you,"

So we were playing "Hide Away" or "Sen-Sa-Shun," one of the two songs he made famous. He was playing and all the sudden I heard a "ching" and something went flying. Freddie he reached into his pocket and, I swear to God, it was as if somebody had a spotlight on him. He threaded that string through the bottom and up through the top, got rid of the other string, and wound the keys on it. I would say it took less than a minute. He was just about perfectly in pitch. I hit one chord just to give him a signal and he turned away once again and just barnstormed it.

It was some night. A few years later, when I was in Panama City Beach in Florida, I drove over to Houston to see him play again. But shortly after that, his health gave out, most likely a result of too many Bloody Mary's and too many nights on the road. Freddie King, one of the all time greats, died in December, 1976 at the age of 42.

We continued playing around Asbury Park for awhile. I'd sit in with other groups sometimes. We played the Student Prince as the Joyful Noyze once or twice. It was a hassle because the B3 Hammond organ was a brute to carry. I also had a Hammond Porta-B organ which was lighter and more compact. So I sold my B3 to somebody and kept the Porta-B, which made it a lot easier to carry.

We also had another horn player in the Joyful Noyze. Back when Russell Warmoltz was playing bass for us, he introduced us to a friend named Ronny Alard. Ronny's father taught at Juilliard teaching some of the greats like Stan Getz. He was the guy you went to when you had a problem in the symphony or an orchestra. Well, Ronnie was his son and he was playing together with Clarence and me. Ronny used to play two horns at one time. He would have an alto and a tenor out and Clarence had the other horn. So on certain songs it was bizarre to the point where I actually was doing Frank Zappa songs in a commercial club. Ronnie was always in demand for session work.

Joyful Noyze: The Album

I felt we had a powerful sound and it was time for the Joyful Noyze to make an album. I picked out nine songs. That was at a time when everybody said, "Norman can't write songs. But, you can't be this proficient on any instrument like a piano or a guitar and not be able to write. I wrote all the melodies, with help on some of the lyrics from Kevin Newton and Eddie Donnally.

Then I took the group to Broadway Recording Studios. By then, Broadway Recording had moved from their four- or eight-track studio to a much larger multi-track studio. But it was still run by my friend, Pat Jaques.

Clarence had not really been in a major recording studio until then. Clarence had his own unique style and Ronny Alard was a monster musician. Talk about a jazz player! Ronny was the Clapton of tenor and alto sax. He could sit right in there with Dave Brubeck and play Paul Desmond stuff and not even blink. So he did the session with us. There are a few tracks like "Time To Move On" where you hear the two different sax solos with distinct styles.

I played keyboards and sang all the lead vocals. When I needed background vocals I had Barry Lynn and Hal Hollander. I also brought in Nicky Addeo for background vocals and I had some help from the Poindexter Brothers who were in the studio. We had to get a bass player for the recording session because I usually played keyboard bass on our gigs. We used a guy named Bob Danylchuk on bass.

There were a lot of people at Broadway Recording Studios that I could call on to help. They were regulars who hung out there. That place was home to Bernard Purdie, Richard Tee, Eric Gale and Cornell Dupree. They were there almost 24 hours a day. All these guys helped when needed. Whenever we got stuck for musicians, we just pulled them out of the studio. I recall asking one day, "Who am I going to use for this?" Somebody in the room said, "Use what you've got! Take a walk across the whole floor, take a walk downstairs and in front of the building. You'll find everybody you need."

There was so many musicians there and some of them didn't even want credit for being on the recordings. It was crazy. One day they called *Atlantic Records* and a bass player came in to play when ours couldn't. There were just a lot of people. I kept asking the owner, Pat Jaques, "What do I owe you?" And he'd say, "Oh, don't worry about it right now." Everything was mixed and mastered there. It was my first really big production. To me, it was big at the time.

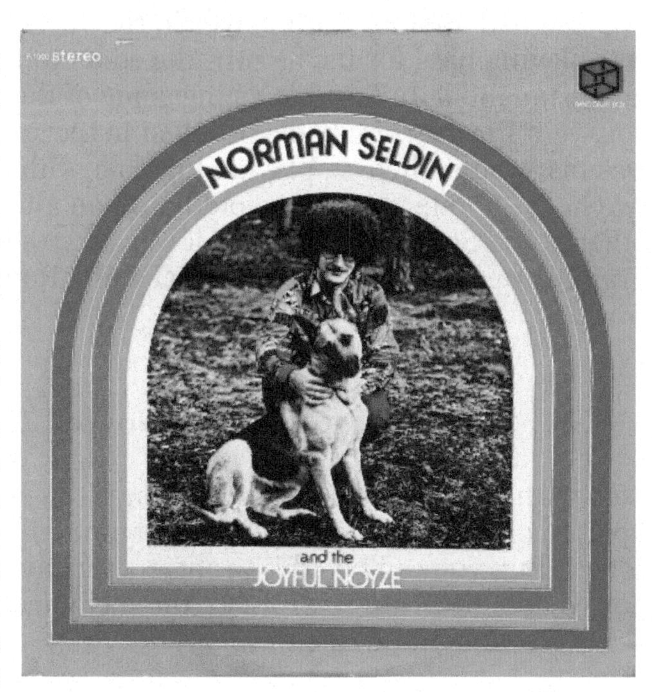

My next concern was who was I going to get to design the album cover? Well, it turned out there was a Latin music entertainment firm there called *Fania*. *Fania Records* was more than just a record label. They were producing artists that revolutionized the Latin music industry. Just about anybody who was anything in the New York Latin music scene was there. I was in the studio with Tito Fluentes and Joe Cuba who recorded "Bang Bang." They had Hector Garrido. the arranger, who was brilliant with strings. Not only did *Fania* change the perception of Latin music, they also changed the way the world perceived album covers artwork. *Fania* had an in-staff artist named Izzy Sanabrio who designed the label's album covers. Sanabrio designed album covers are now coveted as works of art.

Overhearing my need for an artist, Pat Jaques turned and said, "Maybe we can use Sanabrio. He does all of *Fania*'s albums." To my delight, Izzy said, "Sure, I can do your album cover for you." I said, "Well, I'd like to have color." He said, "Just give me the pictures and I'll do it." So I gave him an Earl Stout color photo of me and my dog for the cover and black and white photos of the band members for the other side. Karen Cassidy's picture is on the reverse because she was part of the group but her voice is not on the album.

We pulled off what I thought was a pretty decent album for the time. It was low budget but we got it done. We got it pressed on my own record label, Pandora's Box and released it on April 15, 1972. The pressing was done by Irv Ballen's *Gotham Records* in Philadelphia. They've turned into Disc Makers now. We promoted the hell out of it and sold about 3,000 copies.

By then our bookings were improving as clubs found out how good we were and how many followers we were drawing. We went back into the Bamboo Bar in Seaside Heights and then the Ship Bottom Lounge in the Beacon Manor in Point Pleasant.

The Carlton Theatre in Red Bank

In June, I produced the first of two big concerts in the Carlton Theatre in Red Bank. The Carlton Theatre was built back in 1927 and had seen countless famous entertainers in its day. By 1972, it had seen better days, but renovations would have to wait until 1974, when it was reborn as the Count Basie Theatre.

The purpose of the concerts was to spotlight new talent but I paid all of the groups. The first Carlton Theatre featured the groups Mad John, Abilene and Happy Trails along with the Joyful Noyze. Mad John was an all-original country rock group that I was managing, with three-part harmony and a good guitarist. The other two groups were just ones I was highlighting.

The first show at the Carlton Theatre went well so I did a second one a month later. This time I had a group called Southern Conspiracy, Mad John and the Joyful Noyze. Southern Conspiracy had sort of a country rock, blue grass sound that was different. They were friends of mine.

The Carlton Theatre Concert performers. Members of the Joyful Noyze, Mad John, Abilene and Happy Trails

The Joyful Noyze with Clarence Clemons, 1972

The Joyful Noyze. From left: Clarence Clemons, Norman Seldin, Barry Lynn, Billy Ryan, Hal Hollander

Moving On

We were playing the Ship Bottom at Beacon Manor in Point Pleasant all summer. The Ship Bottom was a basement club with a stone floor and low ceiling. We used to start playing at 10 p.m. and go until 3 in the morning. We'd draw hundreds of people on Friday and Saturday nights. A couple of times Bruce Springsteen came by and sat in with us to sing either "Johnny B. Good" or "Route 66." I think Karen Cassidy was friends with his girlfriend or something and might have invited him. Bruce had just signed with *Columbia Records*. He was assembling a band and had begun recording with the advance the record label had given him. I didn't think much of it at the time. By then, Karen had left the band and I brought back Billy Ryan as an additional guitarist.

In the fall, the Joyful Noyze moved into the Club Plaza located in the Beachwood Shopping Center in Bayville. There we played Wednesdays, Fridays and Saturdays 9:30 p.m. until 2 in the morning. We were playing rock & roll, blues and a lot of our own material. We'd take requests and people would see if they could stump us, which they couldn't.

Meanwhile, unbeknownst to me, Clarence had begun doing some session work with Bruce Springsteen. Springsteen had already completed most of the songs for his first album but Columbia wanted a couple more. He quickly wrote "Blinded by the Light" and "Spirit in the Night." When some of his band members weren't available, he recorded both songs with just himself on guitar, Vini Lopez on drums and Clarence Clemons on sax.

Evidently, it was already in the works that Clarence was leaving the Joyful Noyze. I just didn't find it out for about six or eight weeks. Then he offered to give me two weeks notice. Now, I booked eight months in advance, so it was not a pleasant parting, With the kind of work and the kind of promo I did, I wasn't worried about working next week. I was making sure that the right guys had work for five or six months in advance. Losing Clarence hurt the sound of my group because by that time, people were used to me having him as our sax player.

Clarence and I had become close friends. I remember when I first met him he was a custodian at the James Burke Boy's Home. I'd said, "I'd like to come over and see you. Is there anything I can bring you?" He said, "You can bring me three or four pool cues because the kids downstairs break them." That started a real friendship and it cooled for a while at that point. But our friendship never really ended because we had a strong bond. Clarence left his group to join me and he left me to join Bruce. Any negative feelings were soon forgotten. We later played together again and remained good friends until he died. Certainly Clarence was a huge asset to Bruce Springsteen's band.

The Rock & Roll Revival Concerts

So then it was just Barry Lynn, Hal Hollander, Billy Ryan and me. We began getting bookings from Banner Talent Associates. Banner was a booking agency run by David Zaan. They were booking big names like James Brown and Joe Tex. Then they got very involved in Oldies Revival concerts. At first they booked the Joyful Noyze for a job out on Long Island. Then they started using us as the backing band, whenever Bobby Comstock's band couldn't make it. The first one we did was at the Philadelphia Academy of Music, December 15, 1972.

That concert featured the Skyliners, Platters, Freddy Cannon, the Shirelles, Danny & the Juniors, the Chantels, Bobby Lewis, the Five Satins and Johnny Maestro and his Crests (Brooklyn Bridge) group.

All the Banner Talent Oldies Revival concerts were put together by Larry Goldfarb. We always had good acts. Usually I was in charge of the whole stage which meant handling the lighting and rehearsing the groups. Sometimes I'd even have to carry the acts' money for the cash payments.

Some of the acts were a delight to deal with and some weren't. Tony Williams of the Platters was blasted out of his mind. I had him sitting on a chair in front of 3000 people because he couldn't stand up. Jimmy Beaumont, lead of the Skyliners was a gem to work with. All he wanted to do was relax and smoke a nice cigar and then come out and sing. He wasn't as dynamic as Johnny Maestro, but he had a gorgeous voice. It would send you to the moon. We backed all of his songs. Beforehand, Jimmy had said to me, "We might want to do five songs instead of four." I said, "Listen, you guys can do ten if you want." But then somebody screamed, "There's a song limit." I said, "As long as you sing 'This I Swear,' I don't care what you do." He did that and I think he sang "My Lonely Way" and "Since I Don't Have You" too. It was just tremendous. One of the best ballad groups I ever heard.

The Joyful Noyze, December 1972.
From left: Billy Ryan, Hal Hollander, Barry Lynn, Norman Seldin

The concert was emceed by WCAU-FM radio personalities Jim Nettleton and Long John Wade. When they first told us we were doing the Philadelphia Academy of Music, it was originally strictly as the backup band. Then one of the groups, I don't recall which one, was running late so they asked us do a couple of songs. Well, the Joyful Noyze was a music group that could do acappella with the four of us as well as anybody else could. A lot of times we'd stop our show in the middle and sing "The Book of Love" or something like that. Right in the middle of the set we'd do acappella. Once we had a blow-up doll that our guitar player sang "Teen Angel" to. That offended some people because our guitarist threw the doll around so we didn't repeat it.

Anyway, we did so well at the first show that the promoters said, "How about if you open the next Oldies Revival show at the Philadelphia Academy of Music. That's a big deal because backup groups don't often perform their own sets.

The second show took place on March 2, 1973. It featured Chubby Checker, the Angels, Cornell Gunter and the Coasters, the Clovers and Del Shannon. This time it was emceed just by Jim Nettleton.

I had a lot of fun working with Cornell Gunter. His Coasters group was a really magical act. Del Shannon was interesting to talk to at rehearsal. He was such a nice guy. I noticed some strange things about him though. He had done pretty well with hit records like "Runaway" and "Hats Off to Larry" in the early 1960's and was enjoying the bookings on the oldies circuit. But there was just something about him that seemed sad. Years later after he committed suicide and after I'd experienced someone I knew who was bipolar, it rang a bell. He must have been experiencing bipolar disorder even back then.

The Joyful Noyze, March, 1973
From left: Billy Ryan, Barry Lynn, Hal Hollander. Seated: Norman Seldin

One of the things I remember about that night was that we had Muhammad Ali in the guest box at the Academy of Music. I got to meet him and I shake his hand. I knew he had a fight coming up later that month so I wished him good luck. Unfortunately that turned out to be the night where Ken Norton broke his jaw so I don't think my well wishes worked. But he loved the show and he sat up in one of those theater boxes and was acknowledged from the stage a number of times.

I think we did three shows at the Philadelphia Academy of Music and one at Madison Square Garden in New York. We played behind so many groups, I can't begin to remember them all. I recall backing the Teenagers when Pearl McKinnon of the Kodaks was singing lead. She was excellent, by the way. I spoke to Teenagers' bass singer, Sherman Garnes, quite a bit.

To be honest, I can't even recall which groups were on the Madison Square Garden concert. There were just so many and we were just the backup band there. All I remember about the Madison Square Garden show was that some guy wouldn't let me plug in my own organ because it had to be plugged in by a union member. I was in one of those moods. I said, "Just plug it wherever the hell you want and we can get this thing done and get out of here."

I had to run the stage and it was difficult because I was young. I was still in my early twenties running the stage for singers whose records I'd purchased when I was just seven or eight years old. I gained a lot of experience from just those few shows.

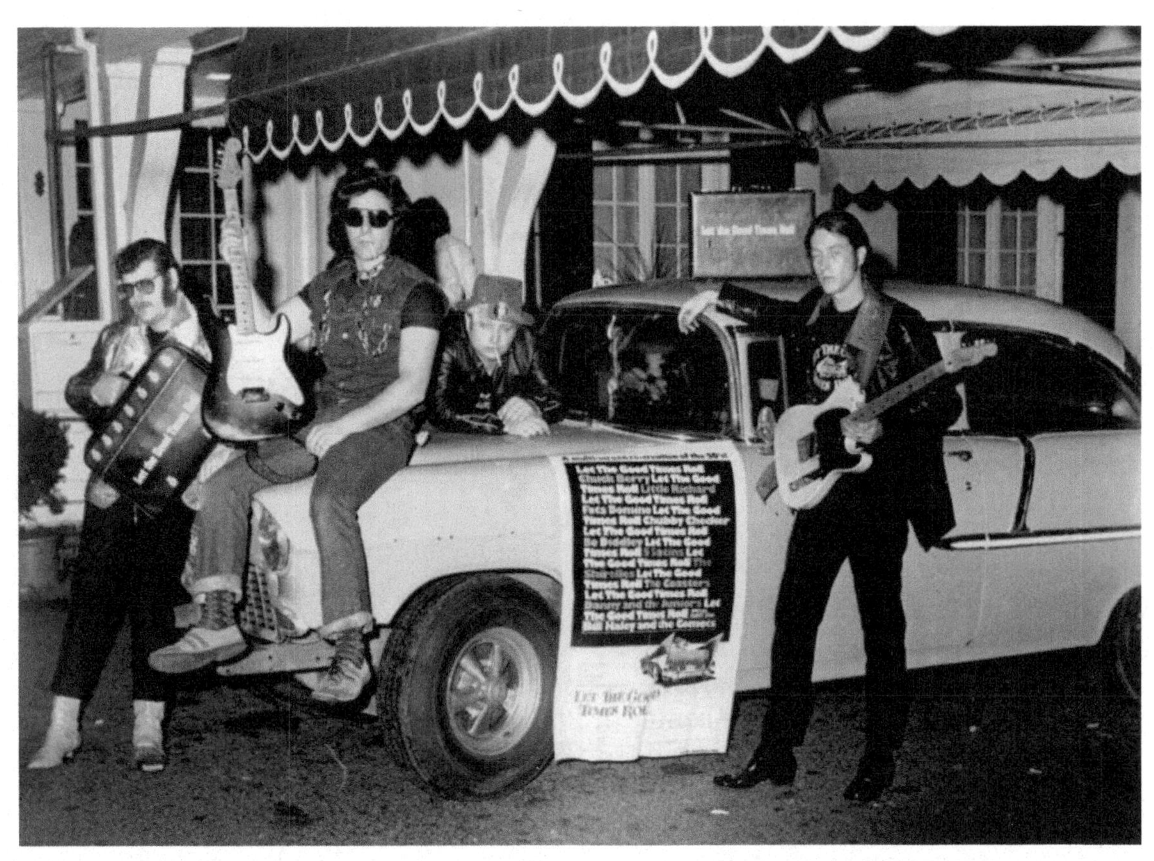

The Joyful Noyze dressed as greasers to promote "Let The Good Times roll."
From left: Norman Seldin, Hal Hollander, Barry Lynn, Billy Ryan.

Let The Good Times Roll

Back in New Jersey, we played Asbury Park's Student Prince in March and then Sweeney's on to Greenmount Avenue in Baltimore. From there it was a club called Jolly Cholly's Lounge on Ocean Avenue at Second Avenue in Asbury Park. Shortly after we started playing there, the club's name was changed to Magic Touch.

On May 25, 1973, the film "Let the Good Times Roll" premiered in New York City. The rockumentary film featured recent concert footage of numerous stars from the American rock & roll music scene of the 1950's including Chuck Berry, Chubby Checker, the Coasters, Danny and the Juniors, Bo Diddley, Fats Domino, the Five Satins, Bill Haley and the Comets, Little Richard and the Shirelles.

Columbia Pictures hired us, the Joyful Noyze, to promote the release of the film through a series of live outdoor concerts performed in front of theaters and at block parties. They made us dress up like greasers and took the crazy picture you see here with me leaning against a '56 Chevy with a briefcase and my hair greased back. They had a "Let The Good Times Roll" banner hanging right on the side of the car. The photo was taken in front of the Shadowbrook at Shrewsbury, which is a historic multimillion dollar restaurant and wedding venue. The Shadowbrook's owner had a fit that we didn't show the name of the place in the picture they were taking. But we didn't. We just pulled the car up under the awning and we all posed with it looking like greasers. They shot the picture and that was it.

The Joyful Noyze, 1973. From left: Norman Seldin, Kathy Scatagglia, Hal Hollander, Barry Lynn

Then Columbia Pictures sent us to North Jersey and all over. I mean they send us to some God-forsaken places. We performed in front of movie theaters and we had crowds because we were a live band.

We played a block party in Philadelphia for "Let the Good Times Roll." They had all the streets blocked off and we played right there in the center of Philly. We did other block parties too. We did so many fifties songs that we added them to our repertoire which had already stretched to more than 400 songs. And for a while, we performed as an oldies band.

We started doing more out-of-state jobs. In June, we played a place called the Warm Up in the Hazleton Shopping Center in Hazleton, Pennsylvania. But then we were right back into central New Jersey playing the Speakeasy in Bound Brook and the Straw Hat in Green Brook.

We also started shuffling personnel during the summer of 1973. Gone was Billy Ryan (again). I brought back Ron Alard and added a new female singer, Kathy Scattaglia. In addition to playing two horns at once, Ron could also play the bagpipes.

We played Fat City in Seaside Heights, the Royal Manor in Wall Township and even a concert at the University of Illinois.

The year 1974 started with more personnel changes. I still had Barry Lynn with me and Billy Ryan was back, along with new members Ken Anderson and Phil Azzam. In times when he was not with me, Billy Ryan had spent time with the James Cotton Blues Band.

We experimented with a number of things. Some worked and some didn't. One time, I think it was for Halloween, we came out in comical costumes, calling ourselves Sonny Switch & the Switch Blades. We dropped that routine pretty quickly.

We spent most of the summer of 1974 at Pier One in Toms River, New Jersey. By then, we had back the classic line up of Barry Lynn, Hal Hollander, Billy Ryan and me.

As of September 1974, Joyful Noyze was no more. A part of me felt sad about breaking up the group, but it was time for a change. We'd been performing for seven years and had been through some great times. But the music industry was changing and I was ready for new challenges. The time came to move on.

Chapter Eight
Music School, Mellotrons & Jewelry

It was the fall of 1974 and I had come to realize there were too many things going on in my life. I'd been simultaneously booking, producing and recording several acts, writing and arranging songs, promoting and producing shows and performing several nights a week. All the while, I was also handling my parent's jewelry store. I often look back at those times and wonder how I was able to do all of those things in an age before there were computers, Internet or even cell phones. On top of that, while I was with the Joyful Noyze, I'd also gotten married. I felt I'd taken the Joyful Noyze as far as I could and it was time for me, at the age of 27, to settle down.

The Roberts School of Music

Back in 1972, I'd also gotten involved as a partner in a music school in Red Bank. I'd run into somebody who always came to hear me play. He taught guitar and had this little music school at 60 White Street in Red Bank called Roberts School of Music. I went in 50:50 with him. I taught piano and I also had Barry Lynn there teaching drums.

My partner added a soda machine and it was making money for us. I said, "Wait a minute. We should be making money on accessories like the strings, not soda." So we created a little retail section in the front of the store. I said, 'We have to get a pegboard and hooks to hold guitars." My partner said, "Oh, we can't get into selling guitars." I said, "Sure we can. You can't have a little mini-school and not sell instruments."

Now up the street from us was Red Bank Music, which was a huge music store. That's where I bought all my stuff that I performed with and took on tours. Red Bank Music must have had four or five thousand square feet of floor space. It was huge and it was exactly a block and a quarter away from us. So I said, "Well, we can't go head-to-head with Red Bank Music on high price musical instruments. We can only get second-line instruments." Now, the Japanese were making copies of Gibsons and Fender guitars. And they made a decent guitar. So that was one option. I saw some ads in a couple guitar magazines and I said, "We need to look into Ovation guitars."

Ovation was a guitar company in Hartford, Connecticut that manufactured guitars with distinctive round backs and carbon-fiber tops instead of the typically wood tops. I'm a pretty big fan of guitars. I called up the company and they said, "Red Bank Music didn't want our guitars because they said nobody's going to buy a guitar that has a fiberglass back that's rounded." I'd heard a couple people play Ovation guitars and they sounded pretty good. Now, one of the salesman was at our store so I said, "Let's try some of them." My partner said, "We're never going to sell these guitars, not with this place up the street." But we went ahead and we were the first dealer for Ovation guitars in Monmouth & Ocean Counties.

That's when Ovation got the endorsement from Glen Campbell who was a great guitar player. Then Mac Davis started playing one. All of a sudden, we went from having one or two pieces on sale in the store to having six or eight of them. That was a huge investment for us at the time. They were not an expensive guitar and people were coming in to buy them. I said, "Look, there won't be any problem with the wood cracking on the back because it's fiberglass." As the first area dealer to have them, we sold the hell out of them.

We got to the point where we were bumping heads with a lot of other acoustic guitar makers. Since our guitars were different, our students were buying them. Some of the pros were coming in to buy Ovations, too.

I continued teaching piano at Roberts Music school for about a year and a half. We gave lessons in piano, guitar and drums. We had 40 or 50 students, both male and female. People couldn't wait to get in there because I was a real player. I was in a band. That made a big difference. I had some pretty damn good students. A couple of them now are major players down in Florida.

Baseball

Roberts Music School had its own baseball team. We were part of a softball league. The first time out I looked at these players, it was like being with a bunch of singers that couldn't sing in tune. I said, "Oh my God! We need this. We need that." They said, “Are you a piano teacher or a ballplayer?” I said, "I know how to run a ball team but this isn't one."

Norman playing softball.

Eventually I turned it into an adult championship team. A little finagling along the way made all the difference and I knew how to finagle. I said, "You're not going to hit a softball 350 feet with the players we have here. But if we have a couple of guys who have played in the semi-pros it would help.” They said, "We can't get them." I said, "Yeah, we can get them. They love to play. They want to be stand outs." So we got some guys who played in the minor leagues with Boston or pitched for awhile. Two players in the Oakland A’s organization lived in Red Bank and Keansburg. I put them on the team and they were pretty heavy duty. I had a lot of fun with it.

I had one semi-pro player that I put in center field. I was playing catcher. I should have played first base because a couple of times I got knocked eight feet away and unconscious in close plays at the plate. I remember one time I was catching and the batter hit a ball so far to center it looked like a sure home run. He was trotting around the bases thinking it was an easy round tripper. Well, our semi-pro center fielder picked up that softball it threw 275 to 300 feet in the air from centerfield on the run. It landed in my glove eight feet in front of home plate. The runner was rounding third. The guy was so in shock, he actually stopped. He never slid. He couldn't believe the ball got there. I just stood there and tagged him out.

The fans of my band from West End Casino and elsewhere used to come out to the games. So, it was like my little personal hangout for a while.

The Mellotron

While working at the Roberts Music School, I started reading about a high-end musical instrument called a Mellotron. I decided to look into selling them through the store.

A Mellotron is a small keyboard instrument capable of producing practically any musical sound. As opposed to a Moog synthesizer which produces synthetic sound, the Mellotron is not synthetic but the real sound of taped instruments. The Mellotron does not fall into any known category. Developed in Birmingham, England in 1963, it is best described as a series of controlled tape machines manipulated by keyboard. Each key relates to, and when played, activates a tape on which has been recorded a single note of an instrument. It offered any sound you wanted, from a symphony orchestra or church choir to samba combo or rock 'n roll drums. If a musician selects a musical instrument like a flute, and one key is pressed, the sustained note of one flute is heard. If a four note chord is played, the sound of four flutes will be heard in harmony. The latest model at that time, the M400, had 100 different instrument sounds available and more than 1000 different sound effects.

The Mellotron M400

Some major rock acts were already using Mellotrons extensively. The first was the Moody Blues who used it on all of their albums. The Beatles used a Mellotron for the string section on their "Magical Mystery Tour" and "White" albums. Mellotrons were also being used in recordings by the Rolling Stones, Elton John, Santana, Chicago, Jefferson Airplane and Led Zeppelin to name a few. A basic Mellotron cost $3,900 and each tape cost an additional $550. On each tape there were three recorded instruments. The purchase price was steep and many musicians were unaware of what a Mellotron could do.

I went up to Dallas Musical Instruments' American headquarters in Mahwah, New Jersey. Back in their warehouse, workers were assembling the Mellotrons because they came in from London as parts. I went into the back where they had different ones plugged in. I'd never played one before, but playing the Mellotron is similar to playing any keyboard instrument. The difficult part is blending two sounds at once and knowing when to bring in one sound and fade out another. I started playing one and an executive came out and said, "Who is that playing back there?" And one of the employees said, "That's Norman Seldin. They call him Stormin' Norman." Well, the executive said, "We need this guy. We need to hire him as a clinician."

So they hired me. I believe at the time they were paying me $1,500 a week plus expenses, which was a lot of money then. Dallas Music Industries Ltd, a British company, wanted me to tour the country giving Mellotron concerts and holding clinics to introduce and familiarize America with this unique instrument. That was really the first job that I had working for somebody else. I'd always been self-employed, working as a performer, running my booking agency, teaching in the music school and working in the jewelry store when I was around.

On the Road

I sold my interests in the Roberts Music School and store back to my partner. I think my original investment had been three or four hundred dollars. I think he gave me back five or six hundred bucks for my share. I gave him the whole store to have fun with. I'd been doing everything including the books, the ordering and the piano teaching. It had begun being a drag for me.

One of my first obstacles was the musicians union. You may recall that I'd been one of the youngest musicians to be accepted into the musician's union. Well, the American Federation of Musicians objected to any instrument that might take jobs away from other musicians and refused to classify the Mellotron as a musical instrument. Further, they forbid union members, meaning me, from using a Mellotron in such situations. As a union member, I petitioned the union to list me as the first Mellotronist.

Well, the union fought it because they thought the Mellotron was taking work from the violin players. But it was just background. There was no way, as a performer, I was going to hire four or five violinists for a gig anyway. But they fought it, not wanting me to perform with a Mellotron. They finally put it in their rule book for one year. But they gave me so much grief that I never paid another year of union dues again. I haven't been a union musician for some thirty some years now.

My first assignment was to demonstrate the Mellotron at the annual National Association of Music Merchants (NAMM) Convention and Music Expo. The 1974 convention was held in June at the Astrodome in Houston, Texas. The NAMM conventions are for member companies that manufacture, distribute or retail musical instruments/products, to display their products. These trade shows are always huge events.

Norman Seldin demonstrating the Mellotron

The company flew me to Houston. I'd never been to Texas before and when I got off the plane, I asked, "Is the Astrodome close enough to walk to?" The guy just laughed at me and said, "The Houston Astrodome? Well, if you start walking now you'll probably get there in three or four days. It's about 35 to 40 miles from the airport." So I took a cab to the Astrodome. Fortunately, the company had the Mellotron and accessories shipped there ahead of time.

They had a booth on the convention floor where I demonstrated the Mellotron. But everything was mass confusion. There were a lot of companies with booths there that I'm sure weren't in business three months later if they didn't get any orders. And we didn't really fit on any grid. They didn't have a separate keyboard area because that was still pretty new then. We wound up next to Hohner harmonicas or Gibson guitars. Eventually, I got around to all the company booths. A couple of them wanted to hire me on the spot. But I really wasn't interested in to getting hired somewhere else.

Still, for me it was really pretty amazing. It seemed like every musician in the world was there. I saw Larry Coryell and Frank Zappa. Anybody who was involved in music was there - so I represented Mellotron. The NAMM show really let me see how big the scope of the music business was. That's when I realized how many manufacturers there were, how many guitars, how many amplifiers.

Mellotron Clinic in Prattville, Alabama

The company showed me things like how to change the tapes. You'd lift the rack out, lift the strings and put them across all the recording heads. I saw how the notes pressed against the string. It was new to me, but it was easy. You could adjust the speed of a motor to get them in tune. If they were sharp or flat, you can turn a knob. I have perfect pitch so it was no problem.

Then I hit the road, giving Mellotron clinics and concerts. A typical clinic would be like this. I'd go into a town and head for a place that they had arranged. I'd explain the instrument; how it's built, what it does, what the advantage would be to having one for a choir or for arrangements. I'd basically open it up and pull all the reels of tape out. The potential buyers were always astounded to see all of the fifty notes it held - pulled out, every sharp or flat that was on there. I'd talk about it and play it for them. Then they'd try it out. People would say. "Well, it doesn't quite feel like a piano." I'd say, "Well, it's not a piano. It's more like an organ." And then they'd say, "But if you hold down these two notes you can only hold them for so long and then they stop." You'd have to let them up. I used to play two at a time and they'd say, "How do you do that?" I'd say, "I have exact timing on all ten of my fingers. I have lots of control from lots of piano playing." So, I could remember my fourth finger was down for seven seconds, my second finger on my left hand was down for three seconds, and I could release in time to make that thing work.

Norman with Mellotrons

The company promoted the clinics ahead of time. They did the kind of promotion I would do for myself. I went all over. But I was pretty much on my own. I had to make my own format and my own program. I had to make up my demos on my own with what I had to work with for the different sounds. It was pretty crazy because I did not understand the premise of it. I'd never been to a music clinic. I'd only heard about them. So I had to make things up as I went along. It was an ad-lib kind of thing.

The company didn't know how to book things logically. They had me in Alabama one day and Michigan two later, then back in New Jersey. They had a need to get as much exposure as they could, no matter what college it was at, no matter what music store. I almost had to look at the newspaper to find out where the hell I was going next.

I gave clinics in Prattville, Alabama; Rochester, New York; Bridgeport, Connecticut; South Bend, Indiana; Elkhart, Indiana; Vineland, New Jersey; and a number of other places that slip my mind at the moment. They just kept me working, flying all around the country. They covered my expenses, but the company was cheaper than cheap. I mean if I wanted to get reimbursed for an expense, they wanted a receipt. If I had a piece of bubble gum they wanted a receipt. I was on the road constantly for eight or nine months.

That tour, with all the constant traveling, really knocked me out. I started feeling really sick. I think I ate some bad seafood or something and I got an infection in my stomach. I was on the road and they got me pain shots because I was in mortal pain. Plus I had all this stress. I ended up in the hospital. There, the doctors did an endoscopy to see what was wrong. Back in those days, they didn't have the tiny tube they use today. It seemed like something the size of a garden hose. They didn't put you asleep for it, either. I had to sit up in a chair and they told me to keep swallowing while they slowly put this thing down my throat. It felt like somebody was trying was trying to kill me. It was awful.

Mellotron Clinic in South Bend, Indiana

It turned out I had a duodenal ulcer. It was bleeding and it was pretty bad. I ended up spending six days in the hospital with it. My company called two or three days into my hospital stay and asked when I could go back on the road. I said, "Well, the doctor says they don't need to operate but it's going to be at least four weeks recovery." They said, "Well, that's not going to be good enough because you got the tour going so well that we're going to have to find somebody else." They fired me. This was early spring, 1975. They let me go, just like that.

I hadn't been with Dallas Musical Instruments long enough to get unemployment. They did cover my medical bills, which I'm sure were pretty hefty. It took quite a while for me to heal and then recover my strength. At one point I showed up at baseball practice to see what I could still do. The players didn't want me to do it, but I was determined to take a few swings at batting practice. I said, "Let me take a couple of swings to see how I feel." I took two swings and I was on my knees. I just didn't have any strength. I was drained.

Pandora's Box

At this point, I had to get some money coming in because I had a wife and two daughters to support. Continuing in music didn't seem to be an option for me. The band had broken up and everybody had gone their separate ways. I had to do something else. So, I decided that I would take some jewelry from the back of the store and try to sell it at a local flea market. The Englishtown Flea Market was huge. It went on for acres and acres. There were hundreds of flea market dealers selling everything you can imagine. I had the van and every morning I'd go and get tables like a dirt merchant. Some of these tables needed me to put my own nails and screws in to make them stand up. At the flea market I had to deal with different brands of people and believe me, they were different.

Among the hottest jewelry at that time were silver and turquoise necklaces, bracelets, rings, watchbands and belt buckles handcrafted by Native American silversmiths in the American southwest. While authentic handmade pieces would sell for $400 to $1,500 or more, the market was awash with inferior fake mass-produced pieces passed off to unsuspecting buyers for $200.

Right away I saw there was a big market for authentic pieces. I became an American Indian reservation jewelry buyer, making trips out west to bring jewelry in. All of my merchandise was authentic jewelry handcrafted by Zuni, Navajo, Santa Domingo and Hopi artists that I brought in from Arizona, New Mexico and Nevada. I starting going out there every few weeks because we sold so many things So, I kept expanding from one table to two tables to three tables. Finally, it got to be ten eight-foot tables. That was a long row and I had all the tables filled with these cases of jewelry. It was massive. I was doing more business with that per day than I had been with the bands. And my bands had made money.

Because Englishtown Flea Market was so big, I needed to distinguish myself from all the other jewelry dealers there. American Indian jewelry was coming in real big and I needed an idea to get the big spenders.

I thought that if I could use my parents' jewelry store as my home base and take the credit card charge machine to the Englishtown Flea Market, I'd be able to take American Express and BankAmericard payments. In those days before the Internet, merchants had to physically swipe a credit card so the information was imprinted on a carbon copied receipt. This was easily done, but for large purchases the merchant had to make a phone call to the credit card company to verify the line of credit. This of course, required a telephone in an open flea market field before the age of cell phones. It was no wonder that none of the hundreds of flea market dealers offered credit card purchasing.

Undeterred, I purchased one of those expensive car phones that were the size of an elephant and had it installed in my van. The phone was powered by the vehicle battery and couldn't be removed from the van but that was OK for me.

I had the van parked by my tables. The van was carpeted and I sat in the middle with my charge machine and could make verifying phone calls and carry out transactions almost immediately. As long as I could get there and put the charge system in, I was set.

People walking past my tables said, "Look! This guy takes charge cards." All of a sudden there were people waited for us when we arrived at the flea market. We used to get there at 4:00 in the morning while it was still dark. That was the only way to get the best location and catch the early bird customers. I used to have two or three girls working for me. We'd park the van behind the tables and pull out the showcases of jewelry. Once we started taking credit cards, sales jumped from $200 or $300 a day up to $1,500 or $2,000 a day. All of a sudden customers were no longer buying

$20 or $30 jewelry. It was $200, $300, $400.

Harry Chapin

I showed a guy a squash blossom necklace one day and he said, "How much?" I think I told him $1,300, which was a fortune back then. He said, "I'll take that," and he pulled out his American Express card and bought it.

Of course, I took cash, too. I always had a big Bowie knife that I carried for protection. I also had something else that I shouldn't have carried. But we had those lock boxes where you put your money.

I named my jewelry business Pandora's Box. This was a time that I started getting into drugs. Nothing too heavy. Just a little pot and coke. I had so many people working for me that I would basically be there for high-end customers. I'd mostly just sit there smoking some weed and watch the people come and go. I had to take all of the merchandise home and then polish it all up every week. There was dust and sun so the jewelry had to be cleaned. Hundreds and hundreds and hundreds of pieces of jewelry needed to be cleaned weekly. That's what I did. I was doing that and then I got back into the horses again.

But the business kept expanding. In addition to Englishtown, the Golden Nugget Flea Market in Lambertville and Cowtown Flea Market, I opened up a regular store in Peddlers Village down in Manasquan. It was a crazy two years. I was just so busy I really didn't think about playing music any more.

That was until the summer of 1976 when I met up with Jeff. I can't recall Jeff's last name but he was Harry Chapin's road manager. Jeff came up to my table at the flea market and said, "You look familiar. Don't I know you from somewhere?"

I told Jeff that he might have seen me play somewhere and we started talking about music. He told me that Harry Chapin, the folk rock singer songwriter who'd topped the charts a couple years earlier with the song "Cat's In The Cradle," was playing the Garden State Arts Center in Holmdel, New Jersey for two nights in late August. "You need to come to see Harry at the Garden State Arts Center," said Jeff. Both shows were sold out but he offered to comp me. He said, "We're still trying to figure out where we'll have the party after the second show." I said, "Well, let's have it at my house in Fair Haven."

So Harry Chapin and his whole entourage came back to my house after the show.. They brought shrimp and lobster and wine. The whole house was flooded with Harry Chapin's band. Vicki Sue Robinson who had recently recorded “Turn The Beat Around” was with them. I began playing the piano and everyone started singing. We had a great time. But then I started to realize how much I missed playing music.

Chapter Nine
Rockin' & Rollin' Again

I guess hanging out with Harry Chapin's band that night, playing and singing, made me realize how much I missed the music. My next thought was "How am I going to get back into this again with no band?"

Fortunately, a restaurant called Lock Stock & Barrel was around the corner from where I lived in Fair Haven and they had entertainment. I spoke to the owner and he said he'd love to have me perform there. The first night I played there I must have had 150 people show up. That was a lot for a piano player with no vocals. People were so glad to see me back performing.

So, I continued performing regularly at the Lock Stock & Barrel. I was bringing in so many people they had me there several days a week. I was also making some appearances at the Sail Inn in Sea Bright.

As word got around, local musician friends like Billy Ryan and Kevin "Bird" Conair started dropping by to jam with me. By January, 1978, Bruce Springsteen's E Street Band had just come off of their eight-month cross country "Darkness On The Edge Of

Norman Seldin and friends at the Sail Inn, Sea Bright, New Jersey, January 1978
Photos by and courtesy of Betsy Ellis Lunney

Norman & Friends at the Lock Stock & Barrel, 1978. Left to right:
Garry Tallent, Max Weinberg, Billy Ryan, Norman Seldin, Clarence Clemons

Town" tour and were back in town. One night Clarence Clemons, Garry Tallent and Max Weinberg came by to sit in and play some tunes with me. All of the sudden, it evolved into a regular event. I basically had Clarence Clemons, Max Weinberg, and Garry Tallent for a house band one or two nights a week.

We had lines of cars backed up with people wanting to get in. I wasn't sure how damaging it would be to me because the audiences were getting used to hearing me playing with them. People were coming to hear members of the E Street Band, not me. Being the promoter that I was, I was promoting the hell out of everything. But at the same time, I knew that eventually Springsteen would take the E Street Band back on tour and I'd be by myself again. Still, it was kind of great while it lasted, and it lasted for some months.

So, Clarence, Max and Garry came to play and it was just like a house band. We actually bought a set of drums that stayed there for Max to play. We bought an upright bass for Garry Tallent as a birthday present. And we put the Mellotron on the other side of the piano. We played and we had ridiculous crowds.

This went on for quite a few months. At the same time, I'd gotten back into the horses.

Norman Seldin, Billy Ryan and Clarence Clemons at the Lock Stock & Barrel, February 14, 1978
Photo by and courtesy of Betsy Ellis Lunney

Open Call

I mentioned earlier that I have two sisters, Sarita and Rochelle. Both are talented musically. I guess it runs in the family. Both sisters play piano but it was Rochelle who decided to make entertainment her profession. Rochelle studied voice and dance and got involved with theater at a young age. She made her way to Broadway where she appeared in shows and sang in different clubs.

In April, 1979, Rochelle invited me to join her for an evening at a club called the Open Call. It was operated by the Beefsteak Charlie's restaurant chain and was located in the old Hotel Edison on 47th Street between Broadway and Eight Avenue in the Times Square section of Manhattan. Back in the day, the Hotel Edison was the first place that Kate Smith ever sang. The Hotel Edison had those old velvet curtains draped all around.

They just had a piano player, but being in the theater district, cast members from the different Broadway shows would drop by and get up and sing. On any given night you'd find cast members from shows like "Dracula," "I Love My Wife" and "Annie." "Annie" was playing at the Alvin Theatre (now the Neil Simon Theatre) and operatic tenor Donald Craig and others from "Annie" were regulars.

Anyone who wanted to sing would give the piano player a slip of paper with a song and he'd accompany them. It could be anything from opera to show tunes. Often the Broadway stars would keep a low profile because they didn't want to scare off new talent. It's not that someone off the street didn't have talent, but who'd want to follow a star like Donald Craig. Often, too, professional entertainers just wanted to relax and enjoy the show.

Well, I just went to the Open Call that evening with no plans of performing. The piano player that night was Houston Allred. Samuel Houston Allred was born in Texas, the son of that state's governor during the Roosevelt Era. Raised by a mother who adored show tunes, Houston chose the life of an entertainer rather than a politician. By the time I met him, he'd built a reputation as a phenomenal accompanist and club entertainer, mixing humor with show tunes.

On that evening, Andrea McArdle from the cast of "Annie" was there and requested the song "Sail Away" by Randy Newman. Houston Allred didn't know it. Now, Randy Newman was my forte at the time so I asked if I could sit in and do that one number. Someone must have warned Houston about me because he said, "I've been told to watch out for you." I assured him that it was his gig and I didn't want to upstage him. I just wanted to play as his guest. Well it must have gone over pretty well. Some of the people were filing out at the time, but when I started to play and sing, they came back in.

Then, shortly after that, the Open Call needed someone to fill in for a while. Allred recommended me. The club was a little nervous about hiring me, but they pretty much took Houston's word. I told them I'd only play the room if I could do what I wanted to do. That included leaving some of the Broadway influence behind and adding some jazz and blues.

Well, on opening night, Clarence Clemons and Garry Tallent dropped by and got up and joined me on some swing tunes. We got a standing ovation! Garry Tallent couldn't believe we'd gotten such an applause for acoustic instruments. I played the Open Call for a little while. Within two weeks I was setting attendance records for the club. And I actually got jobs from that as a solo. But while I liked playing in New York, I really wanted to get back to playing the Jersey Shore. I looked forward to going back to the Lock Stock & Barrel.

The Timmy Hensler Benefit Concert

On July 17, 1979, a friend of ours, Timothy Hensler died. Timmy was a self-employed tree surgeon who had died from injuries suffered after a fall from a tree. He was only 26 and left behind a wife and 18-month old daughter. Prior to being a tree surgeon, Timmy had been a bartender at the Lock Stock & Barrel in Fair Haven and the Hook Line and Sinker club in Rumson. All the musicians knew him. The Henslers were one of the six or seven families that everybody knew. In fact, I think one of them lived on the same street as I did at the time.

Clarence Clemons said, "Why don't we have a benefit for Timmy's wife?" So we decided to have a benefit with me and Clarence Clemons and other musicians who knew Timmy. Word got out that I was looking for musicians to volunteer their talents and the response was overwhelming. I had to be selective because there was only so much room on the stage and the concert had to be limited to two hours and twenty minutes. I know some local musicians were upset that they weren't included, but I had to draw the line somewhere. The final lineup ended up being Clarence Clemons (sax), Barry Lynn (drums), Max Weinberg (drums), Garry Tallent (bass), Billy Ryan (guitar), Ron Alard and Artie Bressler (horns), Phil Garland (violin), Richard Blackwell (congas) and David Sancious (jazz keyboard) and me (piano). Nicky Addeo would handle the vocals. I also had Peter Hartung, Bruce Foster and Kevin "Bird" Conair do opening solos. Danny Federici didn't perform but was gracious enough to work backstage, handling the sound system.

Clarence Clemons, Gary Tallent and
Norman Seldin preparing for the
Timmy Hensler Benefit Concert
Photo by Earl Stout

We paid all the costs for renting the theater and equipment, promoting the concert and providing for security and insurance out of our own pockets. All the musicians donated their talents for the benefit.

We started rehearsing for the benefit concert three times a week at Clarence's home. Clarence and I handled the publicity. We arranged for tickets to be sold at local stores and had posters and tee-shirts printed. We wanted to squelch any rumors that this was a "Springsteen concert." It wasn't. But with Clemons, Tallent, Weinberg and Federici of the E Street Band involved, rumors persisted.

The benefit concert was to be held at the Monmouth Arts Center (formerly the Carlton Theatre and now the Count Basie Center For The Arts) in Red Bank. We wanted to think of a really great way to open the show, because a benefit show like this is very emotional. I asked Ronny Alard, "How can we open this show, just to get the audience settled in?" Ronny said, "Bring me out with the place totally dark playing "Amazing Grace" on bagpipes."

We did that and, I'll tell you, it just left people stunned. They'd never seen anything like that. After a moment of silence, Ronny Alard came walking down the aisle in the middle of the theater playing "Amazing Grace." Then he was joined Clarence and the rest of us playing while Nicky Addeo supplied the vocals. That's what opened the concert.

Held on August 22, 1979, it turned out to be a phenomenal benefit concert. We had over 1,500 people there. It sold out to the brink and that was a big deal. Before the concert really got underway, we had 20 or 30 people yelling, "Bruce, Bruce." Clarence got really annoyed and told the audience, "Listen, y'all. You need to shut up. This thing isn't about Bruce. It has nothing to do with Bruce. It's a benefit for Timmy Hensler's family." Clarence kind of reprimanded the whole audience. After that, the audience toned it down quite bit.

The first set featured the band backing Nicky Addeo as he sang everything from the Miracles' "Bad Girl" to Jackie Wilson's "Higher And Higher." After a short intermission the band rocked a number of instrumentals beginning with Junior Walker's "Shotgun" and moving on to soul, blues and jazz numbers.

Timothy Hensler's widow came on stage to thank all of us and I had her stand by my piano while the band backed Nicky Addeo singing "Over The Rainbow." The song brought the entire audience to their feet for a long standing ovation. In the end we raised almost $16,000 for a trust fund for Timmy's daughter.

Rhythm & Blues at the Paramount

The benefit concert went so well, it wasn't long before some of us got together again on a big stage. In November, 1979, we did a rhythm & blues and rock & roll show at Asbury Park's Paramount Theatre. The show was a mix of rhythm & blues, doo wop acappella and early rock & roll. I again assembled a band that included among others, Clarence Clemons on sax, Garry Tallent on bass, Max Weinberg on drums and me on piano.

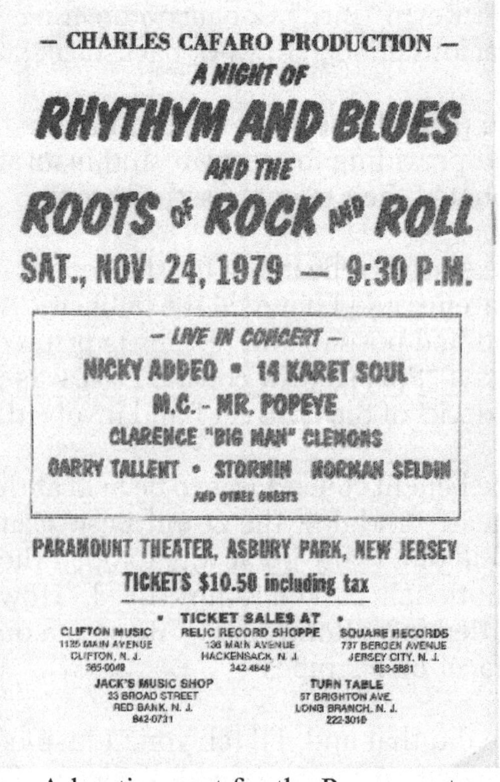

Advertisement for the Paramount Theatre concert. From the Classic Urban Harmony Archives

At the time, rhythm & blues and doo wop acappella music was seeing a resurgence in New Jersey, primarily through Ronnie I. (Italiano)'s Clifton, New Jersey, based United in Group Harmony Association (UGHA). Nicky Addeo had gotten to know Ronnie I. and some of the acappella groups that sang at their monthly meeting shows. So Nicky sang a set as did two young black acappella groups from UGHA: the Attributes from Jersey City and 14 Karat Soul from East Orange. Both of the acappella groups were excellent. The Attributes did cut an album for Ronnie I. but didn't last all that long after that. The group, 14 Karat Soul would go on to greater fame, appearing on "Saturday Night Live" four times and supplying the background vocals for the Stray Cats' "I Won't Stand In Your Way" before an extended stay performing in Japan.

We had Mr. Popeye (Kenny Pentifallo), former member of Southside Johnny's Asbury Jukes doing the emceeing. I recall doing a Ray Charles number which drew a standing ovation. Outside of having a terrible piano to play, it was a decent show. The Paramount Theatre was pretty run down at that time. But we did the show and I think we had a good crowd that night.

I know the advertisements call that concert a Charles Cafaro Production, but my recollection is that we all kind of put that show together. Nicky Addeo was trying to promote that fact that I had these three E Streeters, Clarence, Garry and Max, playing with me. In fact, prior to the Paramount Theatre concert we did a wedding.

Nicky Addeo was friends with Caesar Kimmel, who'd been co-founder of and longtime executive at Warner Communications. Caesar was also a big-time race horse owner who lived in Deal, New Jersey. His daughter was getting married and Caesar wanted a real good wedding band. I said, "Well, we can do that."

So, we had Max Weinberg on drums, Garry Tallent on bass, me on piano and Nicky Addeo singing. I don't recall if Clarence played that gig or not. But it was a very expensive all-star wedding band in Caesar Kimmel's backyard in Deal.

Roy Orbison and the Club Spanky

In 1980, I started gigging at a place called Club Spanky on Ocean Avenue in Long Branch. Club Spanky was started by a couple of my friends back in 1978. Rod Faccone and Ron Rosenzweig were both members of the band Fresh, who'd been playing the Jersey Shore for several years. Ron was the piano player while Rod played drums for the group. They used to leave their big Fender electric piano up there so I wouldn't have to move one. We used their public address system.

Roy Orbison, Publicity photo.

We were getting good crowds so I gradually started getting back into promoting shows. A friend of mine, Stu Rick, was booking all the bands from Holmdel, Howell, and Jackson at the time. Stu called me up and said, "Listen, would you like to promote something with Roy Orbison?" It wasn't cheap, but I had a friend named John Hanneman who helped out financially to do the show.

We brought Roy Orbison into Club Spanky on Sunday, August 10, 1980 for two shows - one at 4 in the afternoon and one at 11 P.M. We, Norman Seldin and Friends, opened up for Roy on both shows. My "Friends" consisted of Billy Ryan on guitar, Garry Tallent on bass, Max Weinberg on drums and me on keys. Roy Orbison had his own band so we didn't get to back him.

This was Roy Orbison's first-ever appearance on the Jersey Shore and, if I'm not mistaken, his first appearance in the state of New Jersey. Orbison was making a comeback after recent triple bypass surgery. His duet of "Getting' That Lovin' You Feeling Again" with Emmylou Harris was his first hit record since the 1960s.

Roy Orbison took the stage looking very pale, yet dressed all in black wearing a large medallion and his trademark red-tinted dark sunglasses. In contrast, his band was dressed all in white. Orbison launched into a string of his hits including "Only The Lonely," "Crying," Runnin' Scared" and "Blue Bayou." He even sang his first record, "Ooby Dooby" and finished with "Oh Pretty Woman."

I'll tell you, he was better than good. He was crazy, crazy, crazy, crazy good with just a phenomenal presentation. We had a good crowd, but not a great crowd. Nothing like we should have had. It was not a money maker. We probably lost a few thousand dollars on the show, believe it or not. But it still was a monster show for me to put on.

After that, I started doing solo gigs and at one point I also teamed up with a fiddler named Tim Ryan. Tim Ryan was a local guy who went to Juilliard School of Music. For a time he was actually a violinist for Hank Williams Jr. In 1980, country rock fiddle music was big thanks to songs like Charlie Daniels' "The Devil Went Down to Georgia." Tim couldn't really find much work on his own so we teamed up. We had a fiddle and a piano and it worked. I started booking the jobs because I had all the contacts.

Norman Seldin and Tim Ryan at Krone's Lavallette Inn

We played a place called the Office Lounge in Toms River as a duet on Sunday nights while I played the same place solo on Monday nights. Tim and I moved on to Krone's Lavallette Inn in Lavallette, New Jersey. We were doing a mix of country rock, progressive jazz and bluegrass music. I started booking a lot of gigs for us but our partnership didn't last very long. We were at one of Art Stock's clubs and Tim Ryan told me it would be our last night playing together. He said, "The manager doesn't want you. He wants me and my band." After I'd booked all these gigs he was kicking me out of my own act. Naturally, it didn't sit very well with me. But I went back to solo work at places like Scruples in Long Branch.

Club Spanky in Long Branch

Creative Force

By April of 1981, I'd decided to go back to a formula that I knew worked. I started a new band called Creative Force consisting of Billy Ryan on guitar, Kenny Pentifallo (Mr. Popeye) on drums, Nicky Addeo on vocals, Les Pennyfeather on bass and me on keyboards. Les Pennyfeather was a wonderful musician and person. He never complained about anything or anyone. He just got there on time and always played the best he could in any situation on stage. He and the others made Creative Force a very special band. They were one hell of a talented band, scary good, as scary as you could get.

Larry Chance
as Geraldo Santana Banana.
Photo courtesy of Larry Chance

Creative Force moved back into Club Spanky in Long Branch. I also started bringing in other acts to Club Spanky. On one occasion, I brought in Larry Chance, who remains one of the most talented entertainers I know. Larry, of course, was and is the lead singer of the Earls, but at that time he was making regular appearances on Don Imus' radio program, "Imus In The Morning" on WNBC-AM in New York City. In 1981, Don Imus was the most popular radio personality in America. On the radio, Larry played the fictitious comical character Geraldo Santana Banana, a routine he did for us at Club Spanky.

Creative Force continued for the rest of the year, playing Club Spanky and other places like the Bamboo Bar in Seaside Heights. In addition, I was doing solo gigs at Danny's Italian Restaurant in Red Bank.

All the while, I was entering a dark and depressing time in my life. On the home front, my marriage had disintegrated. The music scene was changing. There were still clubs around, but it just wasn't the same. And I started getting heavier into drugs - first pot, then pills and coke. In the entertainment business, the white powder was everywhere. It didn't affect my playing but I was rapidly going down a dark path.

As I'd done before when facing tough times in my life, I buried myself in my music. It seemed my only refuge. And I made a dramatic change in music style, away from the music of the Joyful Noyze and Creative Force. I went back into the classic sounds of the 1930's and 1940's. Things like the styles of Liberace, Oscar Peterson and George Schearing with hints of Bessie Smith and Billie Holiday.

The change started quite innocently. I was having dinner at an Italian restaurant in Sea Bright called Mario's Show Room. I was asked to play a couple songs and began with "I'll Be Seeing You." All of the sudden, the room got very quiet and when I finished playing I was greeted with loud applause. So I was offered a full time gig there.

I didn't realize what I was getting into. It turned out I was getting in with the Mob - big time. There was an upstairs room and they wanted to make it my show room. All of a sudden, there was a big piano there and I had my Bose speakers hung up. It was my show room and for the first few weeks, it was okay.

Then things started to get scary. I realized I was dealing with a lot of people who were connected to the Mob. I was getting $50 tips but I started thinking about where the money was coming from. I started to see the wrong kind of people. I'm talking about some really bad people. And the drugs were all around me. My jockey friends stopped coming to see me play for fear of losing their licenses at the track. They were telling me to get out of there. It got really bad. I started carrying a gun in case I got caught in the middle of something that wasn't of my doing. I had moved into an apartment with some friends. And there were pills there - the wrong kind of pills. There were bad things going on in my life. I felt the pressure all around me that some even worse things were about to happen.

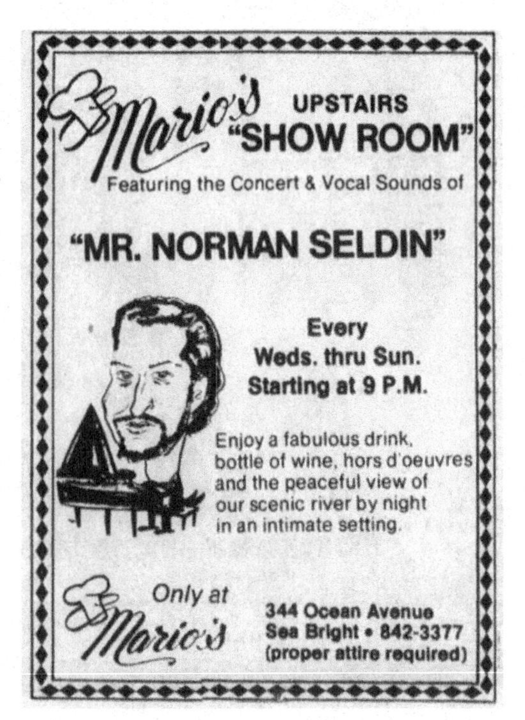

All I knew was that I had to get as far away from there as possible, as quickly as I could. I had a friend who was preparing to move to Mississippi who offered to help. He had a moving van that could transport my belongings and said he could find me work once I got down there.

I had a key to the restaurant and went there when no one was around to pick up my Bose system. I took back my two Bose speakers, my amplifier, my microphone and my microphone stand. My friend's moving van loaded up all of my belongings, including my piano. I made plans to meet him at his place in Mississippi once I got there.

I didn't know what the future would bring once I reached Mississippi. I just knew I had to get away. So I left.

Chapter Ten
Mississippi Delta Blues

The year was 1982. Leaving New Jersey wasn't easy, but I had to get away. My instincts were probably correct. I later heard that the owner of the venue where I'd been playing had abandoned the restaurant and exited the country in a hurry several weeks after I'd left. Something about the Mob having a one million dollar life insurance policy on him in case he fell behind on his debts.

But life didn't exactly start out so well for me in Jackson, Mississippi. It all sounded nice before I left. This fellow I knew was going to help me get settled and find me work once I got there. Well, things got off to disastrous start. I drove down there with a girl I was seeing at the time. Then before a month was up, the guy who was supposed to be helping me ran off with the girl I'd been with, leaving me stranded.

I was in the middle of Mississippi with maybe $1,800 in my pocket and no work. I didn't know a damn thing about the town and I didn't know a damn soul there. I only had my car and my little P.A. system. I didn't have a portable piano and everything available to rent down there was acoustic. All of my furniture and everything else I owned was in storage with this guy. So I couldn't even get to it.

I sank into a deep state of depression. I don't think I've ever been so depressed either before or after. I had to make some calls to get someone to lend me a couple of thousand dollars to get my own stuff released from storage. I finally got back my pinball machines, my furniture and a few other possessions. But they kept all of my clothing, my expensive boots and even my expensive cowboy hats that had become my hallmark. I'm talking about thousands of dollars' worth of clothes. They didn't return them.

What could I do? I just started driving around, looking for work. I found a restaurant in a little shopping center in Ridgeland, Mississippi, just ten miles north of Jackson. The owner of Cassidy's Restaurant and Lounge said, "Well, if you had a piano, you could play here." I just didn't know what to do at the time. Finally, someone rented a piano for me and put it in this little restaurant. I don't think the place held more than forty people. The pay wasn't great but it was a start.

I played at that place for a while and then started getting little gigs on the side. People would come in and say, "Are you available to play?" and I'd say, "Yeah, but you'll have to supply a piano." One guy said, "Somebody told me that you played with the E Street Band." I said, "Well, I played with a bunch of their members and I did some recordings, that kind of thing." He said, "Fair enough. I know some people who would love to hire you."

I quickly learned which music styles went over down there. One guy said, "You need to go with that Southern thing, that nasal thing, old Louisiana." And while I was at that little place, a woman said, "This is my number. I would like you to come to my house and play. I'll have my husband pick you up in his airplane, if you need." Now, I had no idea who this woman and her family were. It turned out they were the original lumber people that made all the wood necks for the Fender guitars. They controlled hundreds of acres in Woodville, Mississippi and they were amazing to me. It was the first time I'd ever eaten deep-fried turkey and food like that.

I kept meeting people and getting more jobs. Once a fellow came over to me and said, "When you get done playing, I'd like you to meet these five friends of mine." They were older men. I said, "Well, are they musicians?" He said, "Oh, no. They run a big club at the Main Harbor.

The Main Harbor was a marina and recreation area on the Ross Barnett Reservoir in Ridgeland, Mississippi. While every bar in the city of Jackson had to close at midnight, the bars and restaurants at Main Harbor could stay open 24 hours because they were in a designated resort area. So, the minute everything closed in Jackson, people headed over to Main Harbor.

The fellow said, "I'd like you here playing two or three nights a week." I played for a number of weeks in the indoor front lounge bar at the Main Harbor. But the crowds and the following got so big, they moved me out onto the Dock Bar, right on the reservoir.

The Dock, Main Harbor, Ridgeland, Mississippi

The Dock was a sizable outdoor nightclub located right on the water. Because of its water accessibility, people could come by boat and party at the Dock. People would listen to music on the deck or float in life jackets in the water.

The Dock had everything from speedboats to houseboats pulling up. They'd usually have 100 to 150 people there drinking. The first show I did, I thought that the whole dock was going to collapse. There had to have been 600 people there. And it got worse, and worse. With the crowds, it was hard to entertain with just the piano so I soon added a guitar player, drummer and bass player. We called ourselves Stormin' Norman Seldin & the Dock Rockers. There was so much talent in the area. The *Malaco* recording studios were in Jackson so you know the kind of talent I was surrounded with. A lot of the musicians that I met in Jackson ended up going to Nashville and becoming very successful.

Each week at the Dock, the crowds grew bigger and bigger. It reached the point where the venue started charging a dollar, just to keep some people away. But people wouldn't stay away. It was the music I was playing. I played Randy Newman stuff and then I starting to do some Delta blues. The crowd just ate it up.

While I was doing the gigs around Jackson. the woman who hired me for that party had a fellow named Timothy McGivaren call me. Tim was a Natchez resident who happened to be an excellent bass player. He loved classical music and he also played banjo and bass. I found out later that he'd gone to Louisiana Tech with pro quarterback Terry Bradshaw.

Tim called me and said, "I hear you're a piano man who can really play." He said he was booking the Eola Hotel in Natchez, Mississippi, which was one of the oldest grand hotels in the area. He was also doing matinees at the Under-The-Hill Saloon there. He said, "I'd like you to come in and see how they like you." I said okay, but first I started playing some local gigs with Tim on bass. Once in a while we'd also bring in a drummer named Fred. Every place I played was packed. It didn't make a difference where I played, whether just myself solo, or with Tim.

The Under-The-Hill Saloon

In Natchez, Tim arranged for us to play at the Under-the-Hill Saloon. Tim told me this was where the riverboats pulled in and people came to drink and hear the music. Now the Under-The-Hill Saloon had quite a history. The exact date of construction is unknown due to a courthouse fire, but it was most likely built in the late 1700s or early 1800s. Natchez had been a stop along the Mississippi River for flatboats and riverboats bringing supplies to New Orleans in our country's early history. This dockside section of Natchez, called Under-The-Hill, had been a transient stopover for river men looking to blow off steam. The Under-The-Hill Saloon was one of the last remaining structures from a time when the area was filled with gamblers, robbers and prostitutes. The area had been a rough place. Legendary pioneer, Jim Bowie, earned his reputation in a knife fight within sight of the Saloon. In the past, the Saloon has been used as a brothel, warehouse, general store and bar.

I'll never forget the first time I went to the Under-The-Hill Saloon. I drove there with my Jersey plates and pulled up in front of the two story brick building. It looked every part the two hundred year old hole-in-the-wall tavern. It looked like something out of the Old West. The doors to the Under-the-Hill Saloon were actually swinging gates.

The first thing I noticed was a guy out front who was just beating on this little blond-haired girl who looked to be about 16 or 17 years old. There was another fellow sitting outside in one of those big, giant rocking chairs. He was chewing tobacco and spitting into a spittoon, seemingly oblivious to what was going on.

I wasn't anxious to interfere in someone else's business but I couldn't just couldn't let this guy smack this girl around like a madman. I jumped out of my car, ran up on the porch and pulled the guy off of the girl. The guy was startled at first but then raised his fist to hit me. So I clocked him! Actually, I knocked the shit out of him. When he finally got up, he mumbled, "You'll be sorry for this." I just thought, "What else could go wrong down here?"

I went back to my car and started taking my stuff inside. I'd never been there before. There was a fellow behind the bar that stood only about four feet eleven inches tall. He had to stand on a stool to be seen above the bar. But he was neatly dressed in a tie and vest and he had a big cigar jutting out of his mouth. He stared at me for a second and said, "You must be Stormin' Norman. I'm J.D. and I'm going to call the police right now." I said, "Why are you doing that?" He exclaimed, "Shit! You've done it now. You have really done it now. That boy that you just beat the shit out of outside,

The Under-The-Hill Saloon, Natchez, Mississippi
Sketch by C. Hudson Chadwick, from the back of the album
"Stormin' Norman: Rock 'N Roll Plus"

his daddy owns a couple thousand acres across the bridge in Louisiana. He'll be over here in a heartbeat." I said, "Oh, well." What was I supposed to do?

Meanwhile, a film crew arrived outside to shoot a television commercial for a firm promoting the riverboats. They had Jerry Lee Lewis there to record the music track as he lived just across the bridge in Vidalia, Louisiana. The film crew was having trouble, though. Apparently, Jerry Lee had been drinking and they couldn't get him calmed down enough to play. He was giving them such a hard time the commercial director said, "We're just not going to be able to shoot this today."

At that point, the guy that in the rocking chair with the spittoon pointed to me and said, "We got a pi-an-ny picker here who could probably make some music for you." The director inquired, "Do you play piano?" I answered yes and he asked, "Can you give me some music for the background of a video we're shooting? We were supposed to have Jerry Lee, but he won't be doing it." I said, "Look, no problem." They put all the cameras up and I played "A Whole Lotta Shaking Going On." I played the living hell out of it.

The film crew had just finished shooting the commercial when a big white a Lincoln town car pulled up outside. A chauffeur opened the door and this big guy got out. This guy must have weighed 300 pounds and looked like the guy from "Smokey and the Bandit." And J.D., the little guy behind the bar, said, "Oh, shit!"

I said, "What's the matter?" J.D. mumbled, "That's that boy's daddy." I just sat there at the bar. The Under-The-Bar Saloon wasn't a big place and there were only a few other people in there. The big guy said in a loud voice, "I'm looking for some piano player." I guess they must have pointed me out because I wasn't the only one in there. I was just sitting there wondering what was going to happen next. And J.D. was standing on the stool by the telephone, ready to dial the police.

The fellow asked, "Are you that piano player?" I said, "I'm Norman." He asked, "Did you just beat up somebody out front?" I replied, "Well, I pulled up and there was a guy about my size smacking and punching this little blonde girl all over the front of this place." He asked, "Was there nobody helping?" I said, "No. Where I come from, we don't permit that sort of thing."

"Well," he said, "Can I buy you a drink?" I said, "Thanks, but I don't drink." He said, "Well, then, I'll buy a drink for everybody else at the bar. And when I find that boy, he'll be lucky that I don't kill him."

I asked, "What happened?" He said, "That was his wife he was beating on and he also punched his mama before he left the farm. I just wish you would have beat the living shit out of him a little bit more." I said, "He's beaten up pretty bad." The fellow said, "Evidently, not bad enough, because he got up." This giant of a man put his hand on my shoulder and said, "I want to thank you. That's a nice thing that you did. If you ever need anything, you just ask. Everyone around here knows where to find me. You have a nice day, son." I said, "Thank you, sir," and he left.

Within four days, the commercial I played in ran on every major tourism network. I was trying to lay low in Mississippi and everybody up North was seeing the damn commercial.

That was my introduction to Natchez, Mississippi. I played there for several months and I learned a lot. They called me the "Pi-an-ny Picker." But everything just kind of exploded from there on. I couldn't do anything wrong. I really couldn't.

While I'd only been in Natchez a short time, they held a big Mardi Gras celebration in February, 1983. It was actually the first big Mardi Gras held in Natchez in 73 years. After the last one in 1909, the people in Natchez were dealing with Prohibition, the boll weevil's destruction of their cotton industry and the effects of two major fires. I guess they just didn't feel much like celebrating. Now, more than seven decades later, the city's economy had been revived by the oil industry and tourism. Mardi Gras in Natchez was back and I was right in the middle of it.

The theme of that Mardi Gras was understandably "A Salute to the Oil Industry" and the designated Rex (King of the Carnival) was oil man John Callon. The celebration kicked off on Friday evening with an "invitation only" black tie cocktail party honoring Mr. Callon. It was held at the recently refurbished grand Eola Hotel and Tim McGivaren and I supplied the entertainment.

The next day they had a big parade with twenty-five floats that wound its way through Natchez' downtown historic district. The parade marshal was actor Ralph Waite, star of the TV series, "The Waltons." Waite was in town along with other stars and a whole film crew from Warner Bros. because they were filming a new TV series there called "Mississippi." After that first night, I got a lot of invitations from the Warner Bros. people to play private staff parties that week.

Ralph Waite had just written, directed and starred in a film called "On The Nickel." The movie was about an alcoholic on skid row (the term "Nickel" refers to the Los Angeles skid row street, Fifth Avenue). The soundtrack featured five original songs composed and sung for the movie by Tom Waits, including the dark lyric title song, "On The Nickel." When Warner Bros. had a party in Natchez, I was the only one who could imitate Tom Waits' garbled guttural voice. Ralph Waite was just amazed that I could sing anything after I sang a Tom Waits song, so we chatted a lot.

Besides local help, Ralph hired off-duty state police officers to work for him in Natchez. When I had to rush back to Jackson for a one night gig, Ralph said, "We'll get you back there in about 55 minutes." I said, "It's an hour and 40 minute drive." But Ralph insisted, "You'll be home in time." He called someone and told him, "Take Norman back to Jackson, then pick him up tomorrow and bring him back here." I got the quickest ride ever and nobody stopped us. I said, "Aren't you going to get a ticket?" The fellow just laughed, and said, "Yeah, maybe next year." So he dropped me off, I played what I had to play and the next day he brought me back.

I got to meet a lot of other celebrity actors involved in the "Mississippi" TV show filming, including Muhammad Ali and Linda Mae Miller who was Jackie Gleason's daughter. They actually filmed parts of the parade for an episode called "Mardi Gras." Ralph Waite directed that episode. I didn't appear in any of the scenes they filmed. I just entertained at the staff parties.

There are a lot of huge pre-Civil War mansions in Natchez and elsewhere in Mississippi. I ended up played a lot private parties in those homes. Very private parties, but with fifty to a hundred people and they'd all fit into the one front room. Those were big homes.

At one mansion in Natchez where I played piano, the owner asked me to come look and at the room ahead of time. I took a ride over there and was in the hallway when I heard a player piano playing Beethoven's "Moonlight Sonata." The fellow said, "You've heard that before, haven't you?" I said, "Yeah, I have, but I think that's either Liszt ..." I wasn't sure whether it was Franz Liszt's arrangement that was playing.

He said, "It's Andre Previn's player piano that was sold after his divorce." The fellow had paid $195,000 for it with the piano roll recordings of all these original artists. That was the piano I played on at the party that night with the trio. I had the tuner come by and told him, "I can't believe I'm going to beat on this piano tonight." But that's what it was. The owner had a whole library full of all the piano rolls that went with the piano.

Vicksburg, Mississippi

Then I was introduced to a restaurant owners in Vicksburg, Mississippi. They rented a piano and I played five or six dates there in Vicksburg. These were not big restaurants, but nice places. I had my Bose speaker, my little one amp, a microphone and the piano.

Someone had told me there was still evidence of the Siege of Vicksburg during the Civil War so I asked, "Are there really cannonballs in the walls here?" They said, "Yeah. Take a walk outside, two blocks down." I walked a short distance and there they were, cannonballs right in the walls of the building. I said, "How the hell close were they?" They said, "Well, they were shooting from across the Mississippi River." I ended up playing a couple restaurants in Vicksburg. There's a lot of history down there

Stormin' Norman:
The Rock 'N Roll Plus Album

Word had gotten around Mississippi that I'd had members of the E Street Band playing with me when I was back in Jersey. Springsteen and the E Street Band were well known at that time but I was doing fine by myself in Mississippi, drawing nice crowds. Still, someone asked if I had any recordings with the E Streeters.

Well, it turned out that before I left for Mississippi, I'd taken members of my different bands into the House Of Hits Studios and recorded some songs. So I had recordings of me with Clarence Clemons, Max Weinberg, Danny Federici, Garry Tallent and Roy Bittan, along with Billy Ryan, Southside Johnny Lyon and others.

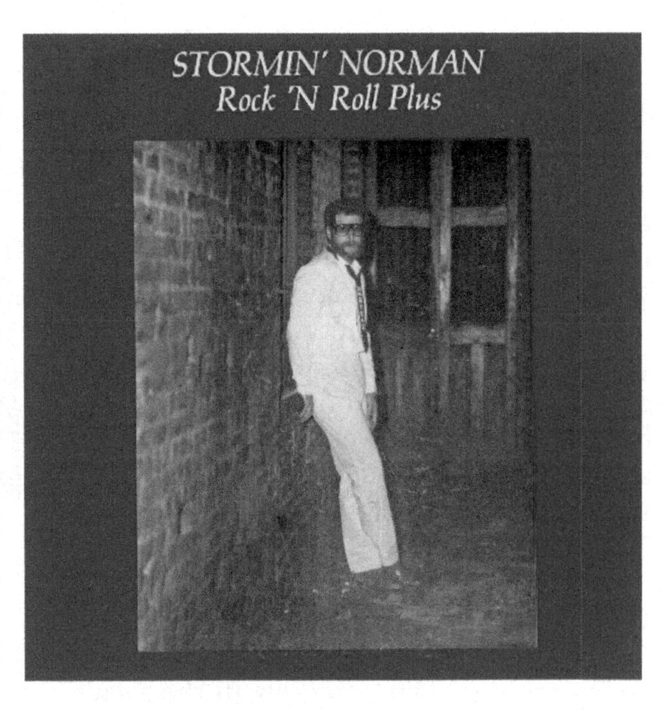

These were all original songs I'd written. I still had the reel of the rough unmixed takes from the sessions. Now, I was on a roll in Mississippi but I was always looking for an additional boost.

Well, this fellow, James Griffin, had a great recording studio and I did a few things there with him. He mastered an LP for me and did a very nice job. We had a local photographer, Sally Durkin, take the photo for the cover. It was actually taken down in the trenches of the Under-The-Hill Saloon, on the steps. We pressed up about 1,000 vinyl copies of the album on my own record label, *Ivory*. And boy, that just set things on fire again. We put copies into the stores and were selling them in the clubs.

During this time I became friends with Bill Simmons. Bill was a Jackson native who spent much of his time in the music scene of Nashville. In fact, he was road manager for Eddie Rabbitt who'd scored a number one record with "I Love A Rainy Night" a few years before. Bill would later go on to play a role in the careers of country stars Brad Paisley and Vince Gill.

There was another guy, Bill Sanders, who used to come to see me play. I recall he'd always request the Freddie King song "Big Legged Woman." Bill Sanders and I became friends. Bill and his partner, Leslie "Bubba" Spencer, owned five restaurants called Poet's located throughout Mississippi and Louisiana. The one in Jackson was called "Poet's in the Quarter" and was on Lakeland Drive. It was a gorgeous restaurant and nightclub. Poet's decor had a Hollywood flavor, owing in part to Bubba's prior background, working with Aaron Spelling in Los Angeles. The club had stained glass windows and a long piano bar made of wood with the upright behind it.

Bill Sanders loved my playing and gave me all the nights that he could. Bill made sure that I was well taken care of; I didn't pay for a thing.

Bill was a multimillionaire. He had an insane business card that read, "Bill Sanders, Millionaire. Hours 10:00 to 12:00, lunch at 12:00. Closed the rest of the day." We became real good friends and I used to hang out at his house. All he wanted to do was drive his Porsches, play tennis and party. He'd throw me the keys to his Porsche and I'd take it for a day or two. He had a woman cook for him and every Thanksgiving she'd make me a turkey with all the stuffing. Bill passed away a couple years ago and I really miss him. I'm still friends with his son.

Ace and Malaco Records

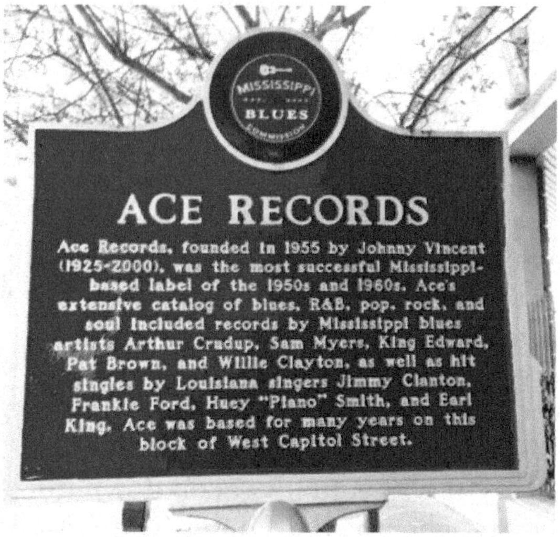

Jackson was a huge music town and there was so much talent there. It was the home of *Ace Records*, Mississippi's most successful record label in the 1950's and 1960's. *Ace* issued records by Jimmy Clanton, Frankie Ford, Earl King and Huey "Piano" Smith. I met *Ace Records* founder, Johnny Vincent while I was in Jackson. Somebody introduced me to him in one of the clubs. A bunch of his friends were going to his house and they invited me to come along. They said, "Come on, we'll show you the old *Ace Records* building."

Johnny Vincent died in 2000.
Long after I left Jackson,
this plaque was installed to mark
the former location of *Ace Records*.

I got to talk with Johnny Vincent there a little bit. He had all these *Ace* label records laying around. We talked about the area's R&B and gospel music and about Vincent's dealings with *Specialty* and *Aladdin Records*. This was before Johnny Vincent had started leasing his records for reissue and he warned me about letting people steal my music. Of course, this was advice I'd already learned from Jocko many years before. Johnny said, "Well, you just watch yourself down here, son, because people have a habit of stealing things." I said, "Thanks but I can take care of myself." He was an interesting man, who was just trying to protect everything he had worked so hard for.

While Johnny Vincent's sway over popular music had waned, the hot record label in Jackson while I was there was *Malaco*. By then, *Malaco* was well established, having produced hits like King Floyd's "Groove Me," Jean Knight's "Mr. Big Stuff," Dorothy Moore's "Misty Blue" and Anita Ward's "Ring My Bell."

But while I was in Jackson, *Malaco* decided to stop trying to compete with the major labels in the pop field and concentrate on niche markets that they excelled in, like blues, southern R&B and gospel. They had artists like Johnny Taylor, Bobby "Blue" Bland, Little Milton and Denise LaSalle. In Jackson, I first realized how popular gospel music was. *Malaco* had gospel groups, like the Jackson Southernaires and the William Brothers, who had huge followings.

Malaco had a solid house band. They had a drummer named James Stroud who I met there a few times. He ended up leaving *Malaco* and going to Nashville where he did really well as a producer. It seems a lot of talented music people came out of Jackson and went right on to Nashville.

I got around quite a bit. Besides Poet's, I played places like Chevy's Lounge, a nightclub that had just opened in May of 1984 behind the Four Seasons Restaurant in Indianola,

Mississippi. There was such music history all around me. Indianola was one of the places that gave birth to delta blues. It was the birthplace of Albert King and the childhood home of B. B. King. Everywhere I went there was music and I absorbed it all, from New Orleans R&B to delta blues and southern rock & roll. I started out more of a single there but after I added a couple other musicians with me. All of the sudden everybody wanted to play with me. I found musicians all over. I developed my styles from playing with all of those players. A piano player stood out down there. I didn't have a B3 organ to carry around, so it was just a piano. Most groups down there didn't have a keyboard player.

Playing Chevy's in Indianola, Mississippi

I started transcribing to piano what other musicians were playing on guitar. Nobody had ever bothered doing that before. They were surprised. I'd hear them say, "That's strange. That's a guitar lick." I'd said, "I know. It sounds pretty good on piano." It took years for me to work that in. I needed to pick up stuff from those guitar players in the Delta and the blues pioneers like Blind Sam Myers. Sam spent ten years playing drums along side of Elmore James and sat in on sessions with everyone from Muddy Waters to Howling Wolf, Little Walter and Hound Dog Taylor. I did a few things with Sam. When I met him, he was just playing small clubs in Jackson. And I needed to get back to that drummer that kept that New Orleans flavor on that kind of stuff. Because you've got piano, but it's still not the same. So, I got a big education down there in Mississippi.

I recall one band called the Tangents that used to play the Dock a lot when I was there. Their front man, Charlie Jacobs, was the son-in-law of famous jazz pianist, and Mississippi native Mose Allison. The Tangents were everywhere. They were very friendly and good players.

I was all over the state of Mississippi. I was in the Delta one week and playing a Jackson Country Club the next. I was busy. I worked five or six nights a week, I was going all the time.

Of course there were always a few jealous people down there that didn't like the idea of a Yankee coming down and getting all the exposure. They thought I was a misfit, but I'm a misfit everywhere I go. It just seems that way. People in Mississippi just took a liking to me. I was playing everywhere. It was just a good place for me, once I got in that crowd. They looked after me like I was valuable. The newspapers started calling me "Jackson's favorite piano man."

Stormin' Norman Seldin
in Jackson, Mississippi
Photo by Charles Griffin

From Mississippi to the White House

I met a guy in one of the clubs. He ran a couple of hotels and he said, "I think I may have something good for you." Well, I'd heard that kind of talk often and didn't think much of it. I thought, "What could he have for me that's so good? I'm already playing at country clubs. I'm playing at places I shouldn't even be in."

But, sure enough, I get a call from him and I found out he was the president of the Mississippi chapter of the Southeast Tourism Society. The STS is a non-profit organization dedicated to the promotion and development of tourism throughout the Southeast United States. They voted to have me represent Mississippi at a festival on the White House grounds. I remember blurting out, "You want a Jew from New Jersey representing Mississippi on the grounds of the White House?" He said, "Yep."

Each of seven southeastern states sent a delegation to Washington, D.C., during National Tourism Week to entertain politicians, bureaucrats, and journalists on the White House lawn. The Southeastern Tourism Society staged this, the second annual "Capitol Hill Hoedown," in May of 1985. There were tents set up with games, prizes, crafts, celebrities, food and plenty of Southern music.

Each southern state had tents where they served up tourist information, food and entertainment representing their state. Georgia sent a bunch of Georgia peaches plus Hank Aaron who was living in Atlanta at the time. Alabama sent barbeque chicken. Kentucky sent the Bourbon and under the Kentucky tent a man in bib overalls was filling glasses with Jack Daniels. Florida sent oysters and a 250-pound key lime pie. Mississippi sent fried catfish and me!

So, there I was under a striped tent on the lawn of the White House, playing for crowds of 500 the first night and 800 the next. The audience consisted of politicians, foreign dignitaries, members of the press, tourist industry professionals and others. I played everything from Jerry Lee Lewis' "Whole Lot Of Shakin' Goin' On" to Carl Perkins' "Blue Suede Shoes" and Elvis' "Hound Dog." I mixed in Mississippi John Hurt's "Candy

Man" and plenty of Delta blues. They crowd just went crazy.

It was a big deal. There must have been twenty or thirty other piano players they could have picked to represent Mississippi, and they picked me.

The "Jackson in June Summerfest"

The following month, I was honored again by being invited to play the first-ever "Jackson in June Summerfest." The four day outdoor festival was held at the Mississippi State fairgrounds and featured top artists ranging from local clubs' favorites to nationally known stars. The entertainers included music styles of blues, jazz, country, rock & roll, R&B, soul, funk, pop and Motown. The headliners that year were the Commodores, the Temptations and Mickey Gilley. There were also carnival rides and food booths.

Diane Pryor

While I was in Jackson, Diane Pryor came back into my life. She sang with me at the Lock Stock and Barrel in New Jersey. We dated a little and were always good friends, and still are. I kind of ran out on her along with everybody else when I left New Jersey in a hurry. She was single and always traveled around a lot. When Diane showed up in Mississippi, she just fit right in. She sat and listened to us and then got up and sang. Diane has that Joni Mitchell or Judy Collins type of voice. Then the bass player said, "Yeah, let's add her to our act." It was only an extra $30 or $40 or something then. And she stayed and sang, and got into things again.

All told, Jackson was good to me. I got a big music education down there. And there were so many gorgeous women down there. I said that if I ever got married again, it would be to a girl from Mississippi. Of course, Jackson also was a big drug market too. Wherever I went I ended up back with the same bad habits. I was doing mostly cocaine and pot. No hallucinogens and no needles. Nothing like that. But I was so ignorant. I didn't know anything about acid or anything like that. One time somebody gave me a big sheet of postage stamps for Christmas I said, "Who the hell gives somebody a sheet of postage stamps for Christmas?"

I was sitting there with the sheet of stamps laying on the table when one of my musicians came in. He exclaimed, "Jesus, God! What the hell are you doing with that?" I said, "Well, I'm curious because none of these stamps say what the postage denomination is." He looked at me incredulously and said, "Don't you know what you have there?"

I said, "They have pictures of an Egyptian pharaoh on them. That's all it means to me." He said, "Each one of those is worth about $20 a piece." I said, "What?" He laughed and said, "Yeah, that's acid." I said, "I don't know anything about that." I could have been the most popular guy in town from that sheet but I just wasn't into that.

I'd been in Mississippi for about four years when a fellow showed up at one of the Jackson nightclubs and said, "I've been sent to bring you to Panama City Beach." I said, "Where the hell is Panama City Beach?"

Chapter Eleven
Florida

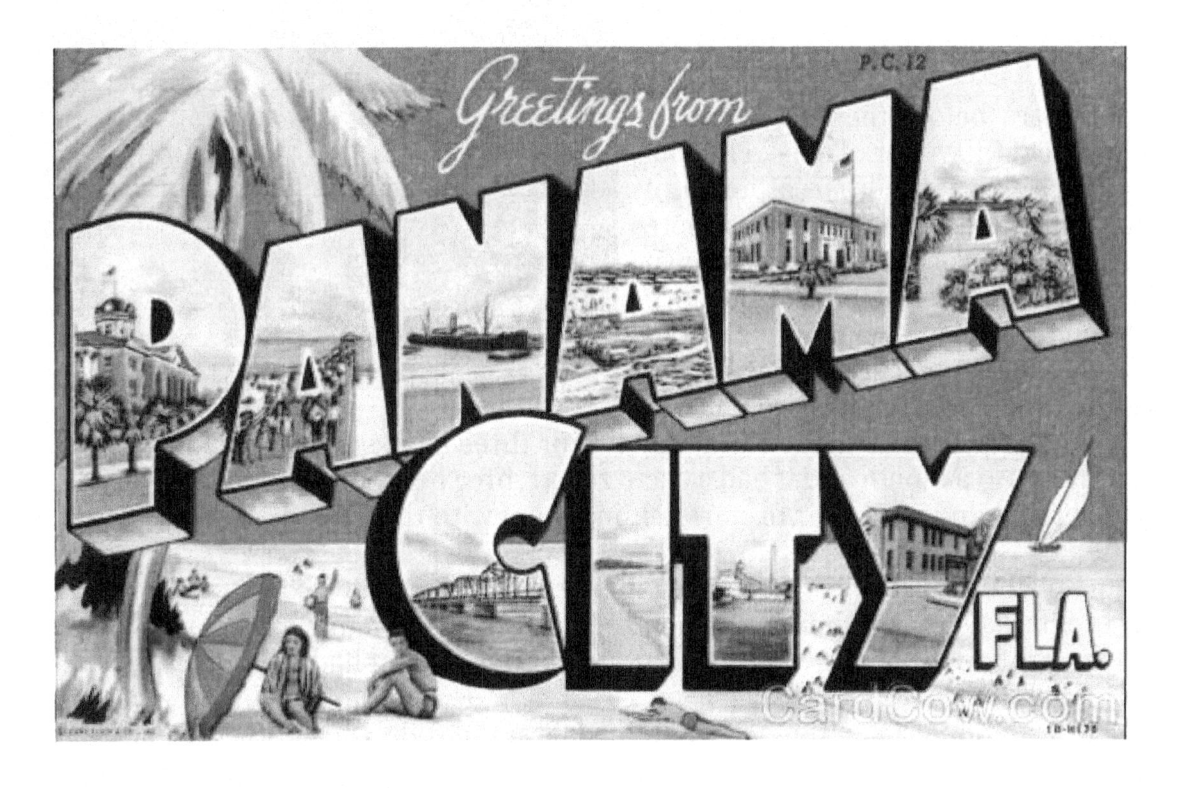

Club La Vela, Panama City Beach

While I was in Jackson, Mississippi, in early 1986, a fellow named Mike Preble came to see me. He'd been managing some Holiday Inns in either Mobile or Dothan, Alabama, but had recently accepted a position at a club in Florida. Mike had heard that there was this really hot entertainer in Jackson and he took the time to drive in and listen to me perform. Between sets he came up to me and asked, "Can I speak with you?" He wanted me to come to a nightclub called La Vela Beach Club & Concert Hall (later known as Club La Vela) in Panama City Beach, Florida, Mike had become the general manager there and he said he'd make me the music director. I would book the bands, be an emcee and play my solo material. I had never really heard of the place but Mike Preble wanted me to come down there and see it.

I mentioned the place to three or four friends and they said, "Oh my God. That place just recently opened. It's the biggest night club in the world." It was, and for that matter, still is, the largest nightclub in the United States. Currently, it has the capacity to entertain 6,000 people but even back them it still held at least a couple of thousand. Panama City Beach remains a favorite destination for college kids during spring break. They'd see 15,000 to 20,000 kids come there every four days.

Mike Preble and Norman Seldin

I went there before the spring break, while it was still winter. To me, Panama City Beach just looked like a bunch of sand dunes and beautiful water where you could see 25 or 30 feet straight down to the bottom. But there must have been fourteen or fifteen huge nightclubs and even an aquarium there. I decided to take the job and I found a nice place to live there. It was on the beach and only two or three blocks from the club. The rent was only $ 400 a month and it had a Jacuzzi and three bedrooms. I moved everything I owned there and went over to start helping them with the club.

The La Vela Beach Club, itself, was even more spectacular than I expected. It was right next to Spinnakers, which was another huge club. As the name says, La Vela Beach Club sat right on the beach. The beach area was so big that it had five volleyball courts on it. Karch Kiraly the volleyball player, coach, broadcast announcer and key member of the U.S. National Team that won gold medals at the 1984 and 1988 Olympic Games used to have beach volleyball tournaments there. The club itself was so big they had 28 bar stations.

La Vela Beach Club did a lot of promotion on WPFM, the local radio station. WPFM-FM had developed an equal following of both locals and tourists and sponsored the big-name Spring Break events in the area. We cut radio commercials for the La Vela and I did all the radio announcing and the overdubs. The commercials were purchased six months in advance. In fact, WPFM did live radio remote broadcasts from the club almost every day.

On my first official day on the job as manager, the general manager introduced me to all the different people. Then he said, "Now, there are a few people here. Just don't let them drag you away down the beach and show you the scenery of the city." I really didn't know what he was talking about. So, that first day I was there making sure everything was set up and sound checked. Everything was supposed to start at 2:00 o'clock in the afternoon and it was only 11:00 in the morning.

Then these two girls, sisters, came up to me and said, "Hey, you must be Norman." I said, "Yes." I figured they must have heard me on the radio. The girls asked, "Can we show around? Come on. Take a walk on the beach with us." I wasn't a big beach person but I thought, "It's early yet. What have I got to lose?" So I took a walk with the two sisters. Well, I ended up spending a couple hours with these sisters in their condo on the beach. I got a little smoked up on weed and didn't quite know where I was. Meanwhile, back at the club, they were on the P.A. System paging all over the beach to try to find me. Finally the girls walked me back to the club to make sure I got there. When I came walking up, the guy who hired me said, "Oh geez. Oh God. What did I tell you?" The sisters said, "We didn't hurt him." He asked them, "Couldn't you two have just given him a break for a week or two?"

Norman on Panama City Beach

Just to give you some history, La Vela Beach Club had first opened on Labor Day 1984, so the year before I got there was their first full year of operation. The club had lost three quarters of a million dollars that previous year. Spring break had started and the first order of business was to find out why the club was hemorrhaging money.

Mike Preble and I went out to the dumpster which had not yet been emptied from the weekend before. We proceeded to count how many cups were in the dumpster. I'd never really done liquor control like that before as there were better ways. But when Mike finished counting, he found that just from that last weekend there around 8,000 or 9,000 cups there. The cash registers only registered about 2,200 drinks. This was being run as an all cash business and the bartenders and the people at the door were stealing from the owners.

The club had to review the entire staff and get rid of some of the employees that were grifting. It was big undertaking. I had to book the bands, but in the beginning I knew none of the local bands. I had to really count on one or two sub-agents to tell me which ones drew the most people. And, of course, some bands were restricted from playing La Vela because of a radius clause in their contracts with Spinnakers next door.

Competition was fierce among the clubs on the beach. In the club next door, they had a guy named Frank playing piano. He had a thing called "Play One, Drink One." Every time somebody requested a song from him, you had to drink. People could hardly walk out of the place at night.

I was just this piano solo guy. I had to change my whole repertoire around. I had to go to Jimmy Buffett and John Prine and songs like that to play on the beach. There was a total turnaround of tons of lyric sheets that they kept there.

They had a huge outdoor P.A. system set up because the back deck was so big. The deck that I was on had the main band. Then, about 200 feet across the deck there was another bandstand with a different band playing at the same time. There were so many people that you couldn't hear the band on the other side. And the band across the beach had 1,000 people. In addition, wc had a disco that held 1,000 people. I never saw anything that big in my life - anywhere.

The parking lot was well over five acres and they charged $10 a car to park. Then to walk in it was $10 and you didn't even get any drinks with your entrance fee. They had a fortune in money coming in, but it was an "all cash" business. They had no system for taking charge cards at all, so we had to rework all of that. The owner, Alois Pfeffer, was from Germany and he had everybody running the club for him. But they put me in the position of performer and also an emcee on all the contests.

Norman emceeing a bikini contest at La Vela

I emceed the bikini contests. We gave away a mink coat for the winner once a week. And the raunchy part of this was, we invented a contest called Jaws. There was a $ 500 prize for the woman could could eat a banana in the most creative way. Young women lined up for this thing and men came by the hundreds from all over. Every Tuesday night we had a Jaws contest. Even the local sheriff came by one night to watch, wearing his two pearl handled guns. He told me, "This is going to be quite a thing to control."

I was the one who early every Tuesday morning would go to the grocery store and get the biggest bananas I could find. I would buy eight or nine big bunches of huge bananas and bring them back for the contest that night. People in town knew me from playing at Club La Vela and would say, "Here comes the banana man." It was probably the biggest contest I've ever seen for almost ten months straight. They crammed the place to watch this. I used to emcee that and other contests.

The Club La Vela also had a lady's night with the male dancers. They had fifty cent shots of Jagermeister. This was a crazy, crazy place.

I would emcee and then go outside and play my set. Then the band that I hired went on. Sometimes I played with them. My music technician and drummer, James Maloy,

Winners of the bikini contests getting their fur coats.

Wild times at La Vela

did all of my sequencer programming and played live drums when I needed them. James was very talented. It was a pretty good job and it lasted well past spring break. It lasted all summer. My pay was $1,200 a week. I worked a lot but I was living right up the street.

But it was a madhouse. We had so many college kids down there for spring break it was ridiculous. The two closest colleges were University of Alabama in Tuscaloosa and Florida State in Panama City. They were bitter rivals. I had Alabama kids on one side of the place and University of Florida kids on the other. One side would yell, "Hell yeah," and the other side would sing “Sweet Home Alabama.” I jumped from speaker to speaker, holding the microphone out while they tried to out shout each other.

Besides the college crowd, we also had the locals from Panama City. Everybody came there including wrestlers from the World Wrestling Federation like Rick Flair. And we had steady attendees like Hank Williams Jr. Panama City Beach was nicknamed the “Redneck Riviera.”

We had fifteen guys on security because the place was so big. They were all football players from Alabama and Tennessee that wanted to work for the summer. It was a lunatic bin, but everybody still wanted to work Panama City Beach. Next door they had big acts like Taylor Dayne and Doctor Hook.

Left: Norman Seldin and Don Barnes of 38 Special.
Right: Norman wearing his "Hottest Piano Man in Town T-shirt"

One time I yelled over the microphone, "There must be some guys here who can sing." One fellow answered, "Would you mind if I came here with my group one night and sat in?" I said, "It depends. Who are you?" He replied, "Oh, I'm Don Barnes, the lead singer of 38 Special."

Well, 38 Special was a very big group at the time. Based in Jacksonville, Florida, the southern rock group was riding high on their recent Top 20-hit. "Like No Other Night." I said, "Sure. How about if we put you all up at one of the band houses?" We had two band houses where the band members stayed. Don said, "We have our own houses. I'll tell you what would be better than that. How about if we just bring our guitars and you give us a free drinks and buy some dinners for the band? How about if we did two publicized shows for free for you?"

We normally would have a line of 150 people waiting to get in. When I said 38 Special was coming, that line grew to 400 people long. We did a matinee and emptied the place out. Then people had to re-park again for $10 and pay another $10 to get in. The club was making a fortune.

Well, 38 Special was a hot number and they were great. They came up there and I did a couple songs with them. Then we took some pictures together.

Left: Male dancers at La Vela with Linda Johnson, Penthouse Pet, February 1987
Right Norman Seldin and friend

Another hot group, the Atlanta Rhythm Section did the same thing. They came and loved the place because it was so crazy and wild. I knew what they were looking for. They were looking for all the women that were there by the hundreds. So they played shows, too, with a different kind of promoting.

That season they told us that we netted over a million and quarter dollars after massive losses the first season. As the winter approached, the Club La Vela shut down until the next spring break. It gave me a chance to perform elsewhere and that elsewhere was Tallahassee, Florida.

I did a couple weekends in Tallahassee at a place called the Peanut Barrel Pub on Lafayette Street. It was a regular bar. I took the digital piano and sang some of the same material that I did at La Vela, but without all the background stuff going on.

Then, they sent me to a place called Norm's in Birmingham, Alabama. I knew nothing about Birmingham at all except that I'd met a few girls from there. It was an after hours club. I didn't know what "after hours" meant down there. Where I came from an after hours place was where you went after dinner.

I had to drive there and get a hotel room. Then I pulled up in front of a place that said Norm's. It was a big place. They had a back room that held about 500 people and a big stage for the band. I was hired to play in the bar area up front.

It was late evening when I entered the place. The manager asked, "Are you Norman?" I said, "I'm Storming Norman." He looked at me surprised and asked, "What the hell you want to do, take a nap for a while?" I said, "What do you mean?" He said, "You don't go on until midnight." I said, "Midnight? I was thinking 10:30 or 11:00." He said, "No. We don't really start getting busy until about 1:00 in the morning. That's when all the other bars close and the bartenders come in. So just set your microphone and your P.A. system up around that piano. I'll get you a tip jar to put out and that's what you'll do."

I looked on the wall and saw photos of people who had sung in there. Delbert McClinton was a regular. The lead singer from the Spiral Staircase had been in the day before and his picture was up.

Birmingham was swinging back then. That was the time they had the American Football League and the Birmingham Stallions football team was there. The area was loaded with people that went to this place. By 2:00 o'clock in the morning there were 600 people there. They'd come up to me and and say, "Coming from the beach, huh? How about a little 'Margaritaville' and a little John Prine. And you can do some Randy Newman." And they started throwing money in the big mayonnaise jar.

It was amazing to see so many people out at that time in the early morning. I'd start playing at midnight and I didn't stop until 6 or 7 in the morning. The sun was always up by the time I left and I'd walk out into the daylight. Then there was nothing to do until that evening at 11:00 o'clock.

Then they sent me to a club in Mobile, Alabama. I played a weekend there. The sound man from one of the heavy groups had told me he lived there and I could stay at his house. So I went there and played that club.

By spring break time, 1987, I was back at Club La Vela in Panama City Beach for the next season. My second year at La Vela went a lot like the first. But at the beginning of my third year there, Mike Preble, the general manager, fell and totally smashed his leg. He went into the hospital and, in the interim, they brought in someone else as general manager. The trouble was, this fellow didn't get along with anybody. He wanted to take over running the contests and he didn't think I had the experience to be doing what I was doing. Things got pretty screwed up. I finished out the summer season there and played a few gigs at the Peanut Barrel Pub again in Tallahassee before returning to Panama City Beach.

Panama City Beach Marriott

All the while, the Marriott Corporation had a resort on the lagoon in Panama City Beach. Someone came over and asked me, "How would you like to come and play at the Marriott?"

Marriott Bay Point Resort

Now the Marriott Bay Point Resort was a five star resort and I walked over to the place in shorts and a t-shirt. Let me say, the place was gorgeous. Overlooking St. Andrews Bay, it had two PGA golf courses with clubhouses, twelve manicured clay tennis courts, five palm draped pools, seven restaurants and a marina. They had tourists and a lot of business conventions. The manager told me that the lounge had been pretty quiet and they wanted to change that.

How could I pass that up? I started playing at the Marriott. I had my sequenced digital stuff and I didn't use a drummer. I had a programmer who was amazing. He added drums to my sequenced material and if you turned your head around you would have thought it was a five- or six-piece band. Then Marriott gave me a grand piano to play. So, I had that around all the digital equipment.

With the Marriott being a destination for business conventions, I got to know a lot of corporate people from all over the country. They would often hear me play and hire me for different business functions.

On one such occasion, Hershey Chocolates hired me for a corporate retreat at the Hyatt Gainey Ranch in Scottsdale, Arizona. It was a big job. I was paid $3,000 or $4,000 just to play piano at a cocktail party. When I got out there, there was nothing for me to do except wait for the show and play the piano for the executives.

That afternoon I was walking down the hallway when I heard a lot of yelling coming from the main concert ballroom. I stuck my head in to see what the hell was going on.

I could see the band rehearsing and on the stage were the Shirelles, the Coasters and Glenn Stetson and the Diamonds.

At that moment, one of the women from the Shirelles recognized me from when I had been booking them years before. She started screaming, "Norman's out there. Norman can do this." I was walking in and she started talking to me, saying, "We know you. You booked us on that show with Johnny Thunder! We need you in here."

I didn't want to interfere as it was somebody else's band but apparently rehearsals weren't going very well. The entertainment director came over to me and said, "The Shirelles apparently think very highly of you. Can you do the show?" I said, "Not alone." He said, "Well, we hired a guy from Memphis and he brought a six piece band with him. But they've been rehearsing for three hours and still hadn't gotten through the first three Shirelles songs."

This guy was a Hershey executive who'd been given the assignment of producing the show. He looked frustrated and very nervous. He asked, "Can you take care of this? This is our main show tonight." I said, "Well, I'm used to doing this but it's somebody else's job." He said, "Your hired. Just go in there and tell him he's fired." I said, "What?" He repeated, "Just go in and tell him he's fired."

I walked in and the bandleader said, "Excuse me. Who are you?" I said, "I'm Norman. I was instructed by the Hershey program director to tell you you're fired. They're paying you anyway so please remove yourself from here and get away from the piano." He said, "Well, these are my musicians." I looked at them and asked, "How many of you want to go home and how many of you want to stay." It was unanimous. They all said, "Listen, we don't want to go home." I said, "Well, I'm your new band leader. Let's see the charts you have here."

I looked at the charts and they were simple enough. I just started laughing. I said, "You guys are musicians and you can't read this shit?" They said, "Well, he kept telling us to change this and change that." I called the musicians together and said, "It's very simple. Here's the way this goes." One of them said, "Well, where do we come in?" I said, "Right there where those breaks are." Those were just chord sheets. There was nothing fancy. I went through the whole thing with them and inside of an hour and half we had the entire show rehearsed.

I met the entertainment director in the hallway and he just muttered, "Hopeless." I said, "No, we go on tonight at 8:30." He said, "You got that to work?" I said, "Don't even worry about it. It's going to work." I guess I took a lot of weight off of his shoulders because he said, "I'll take care of the band members and I'll talk to you later."

Well, the show went on and it was just amazing. It went smooth as glass. I'd worked with those singers so many times before that it was like kindergarten to me. The musicians were easy. They were good players. They were just under the wrong direction.

After the show, the Hershey guy handed me an envelope with $5,000 in it. I said, "What is this?" He smiled and replied, "That's thanks for bailing us out. We paid a lot of money for all these groups and their airline tickets. That show wasn't going on if you hadn't come along." I said, "This isn't necessary. I've already been paid." He said, "No you were paid to play piano. You're a pianist. That's a separate issue." I thanked him and said, "Fine." I was told, "You know, if you want to play golf tomorrow, Alice Cooper's out there playing." I said, "No, I can live without that." Alice Cooper and Kenny G played there all the time.

I started getting calls for more corporate events from that job. It rang all over the south that I received that kind of money. That was like a million dollars at that time.

Meeting Jamey

I went back to the Marriott. One night I was playing my set and looking at the lagoon and the gorgeous sunset that was coming in. I thought, "I'd like to play for two or three more hours and then pretty much be done for the night."

I looked to my right and I saw this gorgeous girl in a sundress come walking in through the sunlight. I said, "Oh good God." I stopped playing in the middle of the song and I went down to meet her. It was Jamey, who would become my future wife. I had to talk to her.

Everybody in the place was going apeshit because they said there was something wrong with me. "What's wrong? Is there something wrong on stage?" somebody asked. I remember saying hello and she said, "Will you be playing Billy Joel?" I said, "No." She said, "You don't play any Billy Joel?" I said, "No, he doesn't play my music. I don't play his." And we started talking.

It was instantaneous. I just could not take my eyes off of her. She had come in from Atlanta and she was with a date who brought her there. I pleaded and begged, "Why don't you come take a walk on the beach tomorrow? We can have lunch." She said, "Well, I'm with somebody else." I said, "Well, tell him you have to do something." So she made up some excuse and met me the next day.

That's how the whole thing started. I found out that Jamey was a retained corporate head hunter living in Atlanta. After she went back home we called and called each other. Back then there were no cell phones so our phone bills between Panama City Beach and Atlanta were getting really big.

It was getting really, really serious. I said, "I'd really like to marry you." Jamey said, "Well, there's two things you have to do." I said, "What are they?" She said, "You have to ask my daddy if you can marry me." Jamey had been divorced and she had a son. And she said, "The second thing is that you can't do these drugs anymore. The crowd you're hanging around with won't work for me." I had no hesitation and gave away all the drugs I had stashed. The next day I called her daddy and he just said, "You can have her, just don't bring her back." I mean, she hadn't been with him for years anyway. Then Jamey actually started managing my career for the next year and a half and got me more money than I ever asked for anywhere.

Jamey Sushinski Curro Seldin

Jamey wrote a new contract for the Marriott. If you had looked at it and you were a hotel manager you would have said, "Get out of my office. I'm not signing this." Jamey wrote it up for four nights a week at $1,500 a week. I had first refusal on every convention for entertainment. Everybody had to be introduced to me and I was to get a percentage of whatever I sold for them. I also got 150 free drinks a month and brunch for four people every Sunday for the entire length of this contract. And if they wanted to get rid of me, they had to give me three months notice or pay me three month's pay. And they signed it. They sent it to their corporate offices in Atlanta and they signed it.

Then, when I walked into the publicity department, the manager said, "We're going to buy fifty billboards and make them hot pink with a caricature of you on them. We'll start them in Alabama and run them all the way through Tennessee up to Panama City Beach." I still didn't believe it until somebody called me and said, "There's a billboard the size of somebody's house in the middle of town." It was a full size billboard, hot pink with a caricature of me with black tails and it said, “Stormin’ Norman at the Bay Point Marriott Lounge.”

Suddenly, people were calling me from all over. They saw these billboards. And I ended up getting the convention from AT&T Microelectronics. I mean, major events. That's where I officially met Bill Pinkney and the Original Drifters. Bill was on the road when he came in and did the AT&T show for me. I got to know Bill. He was an amazing man. Not too many people know he had been in the Negro Baseball League besides being a war veteran. Of course Bill Pinkney was the bass lead singer on the Drifters’ “White Christmas.”

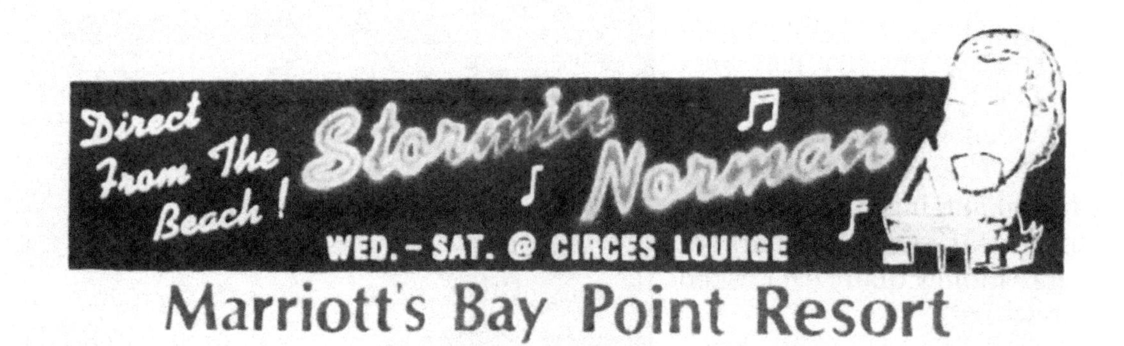

Black and white image of the billboard. These were actually hot pink in color.

Things just kept escalating. We got shows right from the Marriott. The biggest thing I did in Panama City Beach was an outdoor concert that they used to put on. They'd usually had guitar players. But the first year I was at the Marriott they decided that since I was so popular, I should play this outdoor concert. They brought in a big white grand piano and they publicized the daylights out of this event.

I asked, "How many people usually come to this concert?" I was told to expect 200 or 300 but they had over a thousand show up for me. They didn't know what to do with the crowd. I was just a piano player with some sequencing backup, but people loved every minute of it. There were no other acts, just a sound man and me.

Jamey got me a booking for a New Years Eve gig in Panama City Beach. The job was to pay $5,000 for a solo performance. They signed the contract and gave me a 50% deposit. Well, two days before the event they called and said that one of their key people was ill and they were going to cancel. So, Jamey said it would be fine. "Just have the other check for me this afternoon so Norman can pick it up because it's pay or play." I waited until 4:00 o'clock in the afternoon, went down and got the other $2,500. About an hour after I got home, the phone rang. It was one of the other night club owners. He said, "Norman, what are you doing tomorrow night for New Year's Eve?" I said, "Well, they're not going ahead with the gig I was hired for." He said, "Would you like another $1,000 to come play at my club for an hour?" So, I went to his place and played. I picked up $6,000 for the one night. It was crazy because I was special to them down there.

Everybody knew me around Panama City Beach. With how wild the scene had been at La Vela, my act could be pretty risque at times. I guess you could say, my hour of perversion was pretty rough. Compared to what I was doing, Doug Clark and the Hot Nuts would have been considered children's music. I'd get the audience singing along and the people in the condos would complain.

Wedding Bells

Best man, Mike Preble, Jamey and Norman

Jamey used to drive from Atlanta to Panama City Beach. Finally, the drive got to be too much for her so she started taking the puddle jumper. Finally, Jamey moved down to Panama City Beach. We got married in 1990 on the back lawn of the Marriott. We had the reception on the Marriott's own little paddle riverboat. Mike Preble was my best man. We accidentally left the food and beverage manager at the dock. He went back to get some fancy Champaign and we forgot about him and took off while he was standing there.

The biggest problem I had was getting somebody to play the reception. Musicians were afraid that I wouldn't like them or they weren't good enough. I finally said, "Listen. All I need is somebody to just play some Jimmy Buffett songs. Play a few oldies. I don't care what you play, just play some music." Eventually, I talked somebody into it.

While I was at the Marriott, they said, "Listen, we're having a big fundraiser for Bay Medical Center. We usually have a star and they go to the hospital and visit the kids in the there." It was an expensive black tie affair. They said, "You can play the opening 50 minutes to an hour on piano but we need you to book an act." So, I was calling and calling without any luck. Finally somebody said, "I got the perfect person of you, Susan Anton."

I knew of Susan Anton as a film and television actress and as the honorary chair of the U.S. Women's Olympic Volleyball Team but hadn't really heard her sing. The fellow said, "Pal, she can stand next to Aretha Franklin. She'll blow you away."

This was coming up right after we got married and had a little five-day honeymoon. And I said okay so they started running the newspaper articles. They asked me to meet her at the airport with the limo and bring her back to the hotel.

I met Susan Anton at the airport and we started talking. She asked, "We're going to be by the beach, right?" She was a big beach person. I guess that's the volleyball interest. I told her we'd be walking along the beach to get to the club and we might turn a few heads because I'd just gotten married. Susan said, "That's okay. I need to feel the sand." We took a walk along the beach and she took her shoes off to feel the sand under her feet. She said, "Just hold my hand. We're just walking." I knew what the rumors would be about ten minutes later as word travels fast. Susan's a tall gorgeous blond and the minute that we walked in everybody in the place was saying, "My God. He hasn't been married a week and he's with this girl."

Susan went up to her room and I went down to rehearsal after making arrangements to meet at 6:00. Later on she came downstairs in one of those black Donna Karen designer gowns and if you could melt an iceberg, that would do it. The hospital went crazy for her and she was great with the kids. You don't know how the person's going to react in the hospital with a kid's ward. Maybe they don't even like kids. But Susan Anton was amazing. She was the perfect pick.

The only thing I didn't know was if she could sing. I was getting ready and she opened up with Aretha Franklin's "Respect." I turned around thinking that she'd brought in somebody else with her. It was her and she was killing it.

My preference has always been for black artists, but that girl could hang with any of them. That just shocked me. Susan Anton was show and a half. She sang standards and some blues. She just sang it all and the audience just ate it up. They made a lot of money on that show, all for a good cause. The show sold out in about an hour.

When Susan came off of the stage, she said, "I think we had a good show." I said, "Good?" She said, "Well, I've heard you like black music." I said, "Yeah, but I'm not used to a 6'2" blond coming out here and doing that." And I wasn't. It was just shocking. She sang better than she looked and on a scale of 1 to 10 she was a 12. So, those kind of things happened in Panama City Beach.

Chapter Twelve
Back to Jersey

It was late summer, 1991, and we had just done a corporate event for a big insurance company in Hartford, Connecticut. We took either Glenn Stetson & the Diamonds or Danny & the Juniors, I can't recall which, as both groups were based in Florida. I had booked each at different times. The event went well and Jamey and I stopped off in Red Bank to visit my parents on our way back home.

While I was in Panama City Beach, my mother had died. My mother was a beautiful, talented person but she suffered in an abusive marriage. After her passing, my father remarried. My father and stepmother continued to run Seldin's Jewelry Store. They had come down to Panama City Beach for Jamey's and my wedding the year before. My father and stepmother explained how they were getting older and would be retiring soon. They wanted to turn the store over to us. Jamey was already very familiar with jewelry, having been a purchaser for a big firm in Atlanta. My daughter Melody, who'd been living with us, had begun school at the University of Florida so the idea of returning to Red Bank and running the jewelry store was appealing.

I should explain, that my stepmother and I didn't always get along. I wasn't alone in that respect as I knew a lot of people that had difficulty dealing with her. But both she and my father were being nice at the time so we thought we'd give it a try. We packed up our belongings in Florida and in November 1991 moved back to Red Bank, New Jersey.

My parents were supposed to have an apartment above the store totally remodeled for us but when we arrived, nothing had been done to it. The old 1938 light fixtures were still hanging from the ceiling. That should have been a clue that things were not going to work out but since we'd moved back, we did all the remodeling ourselves. Then my parents decided they didn't have a position for Jamey to work in the store. They said there wasn't enough money coming in to support her.

Fortunately, Jamey had her real estate license and was able to find work outside the store. I was getting ready to start playing music again but continued working in the store. In the meantime, we had to live upstairs above my parents' store and home.

One time, we were having dinner and Jamey expressed concern about what we would do if something happened to them. My stepmother exploded with an explicative laced remark and Jamey and I both got up and left the table. From that point on we really didn't talk to my parents very much. We had a separate entrance to our apartment and we spent all of our money fixing up the place. But things kept going downhill.

After remodeling the upstairs of their building, we were told we should start paying rent. One weekend my parents shut off the hot water to our apartment and changed the locks to the jewelry store downstairs which I ran for them. I had to call my uncle to let me in because he had a key.

It was just a terrible time. I was also dealing with some IRS problems from my time in Florida. In my wilder times down there, I didn't file my income taxes for three or four years. That was a serious offense that I could have gone to jail for. We went through a lot of legal trouble before getting that resolved.

Rockin' & Rollin' Again

Throughout my life, whenever times were hard, I've always had my music to carry me through. I'd been away from Jersey for ten years playing blues clubs in Mississippi and Rock & Roll in Florida. But it was time to come home and get back in touch with the music scene I'd left behind. Unfortunately, what I found was a far cry from the Shore music scene of the late 70's and early 1980's. Asbury Park was in a shambles. They had not built back up from when I left. There just weren't as many clubs that featured live music. There were a few people playing but it was totally different so I had to reacclimate myself to what was going on. It was a big change. Promotion wise,

Norman Seldin playing
Danny's Italian Restaurant, 1992

most of the big agents I had worked with were either very, very old or had passed away. The new ones were backstabbing each other. I pretty much had to start over again on my own, but I thought, "At least it will be easier now that cell phones have been invented." I knew I needed to re-establish myself but musically it felt good to be back home.

I started playing solo again nearby at a place called Danny's Italian Restaurant on South Bridge Avenue in Red Bank. I'd known the owner since before I left for Mississippi. In fact, I'd played solo there back in 1981. He was glad to have me back. I started back playing my mix of rock, blues and jazz.

It took a little while for word to get around but pretty soon friends I hadn't seen for years started coming in to say hi and hear me play. It made me feel good to know that people still remembered me. I was playing a couple nights a week and started packing the place. I was also playing LT's Restaurant and Nightclub in Brielle on Sundays.

Eighty Eights

I mentioned earlier that I had two musically talented sisters. Both of my sisters play piano pretty well. My sister Sarita graduated from the University of Cincinnati and became the international buyer for the Lazarus Shillitos department store there. My sister Rochelle was very involved with Broadway shows. She attended the Performing Arts High School in New York. She has a wonderful operatic soprano voice which eventually brought her to Broadway. Rochelle has the ability to make people just stop what they're doing and listen to her sing. She can sing some difficult material and has the personality to really sell a song.

In 1988, Rochelle, Erv Raible and Karen Miller opened a piano bar cabaret on 10th Street just below Bleecker in New York City's Greenwich Village. Called Eighty Eight's, it quickly became a popular hangout for piano bar fans and Broadway show personnel.

Eighty Eights had a long bar and open piano bar space where vocally talented patrons and bar personnel could get up and sing. The club had velvet banquettes, smoked mirrors, plush carpeting, a baby grand piano and a two-story atrium. Up the elegant, curved staircase was a cozy cabaret showroom. On that floor they had an act and they would charge so much with half going to the performer and half to the house.

Norman's jacket from Eighty Eights

Eighty Eights was packed every night. So many Broadway stars and future stars would stop by and sing. Liza Minnelli was a friend of Rochelle's and frequented the club as did many of the Broadway people. It was special. I would play there quite a bit when their main pianist was gone or on the road with a Broadway show. My material used to change a lot because certainly Broadway's not my forte. They had so many great singers there. Elena Bennett, the world-renowned singer and entertainer, used to come by and sing. My sister says Elena Bennett probably knows more lyrics to songs than any 20 people. Whether it's Edith Piaf or Linda Ronstadt, she knows them all and she can sing them all.

Stormin' Norman Seldin playing Eighty Eights with special guest Elena Bennett and Danny's Italian Restaurant, 1992

Everybody there sang. Jay Rodgers was working as a waiter at Eighty Eights when he was discovered and cast as one of the stars of the Off-Broadway show, "When Pigs Fly." The girl tending bar there was Terri White who'd appeared on Broadway in "Barnum" and starred in "Finian's Rainbow." She was off the road and tending bar, and she started singing behind the bar. They didn't work with microphones. They were all singers. It was very interesting.

I thought I'd be working at Eighty Eights once or twice but I ended up being there eight or ten times. Eighty Eights was not really my crowd but everybody from the female impersonators to the gay crowd took a liking to what I played. It was very interesting and very musical. There were some extremely talented entertainers there that really studied their craft. They could dance. They could sing background. They could sing lead and they could act.

I continued playing Danny's from November 1991 until March of 1995. At first I was playing solo and the crowds started getting bigger. Then, I just started playing other clubs and bringing extra musicians in with me. I brought Billy Ryan back and by the summer of 1993 I had enough musicians to bill us as the New Orleans Jam Band. I rotated different musicians in and out of my group. When I had Billy Ryan with me we were called Stormin' Norman & the Party Band. We played Briody's in Rumson as Stormin' Norman & the Half & Half Band. As the New Orleans Jam Band we played the Bayfest Food Festival in Keansburg.

Left: Norman Seldin and Bruce Springsteen,
Right: Clarence Clemons and Norman Seldin
Performing with the Red Bank Rockers at the Trade Winds, June 29, 1993

Clarence Clemons and Friends

In the summer of 1993, Springsteen's E Street Band had temporarily dissolved and Clarence Clemons was touring with his shore area band, the Red Bank Rockers. The group had just appeared at the Sands Casino in Atlantic City. Clemons' band's next stop was a club called the Trade Winds in Sea Bright, New Jersey. The Trade Winds had just been renovated after being pounded by storms the previous winter. Clarence asked me to perform with his band as a special guest. In addition, Bruce Springsteen also made an unannounced guest appearance, performing five songs with us. It was the first time Bruce Springsteen, Clarence Clemons and I shared the same stage since Bruce sat in with the Joyful Noyze some twenty years earlier.

Pam McCoy

Then I was introduced to Pam McCoy and from the moment I heard her sing, I said, "Oh, this is it. I have to have this girl in my band." A friend of my family's named Jan Eisner, whom I'd know since I was eight years old, recommended her. Jan said, "I have a friend who is just out of college and she's got an amazing voice." I said, "I'd like to hear her." Pam came up to rehearse and I listened to her sing. I said, "This girl's got talent." Pam was already married at the time and had young kids. But she made the effort. She just wanted it. In the beginning, she sang and played tambourines and things like that. Over course of the next 30 years that she's been with me, Pam McCoy has developed into a real powerhouse. She made the effort. I mean, she just had the drive.

Briody's, 1993. From left: Norman Seldin, Stuart Hooten, Pam McCoy, Billy Ryan. Out of photo, Vinnie Roslin. Photo courtesy of Pam McCoy

Seldin's Trinkets

In April, 1994, Jamey opened Seldin's Trinkets on Broad Street in Red Bank. It was just a couple blocks from my parents' jewelry store and the two establishments complimented each other. Jamey's store specialized in silver merchandise while my parents' store, which I still worked in, dealt in traditional gold and diamonds. I helped Jamey out with purchasing merchandise and handling the visual displays.

Norman and Jamey in Seldin's Trinkets

Just before I'd left New Jersey for Mississippi, we had had a dog that bit a girl in the arm. We took her to the hospital and she got her shots. I didn't hear anything more about it. I didn't know anything about it but while I was in Mississippi and Florida this girl filed a lawsuit against me for damages to her arm. While I was playing in Danny's Restaurant in Red Bank, I had a state-of-the-art bandstand that I'd brought back from Panama City Beach. All of a sudden, there were all kinds of police officers raiding my band-stand. They served papers saying that they were taking all my equipment on a lien to pay back this girl. They stripped everything I purchased in Florida and took it away for public auction. They didn't have much luck with the auction because a lot of the musicians refused to go and bid on it because it was mine. But a few did so I had to start all over from scratch. I remember having to call Nicky Addeo to borrow a mixer. We pieced it together because Pam McCoy sang with us then and Billy Ryan used to sit in.

Norman in Seldin's Trinkets

Mexico with the Rolling Stones

In December 1994, Jamey gave me a Christmas present of a box of rocks. I asked, “What's this.” She said, “Stones!” I answered, “We have plenty of stones. We run a jewelry store.” Jamey said, “We're going to Mexico City with the Rolling Stones!” A friend of Jamey's had married the woman who was booking the Rolling Stones' transportation and accommodations. So we were going to meet the group and travel in their limo to the hotel and everything as a part of their entourage.

We landed in Mexico City and rode in the limo to the Ritz Carlton hotel. There weren't as many people traveling with us as I'd expected, just the Stones and their background singers and a couple musicians. The concert was to be at Foro Sol, a huge sports and concert venue that held 50,000 people. The Rolling Stones were scheduled to do four nights of sold out concerts there. Of course, the sound people and the stage crew were separate. They got there four or five days in advance as setting up that stage was a four or five day ordeal.

I was signing in at the desk when I heard a voice say, "Stormin' Norman! What are you doing here?" It turned out to be one of the big drug dealers from the States that I'd run into during my previous life. Here I was, my first day in Mexico City and I had this guy right next to me. Of course, the drugs followed the rock & roll scene in those days and the Stones tours were no exception.

We were hanging out with the Rolling Stones for about a week. We had meals with the Stones. They were all pretty laid back. Keith Richards could be found reading a book during the day. He was a huge reader.

They were unloading a guitar rack and there must have been 25 guitars. I knew they weren't Keith Richard's so I asked Ron Wood, "Whose are those?" He said, "Oh, those are Mick's." I said, "I've never seen Mick with a guitar." Ron said, "No those are his guitars. Sometimes, he'll bring out a Telecaster or something and he'll play for a while." There was a guitar in every damn color you could think of. Mick had his own guitar tech but I never saw him play a guitar the whole four days.

It was a great tour. I mean, just watching the rehearsals and sound checks was exciting. I'd seen big mixer boards, but I'd never seen concert boards that big. They were the size of cars and that was just for the monitors.

I don't know how it is now, but Mexico City in those days was not safe. It was very strange when we pulled up to the hotel and it looked like we were being guarded by the Mexican Militia. Someone told me there were over fifteen bank robberies a day in Mexico City, though I never confirmed that. When I walked down the street, every bank had a guy with a sawed off shotgun standing outside. I wanted to go out and buy some jewelry for the store. The hotel had to arrange for a driver to take me and they waited for me. They actually walked me inside. It was an experience.

One night I couldn't sleep so I went downstairs and began playing on the grand piano. Bobby Keys one of the musicians with the Stones came downstairs and was listening. He said, "What group are you with?" I said, "Well, I'm an artist from New Jersey." He said, "I haven't heard playing like that in a long time. I could listen to you all night long." It was quite a compliment as I know he was a really good musician or he wouldn't have been with the Rolling Stones. I played for forty minutes and we shot the breeze. Then I went back upstairs to sleep.

The next afternoon we went out to the concert. We went to the stadium in limos. The police blocked off the major highway all the way out from town to venue. No one could get on or off except for us. I'd never seen anything like that. I'd seen big concerts, but when you block off an entire city and surrounding area from entering a highway to the next 25 miles, that's the kind of security we had. You couldn't even squeeze a motorcycle on along the whole route.

When we pulled up to the stadium for the show there were armed guards across the whole roof and machine guns and shot guns inside the Voodoo Lounge where all the stuff was for the Rolling Stones. They had arcade games there and Jamey ended up playing games with, I think it was Keith Richard's kids. The Stones were playing snooker. They had to have a snooker table wherever they went.

The concert itself was crazy good. They released balloons and had fireworks. A local Spanish rock group called the Caifanes opened up and then the Rolling Stones came on and were spectacular. The funny thing was when the Stones finished their set everyone started calling for an encore. All 50,000 people were standing and the fireworks were going off. All the sudden the group turned around and said, "Come on. It's time to get in the limo." I said, "What about the encore?" They said, "Oh, they only think they're getting one. They're not." That was just a tactic to get out before the crowd did. So we left. We were in the car with them and we we're leaving in three limousines. The place is still packed and they were going, "Encore." or whatever they yelled in Spanish. We were already on the highway and again, the highway was completely blocked off for us. All the way back to Mexico City there was not a car on the highway except us and the police.

It was that way for all four shows. Of course Jamey and I went to a jewelry show there to buy stock for the store. We were told there'd be no problem taking jewelry out of the country. Then when we got to the airport, they wanted to send us back to the embassy or something. The customs guy said, "You take care of me, I take care of you." I had to throw 50 or 100 bucks to the guy with all the gold bracelets we had. So he let us go through with all the jewelry after I threw him cash at the counter. Otherwise, we would have been backed into chicken cages going to the embassy and we would have missed our flights and everything.

Joe Amiel & the Old Mill Inn

I'd been doing a lot of solo work and occasionally bringing in another musician or two. One night in 1996, Jamey and I went to dinner at the Old Mill Inn in Spring Lake Heights. The Old Mill Inn was a pretty big place. They'd had the Knockouts there and the Duprees. Larry Chance had played there. The Old Mill Inn was owned by Joe Amiel. I had met Joe years before but he never showed much interest in hiring me.

Joe Amiel

That night we were dining and I heard someone say, “That's Stormin' Norman over there.” I went over to introduce myself. I said, “Hi. I'm Norman.” Joe Amiel asked, "Why won't you play for me? You've been all over the place. Why won't you play for me?" I just said, "You've never asked me." He just started laughing and said, "I didn't, did I?" I replied, "No. You may have thought you did ten years ago, but you never asked me." So he said, "I'd like you to come in and play."

Well, the minute I started playing there, the crowds increased dramatically. And they kept increasing. They had a showroom upstairs where they catered weddings but I was downstairs doing solos and just really packing the place. I didn't play the Sinatra stuff that Joe liked. I played a lot of nice piano, but I was doing my Randy Newman material and my Golden Oldies. Sometimes Joe would come over and sing with one of his maitre'd's. They would sing "Sh-Boom, Sh-Boom." At best they were terrible, but people got a kick out of that.

Postcard of the Old Mill Inn

Danny Aiello and Joe Pesci were regulars at the Old Mill Inn. So were Ray Liotta and all those people. Joe Amiel had a huge Hollywood connection because I think Danny Aiello was one of his partners. I'm a stickler about pianos being dusted and cleaned but one night no one had dusted the big grand piano. The lid was up, and I was playing my set. Joe just had this quirk in him. He came over and wrote in the dust with his finger, "The Stormin' Norman Band, next Friday night." I just thought, "What the hell is he talking about?" I was solo then. I didn't have a band.

When I finished the set Joe Amiel was laughing. He said, "Well?" I said, "Well, what?" He said, "Where's my band?" I said, "What band?" He said, "The band you're going to have here next Friday night." I remembered that he told me it was good money for him. He said, "Get yourself a drummer and a bass player and start next Friday night." I said, "Oh my God."

I found my regular drummer and a couple of different bass players. You couldn't have an upright bass there because you couldn't really play that loud. We put together some material and the band went over real big. The place was packed. That really got me to start working with the groups again. The Steel Breeze eventually formed out of that.

While I was playing at the Old Mill Inn I became very ill. I caught some kind of infectious flu that got into my lungs and my stomach. I lost 30 pounds. I was going to play New Years Eve at the Old Mill Inn but I couldn't stand up. I didn't want to lose my job there because it was really steady work.

I went to see Joe Amiel and I looked pathetic. He took one look at me and said, "You look like you're half dead. You can't play in that shape." We both knew I was going to be out of action for a while. Joe put a stack of money on the table. He said, "You take this and don't come back until you're healthy." I mean, it was a sizeable amount of

Norman Seldin and Joe Amiel

money, something like $10,000. He said, "You take care of your bills and you can pay me back later when you're able. I don't want anything to happen to you."

I said, "Look, Joe, I don't know." He said, "I don't care if it's two weeks. I don't care if it's two months. I don't care if it's three months. When you're ready to come back everything becomes yours again." I have never had anything like that happen in my life before.

So I took some time off. That was the first New Years Eve I missed. I was physically unable to play it. I did come back to the Old Mill Inn and then in the interim I'd gotten back into booking corporate events and even some of the wedding receptions.

Joe Amiel had a lot of wedding presentations at the Old Mill Inn where small businesses offer photograph booths, wedding invitations and things to engaged couples planning weddings. I played at those. And every year, Joe ran "Feed the Hungry" events with all the different local restaurants. I wound up being one of the entertainment directors there. Joe automatically gave me just about everything that came in there. I did happy hours for the weddings. I'd make $175 to play solo and then all of a sudden I was playing a wedding cocktail party for $350. I charged double but people didn't mind. They just wanted to hear me play.

Joe made sure I got extra jobs and he took care of me. I eventually paid him back but he always backed me. He'd show up at the Wonder Bar and places where I wouldn't expect him, just to hear me play. He was pretty special.

Stormin' Norman Productions brochure
ca. Early 1990's

Stormin' Norman Productions

I was still booking acts for corporate events which kept me going financially during rough times. Major promoters would sometimes get requests for private parties and they would recommend me. Clients would call me at Seldin's Jewelry and I'd find them acts and sometimes play their events myself. One time I received a call from a Wall Street broker named Jerry Farber who was looking to throw a surprise fiftieth birthday party for his wife at the Water Club in Manhattan. Well, the Water Club was, and still is, a world-renowned New York City event venue. It has a massive party space right on the East River with sweeping panoramic views of the Manhattan skyline. Right away I knew money would not be an object for this fellow.

I said, "Yeah, I can put something together for you. What would you like?" Jerry said, "My wife really loves Frankie Avalon. Could you see if you could book him for me? Beyond that just book a second known act and supply a band."

I called Dick Fox who was managing Frankie Avalon at the time. Dick didn't think Frankie Avalon would be interested in doing a private party. He said, "Frankie's turned down $20,000." I said, "Offer him $25,000 plus plane tickets and everything." Dick called me back about an hour later and said that Frankie Avalon really didn't feel like doing the job. I said, "Okay, who else have you got?" Dick replied, "How about Bobby Rydell?" I said, "Okay."

I told Jerry and he said, "Well, Bobby Rydell would be a good substitute." I said, "Good substitute? Bobby Rydell will give you a great show." Jerry said, "But you'll have to bring horns." I said, "I'll have a whole horn section."

Dick Fox also supplied the Shangri-Las. So we hired my band, Bobby Rydell and the Shangri-Las. Bobby wanted to travel in by train so I got him a ticket. His music director and drummer was from Chicago. We had to have somebody meet the guy as he had all these trunks with the arrangements. There must have been arrangements enough for 80 pieces.

Norman Seldin on Bourbon Street
Playing a corporate event in New Orleans

I brought my band in. I said to Pam McCoy, "Feeling good? I hope so because we're going to The Water Club in New York." Pam said, "That's a pretty nice place." I said, "Yeah, we're going to be on a show. I'm putting Bobby Rydell in there with the Shangri-Las. Are you ready for prime time? This is it."

We had to bring a piano up to the Water Club and set everything up like it was a cocktail party as the real event was a surprise. I played the cocktail hour. Bobby Rydell walked in like he happened to be a guest at the cocktail party where I was playing.

I took Bobby over to Jerry's wife and he said, "Hi, I'm Bobby Rydell. Happy birthday." She said, "Oh my God! What are you doing here?" He said, "Well, if you don't mind I'm going to sing for you later." She almost fell on the floor.

I had my own sound people there. We had motorcycles for when the Shangri-Las sang "Leader Of The Pack." I think I had a ten-piece band that night. I brought a horn section in and it was an amazing show. Oh my God. What a show Bobby Rydell did. Jamey watched the whole thing and said it was unbelievable. And we did it all with only one hour rehearsal.

Later on, Jerry hired me to book a disco party as a surprise for his daughter. I hired Louise "Angel" Clivilles," the former lead of the Cover Girls and a big disco cover band called Mantis. Then I booked the Trammps. To this day, if I ever had to follow the Trammps, I would have probably quit. They had Bunny Sigler singing lead with them then and they just ripped that place apart. I was so impressed by the tracks and their vocals were tremendous.

By then I was on this little run. All of the sudden I was getting these big shows. They were big money too,

$30,000, $40,000, $50,000 shows. Jerry booked another one at the Shackamaxon Country Club, the century-old private golf course and country club in Scotch Plains, North Jersey. Jerry said, "We're going to have an anniversary party there. Let's do something big." I said, "Okay. What do you want to do?" He said, "Let's have the Temptations with your band." I said, "Okay. I'll get a hold of Dennis Edwards."

Norman Seldin, Pam McCoy, Billy Ryan

Dennis Edwards had been touring through the 1990's as Dennis Edwards & the Temptations but in a legal dispute with the other Temptations group in 1999 had been forced to rename his group, "The Temptations Review featuring Dennis Edwards."

I also booked the girl group, Musique, who had hit with the song, "Push, Push in the Bush." I had wanted to book Vicki Sue Robinson but she passed away a few months before the show so I booked Musique. And I had my band with the horns and Pam McCoy and everybody.

The demands of putting that show together constituted an enormous task. Between just the air flights, limos and meals, Jamey and I worked on it night and day to get everything set. I was on my way to the country club to check on everything that Tuesday when the plane hit the first tower. It was 9/11/2001.

I was in the car half way to Scotch Plains when Jamey called. The second plane had just hit the World Trade Center. When I reached the country club all the executives from the big stock brokerage firm were out on the golf course. I went to see the maitre 'd and while they had a little TV, nobody seemed very concerned about what was happening. I don't think the seriousness of what was happening had sunk in yet. I asked, "Is there anybody from the stock brokerage firm here?" They said, "Yeah, they're out playing golf but we can't bother them." "Bother them," I said emphatically. "And bring one of them in here."

They brought the guy in and I introduced myself. He said, "Oh, yeah. You're the guy who's producing Jerry's party. We'll be attending it this weekend." I said, "Take a look at the TV." He said, "Oh my God. That's my building." He was the CEO of the company that lost all of those employees. I thought he was going to pass out. Evidently everybody that was on that course that day had taken Tuesday off. They didn't even know those planes hit.

We had to turn around and cancel everything, rebooking it all for a later time. That of course, was insignificant compared to what our country was going through. Jerry was stuck in France. They wouldn't let him fly home because there was a no fly zone.

Idyll Point

Let me backtrack a little. All the while that I was booking shows, a lot was happening in my life. In 1997, I released an new CD called "Idyll Point." On it I experimented with new age piano. I had been doing a lot of material for Joe Amiel - some blues piano and vocals, but mostly piano. So I put together a few originals and standards that I had thought about. It was all piano, no vocals. I went to a nice studio over in Rumson that Burt Szerlip had.

Burt had previously written, arranged and played guitar for blues singer Z. Z. Hill. Burt is a good guitar player but he's not really a blues player He is a good technical engineer. He has good ears and he has put a fortune in a well-equipped studio in his house in Rumson. I think it's 32-track and he did a great job on it. The album required a lot of production work but Burt wanted all the publishing in exchange for the use of the studio, which I gave him.

The piano I used for the CD was the original piano from the House of Hits in North Jersey. Burt had purchased it and it was a big piano. It wasn't a Steinway but it was a nine-footer, probably a Yamaha. It had strings set up so I was actually almost able to play it like the keyboard Moog. It had strings in the background that played along with the piano.

The "Idyll Point" CD became very popular for some reason. Maybe it was because I was at the Old Mill Inn and had that kind of audience at the time. It was a moneymaker for me. I pressed up 1,500 copies and sold them for 15 or 20 dollars a piece. I always got top dollar for my CDs, whereas everyone else would be selling them for two or three bucks above what they paid for them. I guess it was the places I was playing. A 20 dollar bill was like a dollar in those places.

Joe Amiel called up one night and said, "Listen, I've got some guests coming in and they're having a table of thirty. You need to bring thirty copies of 'Idyll Point.'" I said, "Thirty copies?" Joe replied, "Don't worry. The guy wants thirty copies so everyone at his table can have one." The fellow paid me cash for them and then gave me a hundred dollar bill on top for bringing them. He was serving everyone at the table expensive champagne. I think it was a vintage Perrier-Jouët at a couple of hundred dollars a bottle. He told the waiter, "Make sure there's a bottle or two there for the pianist." I said, "Well, don't open them because I don't drink but I'll take them home for my wife." He put two bottles up there for me to take home.

In 1998, while I was playing solo on Friday nights at Rooney's Ocean Crab House in Long Branch and the Fairway Manor in Eatontown, my father and stepmother closed Seldin's Jewelry and retired to Florida. The store had been an institution in Red Bank for 53 years.

The Asbury Park-based *Halycon Records* included my recording "Misery Loves Company" on a 1999 anthology CD called "The Spirit of Asbury Park: Rockin' the Jersey Shore." The song had come off of my "Rock 'N Roll Plus" album, recorded by my Stormin' Norman Seldin & Friends band consisting of Billy Ryan and the E Streeters, Garry Tallent, Max Weinberg, Danny Federici Clarence Clemons and me. The CD and the accompanying newspaper reviews finally started to give me recognition for my contributions to the birth of Jersey Shore Rock music.

Steel Breeze

Late in 1999, I ran into a steel drum player named Desi Norman. I was always open to trying new sounds and I wondered what it would be like with steel drums and piano. We called ourselves Steel Breeze started playing Caribbean island music. We played the Oakland Street School Restaurant in Red Bank one night. I sent a notice out to my mailing list and all of a sudden this place was wall to wall people having dinner and listening to us.

I just used the piano there. I didn't use the sequencer with bass and drums. It started getting to the point where I said, "We can't do this with just two people." So I got a guitar player named Matt O'Ree. Matt was young and everyone said, "You can't use that kid. He's a blues player." I said, "No, he's a great guitar player." I added Burt Szerlip as a second guitar player to the bd. Steel Breeze started growing. We played the boardwalk in Avon on the "Walk to Cure Diabetes" benefit and numerous other places.

House Special

Matt O'Ree

Then I had the idea of doing an album on Steel Breeze. We called the CD "House Special" and I loaded it up with talent. Matt O'Ree did all the guitar work including solos and a sparkling version of the Freddy King classic, "Hide Away." Burt Szerlip (stage name Burt Conrad) played guitar on "The Island Song." Bruce Foster played 12-string guitar on "Little Boy." I added my old friend and legendary drummer Bernard "Pretty" Purdie on drums, Rob Paparozzi on harmonica, Tommy LaBella on saxophone and Buddy Savino on bass. Lew Longo did all the vocal arrangements and sang on all the background vocals that also included Pam McCoy, former Springsteen backup singer Delores Holmes and her daughter Layonne Holmes.

The album was recorded and mixed by Burt Szerlip who helped me produce it. We put in a lot of time on it and it was mastered by Les Paul's son, Gary Paul. Most of the songs were my original compositions with the exception of a couple r&b and blues songs I added.

The most emotional song on the album was "Little Boy." I wrote it with help from Pam McCoy and my daughter Melody Seldin. The song is about my nephew, Jamey's sister's child, five-year-old Tyler Mills. Tragically, Tyler had just been lost to a terrible accident.

Bernard Purdie and Norman Seldin
Together again!

"Little Boy" was a beautiful song, but it was hard to put across to an audience, especially in a bar that was jumping. All I had to do was sing the lead as we put the tracks through the sound system. But when I sang the song there'd be sixty people with the water running out of their eyes because they knew the story. I had to stop playing it. My friend Doc Holiday said,

Left: Norman Seldin, Bernard Purdie, Buddy Savino, Burt Szerlip in Burt's home studio working on the album. Right: the "House Special" CD.

"Norman, it's really too personal to really get it across to an audience."

Jenkinson's Boardwalk

While we were working as Steel Breeze my attorney, Frank Mandia, hooked us up with the people that ran Jenkinson's Boardwalk in Point Pleasant Beach. Frank made one or two phone calls and all of a sudden I was booked with Steel Breeze at two of Jenkinson's restaurants - Jenkinson's Pavilion and Jenkinson's Inlet. The main venue is Jenkinson's Pavilion which is huge. Then there's the smaller Jenkinson's Inlet that is at the other end of the boardwalk. Frank also got us booked into the Parker House in Sea Girt. They were all connected as the owners of Jenkinson's and Parker House were friends.

The Budweiser banner

Then I met with the people from Budweiser and they wanted to sponsor us. They paid for a banner and spent thousands of dollars on beautiful color posters. The Budweiser money allowed me to purchase a real state-of-the-art sound system.

I still had to put up money out of my pocket but I loved the advertisement of the posters. They ran publicity sheets and wrote us up in the press. From Farmingdale to

Steel Breeze. From left, Desi Norman, Norman Seldin, Link Davis

Point Pleasant and Seaside, we were it. You couldn't book a date with Steel Breeze. We were totally booked up. We did the Water's Edge in Bayville on Fridays; Saturdays at Jenkinson's Inlet on the Point Pleasant Beach boardwalk; Sundays at the Parker House in Sea Girt; Tuesdays at Jenkinson's Pavilion in Point Pleasant; and Wednesdays at The Columns in Avon. It was a brutal schedule. I used to leave Jenkinson's on a Saturday and then go right to the Parker House to set up there. We would set up at 3:00 or 4:00 in the morning and then we'd go home and I'd take a nap for five hours. When we came back, everything would be set up. We'd throw a switch and go on for the matinee. By then we had Link Davis on guitar. Matt O'Ree had left to form his own band.

Link Davis and I had known each other for some time. In fact, he and I had gone to school together. We both went to that one-room school house in Red Bank. I hadn't spoken to Link in a year or so but I knew he played guitar. I called him up and said, "Do you want to play?" He said, "With who?" I said, "With me!" Link said yes so I said, "You start tomorrow." Link wasn't a lead singer but he was a good harmony singer. He was also great with computers and graphics. He was very handy and did all the artwork for our posters. The posters themselves were gorgeous. Budweiser never saw stuff like what he sent them. They were full 36 inch posters in multicolor on hard plastic. Do you know how expensive they were to print? We had dozens of each one and Budweiser printed them for us. The Budweiser sponsorship was pretty good. When you could make $800 to $1,000 with a trio on an afternoon, you were getting decent money.

Steel Breeze at Jenkinson's Pavilion

Lee Leonard interviewing Norman Seldin on "Jersey's Talking"

Sometimes I would augment it with horns and sometimes with Pam McCoy on vocals.

"Jersey's Talking" with Lee Leonard

Early in 2001, I got a call from a young lady named Ivy Charmatz. She told me that she was program director for the TV show, "Jersey's Talking with Lee Leonard" and they wanted to interview me. Well, I didn't watch much cable TV at the time but everybody in Jersey knew News 12's Lee Leonard.

"Jersey's Talking" was a New Jersey prime-time television talk show seen in more than two million cable households throughout the state on News 12 New Jersey. It was a live, one-hour interview program featured celebrities, musicians and newsmakers of interest to New Jersey residents. The show usually featured three guests per show and frequently featured live music performances. "Jersey's Talking" was hosted by Lee Leonard, News 12 New Jersey's popular news anchor. The show aired weekday evenings and episodes were rerun a number of times after that.

I took Steel Breeze to Jersey's News 12 studio. When I arrived, I looked around the lobby and there were dozens of photos of name artists who had been there. I was on the show with author Harlan Coben and Broadway icon Tommy Tune. Tommy Tune autographed a photo for Jamey. Getting set up there wasn't easy because their studio wasn't designed for playing music. We hung our banner behind us without realizing we were advertising Budweiser. It took a couple of appearances before the TV people noticed. We did three songs and then I sat down to be interviewed. Lee Leonard was very precise with his questions. We talked about where I came from a lot of other things. The stories of my life were so interesting that it became almost personal to him. I found Lee Leonard to be one of the best hosts that you could ever work with. He was a calmer version of Johnny Carson, minus the humor. He asked a lot of good questions and gave me a chance to answer. The episode was so popular it was shown ten times by the station. That one appearance went over so well that I was asked to bring Steel Breeze back to play there in September. I think what drew peoples' attention was a white Jewish kid on multi-keyboards, a black guy on vibes and steel drums and a 300-pound overweight guitar player. But our sound was great. Besides the interview, we again did three songs. I think I actually brought Lee Leonard up to sing something with us. When the second show was over, program director Ivy Charmatz said to me, "We've had some really interesting guests but we never had anything like you." Considering who they'd interviewed, that was quite a compliment.

When I met Ivy Charmatz, I was reminded of the talents I saw in Clarence Clemons and Harry Ray and the honesty in powerful disc jockeys like Douglas "Jocko" Henderson. I envisioned young Ivy as becoming a future super star because she was so dynamic and beautiful. Now, so many years later, she's an Emmy Award winning executive producer and writer. Ivy remains a great friend until this day and I marvel at all she has achieved.

A Brush With Death

For once in my life, everything was going well. We still had that heavy schedule. We were doing Jenkinson's in the big room, the small room in the Parker House and some places down in South Jersey. We were at the Parker House on June 23, 2002 and we always did the matinee. I was on stage during the first set and I felt pretty good. I was just standing there and all of a sudden the whole place started spinning. I remember grabbing the security guard who was a college kid. I said, "You've got to get me some air. I feel dizzy." I don't remember anything immediately after that. I don't know how long I was out but I opened my eyes and I was lying on my back on the back deck. There were dozens of people and EMT's all over the place.

The guy said, "Are you all right?" I asked him what happened and he told me, "You've been out for more than thirty minutes." I said, "What?" He said, "We need to take you down to the hospital." I said, "Oh I feel fine," and I just stood right up. I said, "I got to finish the set." He said, "No. Your equipment has been packed up for quite a while." I felt bad because hundreds of people had waited in line to hear us play. The place was packed.

My guitar player at the time drove me home. I had him call Jamey and explain what happened. I always called her on a break and she was worried when she hadn't heard from me. I walked in and Jamey was livid. She said, "You need to at least go to your doctor and check this out." I said, "I don't want to. I'm fine." But Jamey prevailed and I finally said, "All right, we'll go check it out."

We went to Riverview Hospital and they started running some tests. Of course, by then I was functioning fine. They said, "Oh you probably have pancreatitis." That seemed to be a general diagnosis for everything back then. The doctor said, "I think we need to leave you here tonight just for observation." No one called a cardiac specialist or anything.

They admitted me into the hospital overnight. Jamey was going to the jewelry store in the morning which was right around the corner from the hospital and she came by to see how I was. Just before she arrived, I just decided to go to the bathroom, intending to go right back to bed. I was in the middle of the room when I got the same sensation as I had the day before. It was like hitting my funny bone but a thousand times harder and it ran from my head to my toes. I again felt the room spinning. I don't remember anything, but Jamey later told me she walked in right when the orderly was smacking me and calling for immediate medical assistance. He was yelling, "Come back, Mr. Seldin." But by then my eyes had rolled up into the back of my head.

I'm told that's when the cardiac specialist rushed in and demanded, "Where's the test results on this guy?" They said, "We were waiting to do testing this morning." "Waiting?" he exclaimed, "This guy should have been in surgery last night."

The cardiac specialist made a quick diagnosis. He said, "This is an aortic dissection!" I'd never heard of an aortic dissection at the time, but it usually means an instant death. It's what that late actor John Ritter died from. At the time only one percent survived from that. The doctor was on the phone calling around. Finally he turned red from frustration and said, "I'll call down to Jersey Shore Medical." He did and asked if Dr. Greeley was there. Then he said, "I'm getting scrubbed and ready to do a quadruple bypass." He told them something like, "Don't scrub and don't prep. I'm sending some brain matter to you." I don't know his exact words but I think he it meant I was almost gone.

They had trouble getting everybody on the same page. The cardiac specialist was so frustrated about the delay in getting me an ambulance, he was ready to throw me in his van and personally drive me to Jersey Shore Medical. That's how bad it was. Somehow they got me in an ambulance. My wife, Jamey, was there and somebody that knew Pam McCoy real well had called Pam at home. They told her, "You need to get down to the hospital, Norman might be dying." Pam and I had only been performing together for a couple years but we'd become very close. Pam must have gotten to the hospital pretty quickly because she and Jamey followed the ambulance on its way to Jersey Shore Medical.

Of all things that could go wrong, the ambulance broke down on the side of the road. I woke up just enough to hear them say, "Guys, we've got to get another ambulance." One attendant said, "No, we don't have any time. We've got fifteen minutes to get him there or he's not going to make it." Jamey and Pam pulled over on the side of the road behind the ambulance. They thought I'd died because you just don't stop in an ambulance like that. I don't know how they got me to Jersey Shore Medical Center, but they did.

At the hospital there was mass confusion. They took me to the cauterization lab instead of the prep room. When they finally got things settled, they sent one of the surgeons out as a messenger to explain to Jamey and Pam what was happening. The surgeon asked, "Which one of you is the wife?" He didn't know because they were both in tears. They said something like, "Well we are." To this days I still have two wives as far as they're concerned.

The surgeon said, "We'll try to let you know what's going on but the likeliness of him recovering is pretty much in doubt." He explained that I could die on the table and if I didn't, I might have a total loss of memory as blood may not have been going to my brain. They just didn't know.

Besides the aortic dissection, when they opened me up they found my aortic valve had ruptured and my whole chest was filled with blood. There was doubt as to whether any blood was getting to my brain. They did what's called a Bentall procedure. They took my heart out while they put a synthetic aorta in. They had me on life-support the whole time and then reattached the arteries. The whole operation took more than seven hours and was quite an ordeal.

Then when it looked like everything was working right they shocked me and I woke up. The first thing the doctor did was to tell the nurse to take the tube out of my mouth because he needed to talk to me. The nurse said, "Doctor, he's barely out of surgery." He said, "Take the tube out, I need to talk to him." I looked around and saw some people around there writing something with their pens. Jamey and Pam were there.

The doctor started asking me questions to see if I had any brain damage. I told him how many notes were on the piano and he asked me if I have kids, was I married, what was I doing. I think I answered everything correctly. Then he wanted to know who the president was. Then came the big question. He asked, "Do you know what the date is?" Excuse the language, but I replied, "Are you f***in' crazy?" Everybody standing there just started laughing and the doctor just about fell out. He said, "Oh, he's fine." He asked me, "Are you hungry?" I said, "I'm starving." He said, "Well what do you want to eat?" I replied, "I'd like a McDonald's Double Cheeseburger with Bacon." The nurse said, "Doctor, he can't have that." The doctor turned around and looking directly at her and said, "I'm the doctor here and by all odds, this man should not even be with us now." He reached in his pocket, pulled out a few dollars and said, "Here. Go and get this guy a cheeseburger."

I made every medical journal around. They wrote up everything on my operation because it was amazing that I even got through it. If it wasn't for those Cornell University doctors that happened to be at Jersey Shore Medical, I wouldn't be telling you this now. It was strange because I never had anything like that. Back when I had duodenal ulcers and was in the hospital it was nothing like that. After the operation I didn't have the strength to even walk two feet.

Rumors had actually gone around that I had died. A couple of my musicians dropped by one of our venues and a guy at the bar said, "I can't believe Norman's gone." They said, "Norman's not gone. He'll be all right. He'll be back." But word was pretty widespread that I probably wouldn't return to performing.

I was there about four or five days and there were times I must have had 30 or 40 people squeezed into the visiting room. In fact, Bernard Purdie had just come back from Europe and he came right from the airport to the hospital. He wanted to make sure I was alright and he just didn't want to leave. I had so many visitors that they finally had to disperse the people. It was ridiculous.

Eventually they sent me home to recuperate. When I first went back to visit the surgeon I had scars everywhere from where they'd made incisions. I thank God that Jamey took care of the ones I couldn't see. But I asked the doctor, "When can I start back on stage?" He said, "Oh you're finished for five or six months." I said, "No, I can't do that. I won't have a living anymore." He said, "Well you can't return to the stage yet." It was June and the temperature was hitting close to 100 degrees every day. I had been playing outdoor concerts most of the time. I said, "Doc, I have to be on the stage before Labor Day or else I'm dead in the water." He said, "Well, I'm going to run some more X-rays." It turned out there was no longer fluid in my lungs and my diaphragm was clear. He said, "This is very unusual." I said, "Well I don't drink and I don't smoke." So he said, "We'll take a look at you in another week or two and we'll see."

When I went back a couple weeks later he said, "We can let you try one night, two maximum." I said, "That won't do." He said, "What do you mean that won't do?" I said, "It won't do. I might as well be out of the business. I've got bookings straight through." My doctor basically told me that my going back to work was suicidal. I said, "Let me try it."

Of course, I sent out my mailing list and the first job was an evening gig in Forked River in South Jersey. Unfortunately it would have to be outside. That afternoon it felt like 110 degrees out there. I got a call from the owner who told me, "You got to stop promoting tonight's show because I can only hold 175 people outside and and 100 inside. I've now got reservations for 300 people tonight. What the hell did you do?" I said, "I just told people I was going to play again. I would be back out with the band."

Jamey drove down there with me. The guys unloaded all the equipment. It was still very hot and muggy and there was not even a fan on the stage. I went and I sang. I opened up with a ballad which was really not smart. It hurt. Oh God, did it hurt. It might have been "Love Has No Pride," which was a pretty decent song to sing for an opener. But I thought, "Well you know what? If I couldn't sing that, I might as well turn the switches off and go home because people didn't come there to hear somebody that was unable to sing. They came here to hear me and my band."

Out of the hospital at last!

I looked at the audience and there were people jitterbugging that looked like professional dancers. I did Joe Turner's "Flip Flop And Fly" and the place went crazy. They danced and did twirls and threw each other under their legs. They looked so familiar and I kept thinking, "Where do I know these people from?" It turned out they were nurses from the hospital.

So I continued playing throughout the summer. I had some scary times when on the breaks I'd be spitting out blood but I decided to just suck it up and finish out the season. And there were times at the Parker House when I felt a little faint. But there was a nurse at the Parker House who made sure I was all right.

One time an owner came over to me and said, "You've done plenty. Two sets is enough." I said, "I do three." He said, "Nope, you're done." He pulled the plug out of the wall. He said, "I'm not letting you hurt yourself any further."

It again became a heavy schedule and it was touch and go for a while. But Steel Breeze and I finished the season out and booked the following year. But that's how that went. At the same time, I was back to helping Jamey with her store in Red Bank and kind of went about my regular business. It was a tough thing to go through.. I don't recommend it to anybody, that's for damn sure.

Chapter Thirteen
Piano Man

I gradually got my health back and Steel Breeze was really on a roll. We were playing gigs like the Meadowlands Racetrack on Derby Day. But, after the second year, one of the guys in the band said to me, "I don't think it's right that you get more money than we do." Now, I was the one footing the cost for equipment and responsible for all the advertising plus a number of other expenses. All the other band members had to do was show up and play to get a couple hundred bucks a night, which was good money in those days.

All of a sudden I was dealing with internal dissension in the band. I was hearing complaints about the type of music we were playing and other gripes that probably would have gone away if I'd had doubled their pay. Instead, I just got threats that they would quit the band after our current commitments. Well, we had numerous bookings scheduled including a summer season at the Parker House.

Out of nowhere one day I got a voicemail from the Parker House that one of my band members had called and informed them that Norman Seldin no longer had a band and would not be able to play there anymore. I lost the entire summer's work off of that one phone call.

That was when I said, "You know what? I'm just going back to the Stormin' Norman band." It just going to be me by myself. I'm going to call all the shots. For the next six months to a year I ended up using the sequences and just add a sax player. We did some big affairs. Sometimes Pam McCoy would sing and I had a couple of sax players and a guitar player here and there.

Jacobs Music

It was 2004 and I'd eventually came to the realization that I could not keep up that pace of performing five nights a week. Jamey and I were figuring out whether I should come and help her in the store more or what I would do. We were driving a van up to New York when I got a call on my cell phone. These were days before robocalls so I answered it.

A voice asked, "Is this Norman Seldin? I'm a headhunter and there's a company that very much wants you." Now, Jamey was a retained headhunter for years in Atlanta, but I didn't even know what a headhunter was. I never worked for anybody but myself.. I said, "I don't work for other people." The fellow asked, "Well would you at least listen to me?" The company is home-based in Philadelphia."

I answered, "Look. I don't know. I don't like Philly. You can't drive in that town." The headhunter was persistent. He said, "Do me a favor and go for the interview. Basically just humor them." I don't know why, but I said okay.

I had to put a suit and tie on. While I was getting ready to go to the interview, I went to go to the bathroom and nothing but red blood came out. I said, "Oh my God." I came downstairs and I called my cousin who was a doctor. He told me, "If you're not in any pain you're not going to get an appointment until awfully late today or tomorrow morning so why don't you go to your interview while I try to get someone to see you."

So, I drove to Philadelphia and went to the interview at a piano store called Jacobs Music. The fellow who interviewed me was a big guy who reminded me of Captain Kangaroo. At least he had that kind of haircut. I almost told him that but I figured it wouldn't be corporate-like. During the interview he kept asking me about handling money and doing sales. He said, "Well you know son, we handle big money."

I'm cocky and I said. "I've been selling Rolex watches since I was eight years old. I've been on stages with $50,000 in my pocket taking care of the groups with contracts. Handling money is no problem for me."

He said, "Well you're not going to sell pianos by just playing one." Now, he didn't know anything about my performances, just that I played and I might make a good sales person.

Then he went out into the hallway and I heard him talking to two other gentlemen who seemed to want me. They had a little discussion. Jacobs had a number of locations. Then the interviewer said, "Well the interview was good. We'll give you a call."

Al Rinaldi

They did call and they had me come back. This time I spoke to the owner who turned out to be a really good guy named Al Rinaldi. I didn't know a lot about Al then except that he had all these piano stores, Steinway franchises. Al seemed like a nice guy whom I felt comfortable with. When we met, he didn't know anything about how I played. He never really did know until later. He said, "Your performing days are over now that you're going to be with my company." I looked at him, I said, "I don't think so." He goes, "Oh, I can guarantee it. That'll be the end of it because you'll be busy with the store." Then he went through all the same questions that the previous interviewer had asked. Jacobs Music had a number of stores but the one location that was available was in Lawrenceville, New Jersey. So, I accepted an offer to work for Jacobs Music selling pianos. I'm still working for Jacobs Music today, but it was a rough start.

First of all, I could never find the damn place. I didn't travel very much and most cars didn't have GPS systems those days. I used to get lost every day. I would call home and tell Jamey, "I can't do this." Plus, they want me to wear a suit and tie at work. I can't wear normal ties. They take me back to the time my abusive father almost choked me to death with a tie. He once grabbed me by the tie and literally hung me in the air. He just picked me up and shook me out. I never really wore one again except for a clip-on bow tie or something for a funeral. Al Wright taught me to always have two pre-knotted ties that are ready to put on. But since that time with my father I won't wear any ties but the zip ties which are great. The knot is perfect for any suit. But working for Jacobs Music turned everything around for me. I went from being casual in cut-offs and jeans to being sharply dressed. It took some getting used to. It was a

Al Rinaldi

Al Rinaldi has been such an inspiration to me, I wanted to tell you a little about this amazing man. If anyone had a "rags to riches" story of overcoming adversity, it was Al. Al Rinaldi was born in a tenement in Scranton, Pennsylvania. Abandoned by his mother at the age of nine months, Al was taken in by an alcoholic lady who lived down the hall. That woman was so poverty stricken herself that Al had to resort to begging to have something to eat. He used to go to the deli and ask for scraps for his dog. There was, of course, no dog. The scraps were Al's dinner.

From age six to nine, Al accompanied an older friend to area bars to sing for tips. His friend played saxophone and took 90 cents out of every dollar they made. At age nine, Al was taken in by a kindly waitress who heard him sing. As she and her husband were German, Al was encouraged to play the accordion. Music became Al's refuge. Through high school and the Navy, music remained a driving force in his life.

After his discharge from the Navy, Al began selling organs, a job that first required his learning how to play one. From there it was a steady uphill climb, from selling and demonstrating organs in a store window to managing the organ department in Philadelphia's Gimbels Department store. On borrowed money, Al started leasing Gimbels' piano and organ department. From there he began leasing similar departments in local Strawbridge & Clothier and Wanamaker's department stores. Al also became a founder and director of the Fellowship Bank which was eventually sold to Chemical Bank. From there, he purchased his first stand-alone piano and organ store on Chestnut Street in Philadelphia, representing the Jacobs Music Company.

By 1976, Al Rinaldi had taken over five stores of the Jacobs Music Company while still leasing departments in Strawbridge and Wanamaker's. But it was also a difficult time for him. At age 39, he was stricken with cancer for the second time. Weighing only 82 pounds, Al was sleeping in a reclining chair and walking with a cane. Somehow, Al beat cancer again. In his lifetime, Al would be stricken and survive cancer 11 times.

In 1985, Al Rinaldi achieved another of his life goals, being appointed a Steinway & Sons dealer representative. Under Steinway's rigorous criteria, only about 70 such representatives exist in all of the Americas. Whenever a Steinway artist performs in Southeastern and South Central Pennsylvania, New Jersey or Delaware, Jacobs Music is responsible for providing instruments and services for that artist. Rinaldi has been honored with multiple awards from Steinway & Sons, including Dealer of the Year, multiple Partners in Performance Sales awards, and a Lifetime Achievement Award in 2012, an honor only previously bestowed on John Steinway and Van Cliburn.

Having risen from extreme poverty and overcome enormous adversity to heading Jacobs Music, the leading piano retailer in the Philadelphia, New Jersey and Delaware region, Al Rinaldi died of gastrointestinal cancer in 2014 at the age of 77.

learning curve. It took years because the day I started, a couple of people there said I had an attitude and wouldn't last a week.

I visited and toured the Yamaha piano factory in Georgia. Jacobs Music was a Steinway dealer which was right up my alley. I had to re-educate myself and tried to rid myself of negativity. I really don't have a good tolerance for bullshit people.

Early on, a guy came in to the store looking to buy a decent but inexpensive piano for his child to study on. Now, upright pianos run into the thousands of dollars with high end pianos costing $70,000 or more. But we had a mint condition piano in the back, and it was only $600 including the bench. The man showed up driving an expensive fancy car and could have just said it was more than he wanted to spend. But instead, he started screaming at me yelling "I did not want to buy a house, you idiot. You want to charge me a fortune!" Something snapped in me and I said, "Get the hell out of here." The manager came running out all excited exclaiming, "What are you doing?" I said, "I was going to lose it with this guy so I threw him out of the store."

I had to learn to balance that stuff as it was a heavy-duty store. They have the President's Club which honors those who sell a million dollars' worth of pianos in a year. It took me until my second or third year but I did become Employee of the Year and made that club. In fact, I made that club 8 or 10 times over the years.. That meant fancy dinners, extra checks and people from Steinway starting to notice the way I was demonstrating their pianos.

Now the store had a Steinway upright piano called a K-52 Vertegrand. The Vertegrand has a bigger sound than 5'10" Baby Grand, but no one ever demonstrated it. The manager would tell me, "Nobody wants that. They just don't sell." And I said, "Well, of course it doesn't sell. It's way back in the corner." So I gradually moved it up across from one of the Baby Grands. I'd play one hand on each to show the difference. When teachers came in they'd say, "We don't have much room but we don't want an upright. We really need a Baby Grand." I said, "Listen to this," and I would play the left hand on that K-52 and the right hand on the Baby Grand across from it. These people said, "Oh, my God, it's a stronger piano." I said, "Yes. It has more strength. It has a bigger sound and it's a Vertegrand piano." They started buying them. I think I sold 6 in one year while they hadn't sold but two in three previous years. They started calling me the K-man. Even the guy from Steinway came and said, "Show me the demonstration you did." He said, "Where'd you come up with that?" I said, "It's really simple. You put your left hand here and you cross over and you put your right hand on the other one and this upright devours the Baby Grand."

My piano demonstrations for potential customers were always different. A lot of guys play the same chords and the same scales when they show a piano to somebody. I never knew what I was going to play until I sat down to play. Sometimes a person would say, "Do you know that song from *Casablanca*?" And I'd play "As Time Goes By." I'd start to play and I'd look the age of the person. If they were older, I'd play that straight and they'd be in love with the piano right away. Of course, I'd explain the quality of the piano and everything. That was a part that I had to really get good at. Some people are very impatient and just want to know the best price. I'd try to show them what they were paying for. A lot of times it was the music that sold the piano.

Jacobs Music

I was often asked to teach piano but I just couldn't do it. I had offers amounting to three times greater than many of the teachers were paid. Every time I sold a Steinway the buyer got a free gift of me coming to perform at their home when they had their grand opening. That became pretty popular.

In piano sales, we get most of our business through piano teachers. Whereas all the other piano sales people had 20 to 30 good teachers to work with, I was new to this and didn't know anybody at all. I had to really work to earn the support of some teachers. Jamey was very helpful. She did a big mailing of personal letters for me to every teacher that was in the teacher's guide. People started calling and stopping in to the store. It took maybe two and a half years and I had more teachers than two or three salesmen who had done this for 10 years. I built the business up. In the course, I met some of the best teachers in the world! Professor Ingrid Clarfield, whom I'd known for many years, was at Westminster Choir College in Princeton, New Jersey. Ingrid had the most dynamic private home studio which also included a most talented group of young pianists, period. The thing that amazed me about Ingrid is that if you put ten students behind a curtain that were all wonderful, I could pick out which one or two were her students. Ingrid insists that the entire family be involved with their children and, along with Todd Simmons, holds many fund raising recitals that raise thousands of dollars for the Children's Hospital of Philadelphia and other worthy causes. Her master classes are sought after throughout the United States and even into Canada. I've had the pleasure of attending many of her classes. Not only were her presentations unique and unusual, but they were all different. You heard the students improve right in front of you. It was spectacular every time!

I've been very lucky to gain the respect of many great teachers. Marvin Blickenstaff at age 84, still does master classes all over the United States and until just a few years ago, was doing a steady stream of great pianos performances that were tremendous. I never attended one of his classes where I didn't learn something new and how to apply it to my performing. It is important to list some of these amazing teachers such as Chiu-Tze Lin, who is not only a great pianist, but also is the music director and conductor of the Bravura Youth Orchestra which puts on unique and award winning concerts. I was amazed to find out that her sister Chi Ling Lin, who is one of my favorite performers, also was her first teacher! It's a must to mention my good friends Yining Wang, Charl Louw, Amy Watt Glennon, Todd Simmons, David Leifer, Veda Zuponcic, Ryugin Mikuriya, Rose McCathran, Yevgeny Morozov, Andy Kahn - one of my favorite jazz and American Song Book pianists plus a great teacher and totally off-the-charts teacher and concert performer Kairy Koshoeva. Kairy is the most dynamic pianist I've heard in years, besides being a wonderful individual. Other prominent music teachers include Sylvie Webb and Igor Resnianski. I could go on and on. I just find it necessary to let some of my fans, both old and new, know about these magical educators I have met and am still meeting currently. My life was not all about blues and rock and roll so it is important to recognize just a few of the dedicated music educators that work so hard and love what they do! After all this was the music I started with at the age of three and practiced 6 to 8 hours a day until I was 15!

At Jacobs Music, I had to maneuver a lot of obstacles. We had these boxes in Jamey's store that were like little Baby Grand pianos. When you opened them up, there was a ring inside them. Well, I took the rings out and I bought sterling silver eight notes, put them on chains and stuck them in those boxes. I sent them to all the piano teachers. I paid for them myself, but then I got told off because I had no right to send corporate stuff out without Al Rinaldi's approval. I just said, "Did you happen to look inside?" Al opened one up and saw the sterling silver note. He said, "You sent these all to teachers?" I said, "Yeah." I think that's when Al really noticed that we had a lot in common. He was a really powerful guy with street sense. He'd really worked his way up from nothing to having a little franchise and selling at Gimbels. When a place would close down, he'd take it over. He just built Jacobs Music up to one of the biggest piano sellers in the country.

It was an interesting relationship. Al started calling me at 5:30 in the morning to run his ideas past me. He'd wake up at 4 a.m., thinking of ideas for all the stores. Al would say, "Norman, I trust you. What do you think about this?" I'd reply, "You're the owner." He'd say, "No, what do you think of this idea?" He put a lot of faith on me.

Steinway Spirio Pianos

Al Rinaldi was very innovative. He thought pianos would sell better if they had a player system. Player pianos have come a long way since the days of piano rolls. Magnetic tapes, floppy disks, and now iPads came to replace piano rolls to record and play back the music. Modern computer-controlled player pianos are able to simulate the nuances of a human performer. Thus, a player piano can be played by a musician or self-play recitals of skilled professional musicians.

Under Al's direction, we instituted a Steinway promotion where buyers would get a free player system along with the piano. Damn if it didn't boost the sales about 30-40%.

When someone called to buy a $70,000 piano and they were going to get a $3,000 - $4,000 player system, they bought it right away. I think that's really got the Steinway Company to looking into developing the system they have now where there's no floppy disk. The songs are in the cloud, recorded by the original artist.

In 2017, Norman became a Steinway Spirio Artist

Then Steinway came out with the Spirio. The Spirio is a piano designed by Steinway. It took years to design. It is not a player piano. It's a re-performance grand piano. It plays like a regular Steinway, but is only available in certain sizes. They have a library of Steinway Spirio artists' performances ranging from as far back as Arthur Rubinstein and Vladimir Horowitz to all the latest like Lang Lang and Yuja Wang. The difference is that those are real artists, not the studio musicians all the other lines have on their player pianos. Other piano companies with player piano systems will have a Billy Joel song accompanied by just a studio musician. Only the Spirio has the original authentic artists playing on Steinway & Sons pianos. There's one performance from 1932. Visually you can see the musician playing on the piano in front of you. You can also transfer that video to the big screen. Audibly, the Spirio song is indistinguishable from a live performance.

The natural thing was for me to become a Spirio artist. That actually happened for me in 2017. It was a huge honor for me to be in company with such a select group of the world's finest pianists. Because Jacobs was one of the biggest dealers, they set me up with Steinway and I recorded ten tracks. Many people said they sell Spirios when they hear me play. While Rubinstein was on there or Van Cliburn or Art Tatum and Duke Ellington, they said, "At least half the time it's your stuff that people like to hear.'" Some stride blues or "Vincent (Starry Starry Night"). Just piano music.

Steinway has a Spirio piano that also records. Once you record it, it will play back what you've played on that piano. So if you play guitar or violin and want to play along with yourself, you play the piano and save that. Then you push that button and play along with yourself live. You can mute, mix and regenerate.

Soon Steinway's going to add a feature where I can be back at the studio, sit down, push one button, start playing and you'll hear me playing in every Spirio in the world... London, Germany, you name it. It all works off an iPad and the cloud. Every month

Spirio adds 20 or 30 new songs and new artists. It's amazing. How many people have seen Art Tatum playing George Gershwin? Nobody! And you'll be able to see them coming up in all Spirios pianos. They've got Monk and Bill Evans. These are some heavy players and they're all Steinway artists.

The white piano for which I posed a picture can be seen at the beginning of Chapter One. It is the John Lennon model which he designed for Yoko Ono for her birthday. Inside, it is autographed by John Lennon.

Al Rinaldi was always a big supporter of the musical community through donations to colleges, schools and even the Kimmel Center in Philadelphia. Sadly, Al died in 2014. When he passed away, we did a tribute concert for him in the Convention Center down in Cape May, New Jersey. The venue seated about 2,300 and it was basically sold out. Jacobs Music had never done a production like that before. They had the Horowitz piano there and they also had another one next to it. All the professors from the different colleges were performing to honor Al Rinaldi. They had a woman jazz singer who was in her nineties who was really great. They had all these great players. I was just sitting there in the back listening and they were just killing it.

Now, the Rinaldi family had never heard me play on stage. When it came my time to play they were joking in the back. Greg Sikora, the head piano technician and one of the great ones, looked at the other technicians and said, "We're going to have to really fix this piano on the break because Norman is going to kill this thing."

They introduced me and I went up on stage. I immediately took off my jacket and cowboy hat off and hung them on the side of the Horowitz piano for a music stand. I sat down at the other piano, said hello to everybody and started playing "Send in the Clowns." Then I went into another ballad. People were wondering, "What the hell is he doing?" Then all of a sudden, I broke into a very short passage of Springsteen's "Jungle Song" with the piano. When I heard the applause start, I stopped right away and started doing "Louisiana 1927" by Randy Newman. The place just dropped to silence. Everybody, all 2,300 people, became silent and they were really listening. I think they were just so tired of listening to classical piano. They heard my voice, singing. I closed with a little Jerry Lee Lewis. I think I went right across the whole gamut of songs. It was incredible.

The teachers, the professors, doctors of music that played before me said, "My God, we thought you were a piano salesman." I never played for any one of them. They said, "The touch, the dynamics that you have, when you started to play, it was so beautiful." These were heavy-duty musicians. One professor who was Russian, said, "So glad you did not play before us."

When I finished, the Rinaldi family just looked at me and said, "What?" They were having drinks at the bar in one of those old homes across the street when the event was over. I sat down at the bar and I remember Al's wife, Gabrielle Rinaldi, saying, "You're amazing. I never knew." I said, "Nobody asked."

From that point on, things changed a lot. The Rinaldis started showing me off on the Spirio. We did a concert in their hall. The teachers showed up in droves because I'd always done favors for them. I've helped them all that I could, and helped their students. With Al's passing, a lot of things changed, but the stores kept going.

The Asbury Cares Concert

While I didn't really miss playing the clubs five nights a week, I did miss playing with my musician friends in front of an audience. In January 2005, I took part in a benefit organized and emceed by Nicky Addeo called "Asbury Cares." The concert benefited the victims of the South Asian tsunami of the prior month. It embodied many of the various music styles present in the Asbury Park area. Also on the concert were Vini Lopez & Steel Mill, Billy Ryan & the Bluescasters, the Sonny Kenn Band, Blue Plate Special, Rock n' Rhythm, Streetheart, Leon Trent, Mr. Popeye, Patsy Siciliano, Danny Walsh, Johnny Petillo, Anita Ferrer, Pat Guadagno & the Candle Brothers, Amanda Cashman, Dusty Micale and others. The event was held at the Asbury Lanes.

The Creators of S.O.A.P. Plaque and Concert

In 2006, John Shaw, organizer and drummer of the Jaywalkers died. So many musicians had played with the Jaywalkers including Mickey Holiday, Billy Ryan, Garry Tallent, Doc Holiday and others. John Shaw had an organized group. Believe me, when you heard the Jaywalkers do Gary Puckett or Ray Charles, you thought you were listening to the record. They were that good. You may recall, I recorded the Jaywalkers for my *Selsom* label back in the day and had sat in with them on occasion. When John Shaw died that started former Soul Set and Jaywalkers member Doc "Fast Eddie Wohanka" Holiday to thinking about honoring the pioneers of the "Sound Of Asbury Park" or S.O.A.P. for short. The idea started with Doc Holiday and Garry Tallent also got involved.

The S.O.A.P. Plaque honoring those who created the "Sound Of Asbury Park."

Doc Holiday planned a black soapstone monument with a brass plaque with the names of 32 of the significant S.O.A.P. pioneers that would stand forever on the Asbury Park boardwalk by the Paramount Theatre. The list of honorees was

Photos from the S.O.A.P. pre-dedication reception at the Berkeley Carteret Hotel.
Top: Norman Seldin, Vini Lopez, Doc Holiday.
Bottom: Garry Tallent, Norman Seldin

whittled down from 271 nominations. These on the S.O.A.P. plaque are Johnny Shaw, Billy Ryan, Bruce Springsteen, Garry Tallent, Steve Van Zandt, Mickey Holiday, "Stormin'" Norman Seldin, Vini "Mad Dog" Lopez, Fast Eddie "Doc Holiday" Wohanka, Billy "Cherry Bomb" Lucia, Clarence Clemons, Nicky Addeo, Donnie Lowell, Jim "Jack Valentine" Cattanach, Ken "Mr. Popeye" Pentifallo, Jay Pilling, Jon "Cos" Consoli, Gary "A" Arntz, Larry "The Great" Gadsby, Steve "Mole" Wells, Ray Dahrouge, Johnny "A" Arntz, David Sancious, Margaret Potter, Tom Potter, Sonny Kenn, Tom Wuorio, Rick DeSarno, Southside Johnny Lyon, Leon Trent, Buzzy Lubinsky, Danny Federici, Bill Chinnock, Patsy Siciliano and Sam Siciliano. My name is right below Bruce Springsteen's. When people ask me, "Are you on the plaque?" I say, "You see Bruce Springsteen's name? Look right underneath."

At the Stone Pony for the 2006 S.O.A.P. Concert.
From left: Mark Love from Jacobs Music, Jamey Seldin, Jamey's brother Michael, Norman, Norman's daughter Rebecca Photo by John Cavanaugh

Along with the plaque dedication, a reunion concert was scheduled at the Stone Pony. Proceeds would benefit two local charities - the Mercy Center and Interfaith Neighbors. The night before there was a reception at the Berkeley Carteret Oceanfront Hotel for the honorees and their families. We had a chance to relive old memories of performing in the 60's and 70's. They sold T-shirts that read "They came back and they rocked."

2006 S.O.A.P. Concert at the Stone Pony
Norman Seldin on left.

The next afternoon they unveiled the plaque in a small ceremony as about a hundred music fans looked on. Asbury Park City Manager Terry Reidy welcomed the crowd and told them, "Today is an amazing day. We're here to honor people who provide us with spirit, energy, history and culture. This is what Asbury Park is all about."

Then it was on to the Stone Pony that evening for the concert. We only had a couple hours rehearsal. Tickets for the concert were only $15 and the Stone Pony sold out immediately. Just before the concert tickets were being scalped for $1,500. Some people thought that Bruce might show up and he didn't but we never advertised that he would be there. But people certainly got their money's worth. About thirty of the honored musicians took part in a big jam session. Besides me, on stage were Doc Holiday. Vini Lopez, Garry Tallent, Billy Ryan, Nicky Addeo, Mickey Holiday, David Sancious and many others. They had two drummers, Vini Lopez and Craig Krampf from the group, Journey, and they had all of those guitar players. Some of them hadn't played for a long time, but it was still a hell of a production. Garry Tallent and I kind of anchored the whole show. We really had the crowd dropping back to the old harmony stuff. After a few hours of jamming, Garry was looking over to me as if to say, "Are we going to take a break here, or what?" It was an amazing night.

Local Heroes

Shortly after the S.O.A.P. concert, I was approached by two Swedish journalists, Anders Martensson and Jorgen Johansson. They were writing a book about the Asbury Park music scene called "Local Heroes." The book was to contain original interviews with about thirty S.O.A.P. pioneers telling their stories about the Jersey Rock Sound.

Book "Local Heroes" and photo of Norman Seldin and author Ander Martensson
Photo by Jamey Seldin

So, these two journalists traveled to the United States and tracked down all of us musicians. Martensson, a writer, conducted the interview and Johansson, a photographer, took the pictures. The book was published in Swedish in Sweden and in English by Rutgers University Press. It came out here in 2008 and had a chapter about me. Jamey started carrying it in the store and it drew a lot of attention.

Asbury Park Then and Now

In mid- 2008, Doc Holiday and Garry Tallent planned a second S.O.A.P. concert at the Stone Pony. I decided to time the concert with a project I had long thought of doing.

Jamey was sitting with me and I started playing songs for her from early in my career that she'd never heard before. She said, "How many more of these do you have?" I said, "We could keep going for hours." I thought, “Wouldn't this be something nice to put out for sale at the S.O.A.P. Concert?” I ran it by Doc Holiday and he said, "Buddy, you're free to do whatever you want. Whatever you sell, you keep." I said, “So let me get this straight, I can make my own multi-color graphic T-shirts?” And he said, “Yeah.” “And the book, ‘Local Legends’?” Doc OK’ed it and cleared it with the people at the Stone Pony.

So I put out a double-CD, “Asbury Park: Then and Now.” featuring 40 years’ worth of Jersey Shore sounds, both released and unreleased, that I’d recorded. In short, it was my life in music form, a record of time spent honing my craft with the help of some very good friends on the Jersey Shore. It contained everything from acappella gems to soul singles to rock and rhythm & blues. As a musician, singer, songwriter, bandleader and producer, I was the thread that connected all of these songs.

The CD set contained 45 recordings that I had done with Barbaroso & the Historians (actually Nicky Addeo, Ray Dahrouge & the Darchaes), Nicky Addeo solo, Nicky Addeo & the Uniques, Harry Ray & the Valtairs, Mickey Holiday & the Jaywalkers, Tony Maples, Stormin’ Norman & Steel Breeze, Stormin’ Norman solo, the Motifs, the Soul Set, Stormin’ Norman & the Joyful Noyze (featuring Clarence Clemons, Barry Lynn, Hal Hollander, Ron Alard, Bob Danylchuk, Nicky Addeo) and Stormin’ Norman & Friends (Garry Tallent, Clarence Clemons, Danny Federici, Billy Ryan, Max Weinberg, Jody Linscott, Jude Johnstone, Roy Bittan, Artie Bressler and Southside Johnny). Some of the songs had to be transcribed from vinyl because the tapes weren't there anymore.

So between the CD set, the T-shirts and the book, we had three products to sell at S.O.A.P. Concert #2. I think we sold $6,000 or $7,000 worth in two days. People jumped all over that book. I know I sold at least 250 copies of the CD there, which was a lot. We were the only ones selling things. I think we've now sold over 4,000 copies. We always set up a display and do signings. At the S.O.A.P. Concert, people were coming up and buying the T-shirts four and five at a time at $20 a pop. I was getting in colored T-shirts at about $4 a piece and they were gorgeous. The other musicians never even thought to sell merchandise.

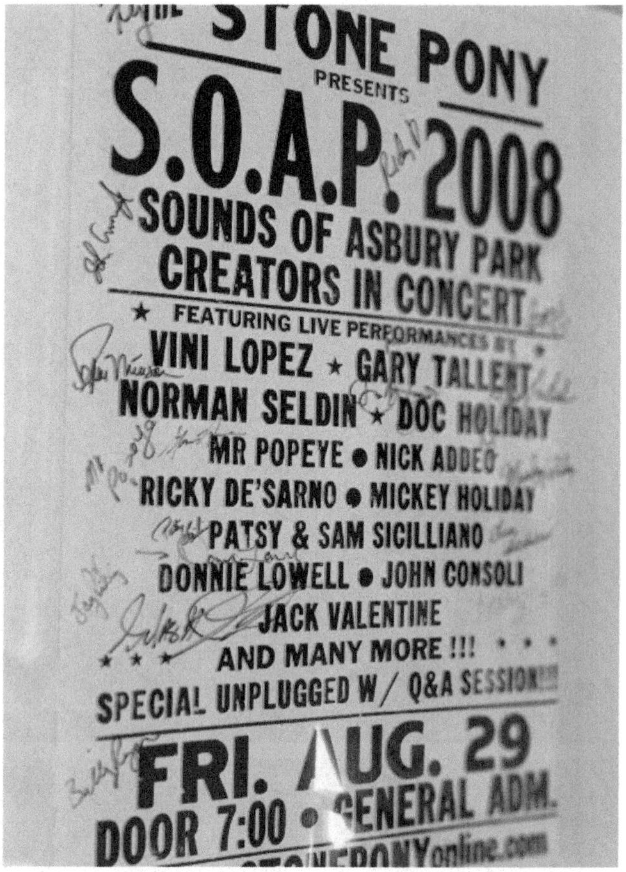

S.O.A.P. Concert #2

S.O.A.P. Concert #2, again held at the Stone Pony, was another huge success. On the concert I was joined by Vini Lopez and Steel Mill, a reunion of Moment of Truth featuring Garry Tallent and a cast of Asbury Park legends including Nicky Addeo, Leon Trent, Doc Holiday, Mickey Holiday, Donnie Lowell, Tom Wuorio, Billy Ryan, Jack Valentine, Ricky DeSarno, Patsy & Sam Siciliano, Johnny Petillo, Anthony Mirabile, Ken "Mr. Popeye" Pentifallo and Mark Hernden (drummer for the country rock group, Alabama from Virginia Beach, Virginia). Proceeds again benefited local charities.

Later that year, Nicky Addeo assembled a primarily doo wop concert at Matawan Regional High School in Aberdeen, New Jersey. By then Nicky had a talented group of background singers called the Nite Owls, consisting of Kenny "Mr. Popeye" Pentifallo, Bobby "Blue" Castellano, Warren Tesoro and Danny Ugarte. I backed the group on keyboards along with Vini Lopez on drums, Les Pennyfeather on bass and Harry London on guitar. Other acts on the show were Kenny Vance & the Planetones and Sammy Sax & the MD's.

Over the next couple of years my work at Jacobs Music kept me pretty busy, but I still appeared solo at places like Mr. C's Beach Bistro in Allenhurst and Doolan's Shore Club Grille and Bar in Spring Lake Heights.

S.O.A.P Concert #2 at the Stone Pony, 2008. Top photo from left:
Pam McCoy, Sam Siciliano, Mickey Holiday, Norman Seldin.
Photos courtesy of Pam McCoy

Clarence Clemons

Norman performing at Doolan's in 2009

In October, 2009, Clarence Clemons published his autobiography, "Big Man: Real Life & Tall Tales." In it he wrote about how he joined my band, the Joyful Noyze, and how I lost bookings because some club owners were fearful that his presence would scare the white kids away. He rightfully pointed out that I didn't care and that the most important thing to me was the music. He also wrote about how hard it was for him to leave me for Bruce. I guess he did all right for himself.

As part of the book promotion, Clarence had a book signing at the Barnes & Noble store in Princeton. He invited me there and we had a good time talking about the old days together. At that time, Clarence was performing with the E Street Band and was scheduled to play Madison Square Garden the next month. He gave Jamey and me tickets to a couple of great seats and invited us to come back stage and attend as his guests. We did and had a great time. As we were leaving, Clarence yelled to the car, "Watch Jon Stewart's Show tonight." I couldn't imagine why he'd tell us that but we did tune into "The Daily Show with Jon Stewart" that night. As it turned out, Clarence was Jon's featured guest and he talked all about me and his time with the Joyful Noyze. The next day when I got to Jacobs Music, everyone told me they learned all about me on TV the night before.

Norman Seldin and Clarence Clemons at Clarence's book signing in Princeton, 2009

In June of 2011, I received the sad news that Clarence Clemons had died of complications of a stroke. It had been forty years since Clarence had played with my Joyful Noyze. Back then there were no black or integrated bands playing places like Mrs. Jay's and the Wonder Bar. When I invited Clarence to join my all white band we integrated a segregated music scene. It broke barriers but we had to pay hell for it. Though Clarence left to join Bruce Springsteen's E Street Band in 1971, we remained good friends and even played

Norman, Clarence and Jamey backstage at Madison Square Garden, 8 November, 2009

together a number of times since then. His passing signaled the end of an era and saddened me greatly.

In 2014, Clarence and the rest of the E Street Band were inducted into the Rock & Roll Hall of Fame in Cleveland. For Clarence it was three years too late.

Chapter Fourteen
Encore

Funny how things can go full circle. My friend and road manager Butch Gregoria and I had a chance to go see my old friend Johnny Thunder when he played Richard Nader's Summer Doo Wop Reunion XXII concert at the Meadowlands Izod Center in June of 2011. It seemed like just yesterday when I had Johnny performing at some of my teen dances back in the 1960's. Johnny and I had always stayed in touch.

Norman Seldin and
Johnny Thunder, 2011

Meanwhile, besides my work as "Artist in Residence" at Jacobs Music, I began playing, along with Pam McCoy, at Sallee Tee's Grill in Monmouth Beach, New Jersey. Sallee Tee's was owned by my old friend, Joe Amiel, formerly of the Old Mill Inn.

At the same time, I performed at other occasions like the Jersey Shore Jazz and Blues Foundation's Reckless Steamy Nights series. There, I played at the Red Bank Women's Club along with Pam McCoy. About that time I also started playing the annual Light of Day concerts in Asbury Park.

Light of Day

The Light of Day Foundation, Inc is a 501(c)(3) non-profit organization that uses the power of music to raise money and awareness in the battle to cure Parkinson's disease and related illnesses. The organization's primary activities started as a series of annual concerts held in Asbury Park every January, though this has now grown to approximately seventy shows in thirteen countries.

In January 2012, Pam McCoy and I played one of the Light of Day benefit concerts at the Stone Pony along with Vini Lopez and members of Steel Mill. Playing the Light of Day concerts became an annual event for me.

Norman Seldin and Pam McCoy

About a month later, word came that Vinnie Roslin had passed away. After the Motifs, Vinnie had co-founded Steel Mill with Vini Lopez, Danny Federici and Bruce Springsteen. I joined Vini Lopez, Gary Cavico, Blue Plate Special, Nicky Addeo, Rob Brooks, Sonny Kenn, the B-Street Band, Bobby Bandiera, the Upstage Jam Band and others in a tribute concert to Vinnie at the Headliner Pub in Neptune. A few months after that we lost Barry Lynn, my stand up drummer from the Joyful Noyze. Barry was so good and we'd had such great times together.

On the positive side, people were finally beginning to give recognition to the Rhythm & Blues roots of the Jersey Shore Rock music scene. The previous November the Asbury Park Historical Society and Asbury Park Press co-sponsored a "Soul of Asbury Park" concert at the Paramount Theatre, put together and emceed by Nicky Addeo. It was a reunion for Asbury Park West Side artists Billy Brown and the Broadways who had not performed together in over 40 years. The concert also featured Lenny Welch, Bobby Thomas and Billy Brown singing with Ray, Goodman & Brown, though Harry Ray and Al Goodman had long since passed on.

The resurgence of interest in Asbury Park R&B led to Ray Dahrouge and Sam Siciliano reuniting the doo wop group, Ray and the Darchaes. Ray Dahrouge, Sam Siciliano, Louie Scalpati, Denny Testa and Patsy Siciliano were back together again, if only for a short time. It had been 48 years since I'd recorded them along with Nicky Addeo as Barbaroso & the Historians. Since that time, Ray Dahrouge had become a highly-respected singer, songwriter, arranger and producer in the soul music field. Sam Siciliano had continued singing while also working for the Asbury Park Press. Sam had an extraordinary talent for arranging vocal harmony. He passed away in 2015.

Sallee Tee's

Ray and the Darchaes joined me at Sallee Tee's one evening where I backed them on a few of their old songs. It was a historic reunion. That's where I met this book's co-author, Charlie Horner. Charlie and his wife Pamela are noted music historians

Norman Seldin and Ray & the Darchaes at Salle Tees, 16 February, 2012
Photo by Charlie Horner

and are, for a large part, responsible for the new respect given to Asbury Park's black music legacy. They interviewed me at Sallee Tee's the following week for an article on Asbury Park's West Side music that they published in "Echoes of the Past" magazine. The Horners were also deeply involved in preserving the legacy of Monmouth County's black music through museum exhibits. They assembled and curated four museum exhibits on shore area black music, in which I was featured. They continue to work as trustees of the Asbury Park Museum.

By the summer of 2012, I was back performing with my band of all stars at the Jersey Shore Jazz & Blues Foundation event, this time held on the grounds of the Middletown Arts Center.

Hurricane Sandy

Then, in late October, Hurricane Sandy wreaked havoc on the New Jersey coast. The state suffered unimaginable damage. Joe Amiel's club, Sallee Tee's, where I'd been playing much of the year was damaged beyond repair. So too were many of the shore venues. Still, the cry went out that we were "Jersey Strong" and we would recover.

Melody Seldin

Fondness for the entertainment business seems to run in the Seldin family and I'm proud to say that my daughter Melody has also distinguished herself in that field. Melody was with me in Mississippi and Florida before enrolling at the University of Florida. I'll let Melody tell you a little about her career in this sidebar.

Early in 1995, I joined the University of Florida student government group SGP (Student Government Productions) after meeting a fellow student in the hallway of the College of Journalism who suggested I apply. I did, and started supporting marketing and production for them. Around that time, SGP brought bands to campus including Phish, Violent Femmes, Billy Joel, Tori Amos, G-Love and Special Sauce, and Deelite along with comedians including a pre-Daily Show Jon Stewart. The people I met in SGP eventually became some of my oldest friends, and around then I realized the entertainment industry felt immediately comfortable. Maybe spending childhood afternoons helping Dad wrap PA system cables and hanging out at bars drinking Shirley Temples had a hand in that!

SGP was also where I got the opportunity to work Thanksgiving weekend as a production runner for the Rolling Stones on the Voodoo Lounge tour in Gainesville Florida. It's also where I got my first MTV job as a local Casting Assistant while they shot for a week in Panama City Beach. By May of 1996 I was nearing graduation when Dad called to say he met a man working on a Ridley Scott film in Florida. He gave me the guy's phone number and told me to keep trying him. I think I left him about 25 answering machine messages before I eventually got a meeting with the production office staff in Jacksonville. The film was "G.I. Jane" starring Demi Moore and they gave me a production assistant role on their production accounting team. Each day I skipped my last semester classes and drove two hours each way to work in Jacksonville. When I graduated I moved there, rooming with another PA, and when production wrapped in Florida they invited me to travel with the crew to the next location of Beaufort, SC and then Virginia.

I always knew I was going to New York City after school was over, so Dad helped me get set up in a one-room studio under a family's house on Staten Island. I called my contacts at MTV and went to work as a Casting Assistant for a special East Coast shoot of "Singled Out." Every night I went to nightclubs representing MTV and signed up attractive young folks to be on the game show. I would go out - often alone - to a nightclub until 2 a.m., then take the 1 and 9 down to the Staten Island Ferry. I'd grab a slice of pizza at the Ferry, ride back to Staten Island, get in my car and arrive home around 4 a.m. Then I'd be back at work at 10 a.m. to process the people I had met the night before and scan modeling head shots of people who wanted to be on the show. That job ended and I took another role at

MTV, but by then I was thinking about California. Most of my friends had gone to Los Angeles and I felt it was where I should be too. I had never been there and didn't have a job, but I packed up my Honda and drove cross country with a friend.

It was a great decision and started a 10-year run of freelance production jobs with MTV, VH1, and various other television projects. One of my early production "runs" was to drive to Palm Springs the day Sonny Bono died. I drove out there alone with an 8mm camera to make some B-roll footage of Palm Springs. I was to go to Sonny Bono's mom's house to pick up old photos of him for our news show. She invited me in and we sat in her kitchen and she told me stories about Sonny and Cher when they were young, and gave me a pair of early press photos of them to keep. In retrospect it's kind of crazy that this poor woman had just lost her son and there she was talking to a stranger like a friend. I still have the little black and white promo shots of young Sonny and Cher...

Another early assignment was to book and meet an ENG (electronic news gathering) crew at The Whiskey on Sunset Blvd. The limos I was greeting carried the living members of The Doors coming for an anniversary shoot. I remember sitting in my car at 7 a.m. waiting for them to arrive - living legends. It was the first of many great experiences where I met performers like James Brown (he shook my hand and said "God bless you, sister"), Kelsey Grammer on the set of Frasier (we sat on Frasier's couch), Moby (who invited me to his Halloween party - I went and he was dressed as a giant baby in a diaper with a pacifier), Ben Stiller (as he shot a comedy skit in the character Derek Zoolander which became a film a few years later), Joe Rogan, Johnny Rzeznik, and a host of fun folks.

When I was around 28, after a chance temp assignment with Lionsgate in their Publicity Department, I landed in the film industry as a Publicity assistant for MGM Studios. It was an office job with some very interesting and fun elements - I was a "table holder" for Reese Witherspoon at the Golden Globes afterparty, helped design a private plane themed to "The Crocodile Hunter" for the late Steve Irwin, traveled to London for a press junket for "Legally Blonde 2," and worked the premiere of the James Bond film "Die Another Day" with Pierce Brosnan.

Eventually I got married and moved to London. After I got settled there I found work assisting the President of Paramount Pictures International. It felt great to have found "my people" in a new country. When Paramount closed its UK HQ, I went to work for Universal Pictures International in London. I worked on all of the red carpet events for Universal in France, Germany and Italy. I got to work with many major actors including Tom Cruise and Vin Diesel.

I helped organize charity racing tournaments, golf tournaments and things like that. I've worked supporting many Universal films including the Oscar winning "Green Book."

- Melody Seldin

Left: Norman Seldin, Charlie Horner, Pamela Horner at Salle Tees, 2012.
Right: Charlie Horner, Norman Seldin at the Asbury Park Museum exhibit, 2019

In December, I again teamed with Ray and the Darchaes. This time it was on a "Restore The Shore" benefit concert with proceeds going to the Sandy Jersey Relief Fund. Also performing on the benefit were Sounds of the Street and PS4. PS4 was a group consisting of members of the Siciliano family - brothers Patsy and Sam and sisters Fran and Lucrecia. I'd share the stage with PS4 again a year later when the Asbury Park Press launched their 2013 Summer Guide with a concert at the Wonder Bar. Also on that concert were former Uniques and Broadways singer Leon Trent, Ray Dahrouge and Johnny Petillo.

With Sallee Tee's gone, I started playing Zachary's in West Long Branch on Friday nights. Vance Villastrigo and I would have weekly dueling piano matches there. My concept of dueling pianos is a little different from what I've seen a few others do.

Dueling Pianos

I've seen musicians do dueling pianos where they have a bucket in the middle and somebody says, "Play 'Twist and Shout'" and throws in $5. And then after throwing a tip in, they only get to hear a quarter of their request. It's all about making money.

I look at dueling pianos quite differently. I get an as good or better partner playing piano alongside of me. We play our best tunes and we play songs all the way through. We kind of make our dueling pianos really good piano players playing better than each other every time, whether it is rhythm and blues or Jerry Lee Lewis or just a lush ballad on two pianos. It's a lot different. Usually both of us sing. Sometimes we have harmony. Sometimes the other pianist does two lead vocals while I do one. We'll both play solos. It depends on the material but we make it more of a dueling thing than it is monetary. The fact of having two pianos, whether they're digitals or baby grands,

Norman Seldin and Vance Villastrigo, Dueling Pianos
Photo by Katie Murphy

it's still eye-opening for people. Usually people only get to see one piano wherever they go. Sometimes, we do triple dueling pianos.

Vance Villastrigo, my frequent collaborator on dueling pianos, is just an amazing jazz and progressive piano player who can also sing. He'll do Stevie Wonder and Luther Vandross and then turn around and sing Frank Sinatra.

Clarence Clemons Day

In 2014, to mark Clarence Clemons' birthday, the State of New Jersey declared January 11, Clarence Clemons Day. There were celebrations all around the state. I was asked to play at a benefit called the Official Clemons Family Celebration held at Martell's Tiki Bar in Point Pleasant Beach. The event drew about 900 people and a number of bands and musicians wanting to pay tribute to Clarence. I was standing along the side waiting to go on for well over an hour and I thought they'd forgotten about me.

In fact, I was ready to leave, but Vini Lopez went ballistic. He said, "Wait a minute. If it wasn't for Norman Seldin, no one would even know who Clarence was. Norman should have been the first one on stage here." One of the things I've always respected about Vini is his professionalism. He's a huge get-it-right rehearsal man, a great lead singer behind the drums and he understands how the song is to be played. He is always open to good ideas and says the right things when they need to be said. Vini Lopez, in my book, is one of my most respected people in my life. We played very little together, but we always got along so well.

So they brought me on stage and one of Clarence's sons said a lot of nice things about me. I ended up on B3 organ and singing lead with a very nice back up band. With no rehearsal they backed me up on "Flip Flop and Fly" and the place just rocked. I mean, they went crazy.

I've done and continue to do a lot of benefit concerts for worthwhile causes. When the Ashley Lauren Foundation held their third annual Butterfly Ball fundraiser, a formal event at the Ocean Place Resort & Spa, I presented "Dueling Pianos" during the cocktail hour. The event raised money for children with cancer.

Monmouth University

I was also involved in a fundraiser at Monmouth University's Pollak Theatre that benefited the Associated Humane Societies (AHS) in Tinton Falls, New Jersey. June of 2016 saw the Monmouth County Sheriff's Office and the SPCA rescue 276 dogs from deplorable conditions in a Howell, New Jersey house. Many of the dogs ended up in the Tinton Falls AHS which swamped the organization's budget. They asked me to put a show together which I did very quickly. I rounded up nearly 20 musicians who performed for free at the benefit. Even Doc Holiday drove in from Nashville for the night to do the show. Pam McCoy and her daughter-in-law, Jillian Rhys McCoy sang. We had Joe Petillo and some of the local groups sing at it. Accordion artist Bruce Gassman gave an amazing performance. That night we had a horrendous rainstorm and some of the roads were cut off completely. There were literally trees down and people were trying to get into into the main part of West Long Branch but couldn't. Our attendance was about a third of what we had hoped for but we still raised $5,000 with no notice and had a great show. In fact, we let the show run overtime because people were late getting in there because of the weather.

We did a couple of piano concerts at Monmouth University's Pollak Theatre, thanks to the vision of the theater's director, Vaune Peck.. The first in May 2017, was called "Where the Piano is the Main Attraction." Of course, Vance and I did the dueling pianos but I had some talented young pianists, Charlie Liu, Taksh Gupta and Nicholas Budny, open up for us. I always tried to put two or three young, very, very good pianists on before we played our dueling pianos. That way we can expose

The Kids on Keys & Dueling Pianos concert at Monmouth University
Left: Ad for the concert. Right: Left to right: Norman Seldin, Vance Villastrigo, emcee Frank Dicopoulos, and Tim McLoone

them to people. They played all classical, of course, and they were brilliant. They got a standing ovation and they were that good. It was my way of tying in with Jacobs Music. Some of the teachers that had good students let their kids be on a national stage, on the concert grand piano tour.

Kids On Keys

A year later we did a second concert at Monmouth University. This time we called it "Kids On Keys and Dueling Pianos." The dueling pianos were Vance, me, and as special guest, musician and restaurateur Tim McLoone. People hardly ever see a nine-foot Steinway let alone two. They saw three that night. Jacobs Music made sure they were all there. Being a Steinway Spirio artist, Jacobs Music was responsible for bringing the pianos for me into schools and venues. The event was emceed by TV program host and producer, Frank Dicopoulos.

The "Kids On Keys and Dueling Pianos" concert was a benefit for Autism Awareness. I was witness to a young boy with autism who couldn't tie his own shoes but after ten months of piano lessons was playing "Moonlight Sonata" and other compositions. He basically won every award he could win in Pennsylvania and he also played trumpet in a jazz band. So our young proteges on that show were 9-year-old Taksh Gupta who had already been to Carnegie Hall several times, 14-year-old Elizabeth Williams and 14-year-old Andy Milsten who'd been diagnosed with autism at age 3.

Still, most of my playing was done at Bum Roger's Crabhouse in Seaside Park or at Zachary's. My friend, Joe Amiel, having lost Sallee Tees to Hurricane Sandy, eventually

The Stormin Norman Band with five saxophones at the Bruce Wacker Tribute Concert
Photo by Estelle Massey

became the owner of the Bay Pointe Inn in Highlands and I returned to play there. Sadly, Joe passed away in February of 2021.

The Bruce Wacker Memorial Concert

On June 5, 2018, Bruce Wacker died unexpectedly at the age of 61. Bruce was a well-respected guitarist on the Jersey Shore music scene as well as a music teacher. He was an excellent guitar player. He taught a lot of young musicians and he also did a ton of playing with a number of area bands. People loved him. Bruce's sister Susan is a good friend of mine. In fact, she designed the cover for this book. Susan asked me if I could put together a memorial tribute concert for Bruce in Asbury Park.

I contacted the Stone Pony and of course they were booked just about every evening. I asked for a Sunday afternoon and they were skeptical that I could draw an audience then. I told them I would cover the expenses and they gave me the date.

Well, we put together a great memorial concert. We had the whole Stormin' Norman Band with five saxes that day. Matt O'Ree brought his band and we had eight or nine other bands that wanted to honor Bruce. Hundreds of people showed up. Some had

Dueling pianos of Norman Seldin and Ryan Gregg with the Stormin Norman Band at the Wonder Bar for the 2020 Light of Day Concert. Photo by Charlie Horner

played with or been taught by Bruce Wacker. Some just knew him and his sister. And then there were people who just wanted to hear good bands. We charged $15 a head and the concert made its expenses, which were big. It was a memorable event.

Back to Light of Day

I keep doing the Light of Day Winterfest each January as it was for a very worthwhile cause. My performances kept getting bigger and bigger. Light of Day started including my band as part of an "Asbury Blues" day at the Wonder Bar. I kept expanding my band at Light of Day. In the year leading up to 2020 it went from 9 to 10 to 11 members. Of course, dueling pianos between Vance Villastrigo and me was always a feature. In 2020 Vance was replaced by another extremely talented pianist, Ryan Gregg. Ryan has since taken on a larger roll, assisting with production and handling publicity for my band. The Stormin' Norman Band that would perform at Light of Day has, depending on the year, also included Pam McCoy as guest vocalist; saxophonists Vic Cappetta, Rich Taskowitz, Rick Brunermer, Damian Cremisio, and Lee Sanderson; bassists Gerry Gironda and Jon Sebastian Brice; guitarists Ray Johnson and Victoria Warne; and drummer Ed Dougherty. I've also had various guests like Rob Paparozzi sit in on harmonica.

The Light of Day concerts are always one of the highlights of the year. Held at the Wonder Bar, they are always sold out as hundreds of people crowd the stage when we play. The Light of Day concerts are always high energy. I'll launch into Fats Domino's the "Fat Man" or "Blueberry Hill" and follow it with Big Joe Turner's "Flip Flop and Fly" or Jerry Lee Lewis' "Whole Lot of Shakin' Goin' On" and the whole place rocks.

The Stormin Norman mascot, Du Barry actually belongs to my friend and road manager Butch Dezsö Gregoria. Du Barry has his own FaceBook Page with over 800 friends.

When the COVID-19 pandemic hit in the spring of 2020 the live performances shut down. I continued to work at Jacobs Music and business was fine. I guess being stuck at home made people appreciate having a piano. I've always thought that music makes the hard times a little brighter.

The lockdown gave me time to reflect on all that I've gone through. I thought I'd share some of that in a book. It's been an incredible journey. I guess I've experienced the good and the bad that this world has to offer. Through it all, I've made a lot of great friends and played with some incredible musicians. If my music and that of musicians I've influenced has brought some joy into this world, I'm happy. And after reading this book, I hope you can now say you know me. But my story isn't over just yet.

As live music started coming back, I reactivated the Stormin Norman 11-piece band for a big show at the Bar A in Lake Como, New Jersey in June 2021. My band featured the sound of New Orleans and more including "Dueling Pianos" with Ryan Gregg, Pam McCoy, Chuck Lambert, five saxes, drums, bass with sizzling classic's by Fats Domino, Lloyd Price, Big Joe Turner, Little Richard, Jerry Lee Lewis, Bonnie Raitt, John Prine, and even a touch of Linda Ronstadt. The Bar A show was a big success. Larry Chance of the Earls attended and I brought him on stage and presented him with an engraved high end microphone. After that I was hired by the Asbury Park Music Foundation to do an open air concert at Springwood Park on Fourth of July Weekend, 2021. The park was recently created on Springwood Avenue where I got my education in black music. The concert drew several hundred people and the place rocked. Then I was booked into Asbury Park's Wonder Bar for November.

And I'm hard at work on a new CD to go along with this book. It will feature many of the singers and musicians mentioned in this book and some other talented friends including Elena Bennett, Pam McCoy, Diane Pryor, Vini Lopez, Larry Chance, Joel

Stormin' Norman Band playing Springwood Park, 5 July, 2021
Photo by Charlie Horner

Katz, Nicky Addeo, Leon Trent, Doc Holiday, Ryan Gregg, Vicky Warne-DiBella, Doreen Arminio, Christopher Plunkett, Ed Dougherty, Robert Boyd, Rick Brunemer, Gerry Gironda, Bobby Byrd, Lee Sanderson, Damian Cremisio, Chuck Lambert, Rich Taskowitz, Vince Cappetta, Jon Sebastian Brice, Gary Cavico, Bobby Vaccarelli and Tom Timko.

In Memory of Sam Siciliano

I only wish Sam Siciliano could have been here for this recording session. Sam passed away in 2015. He would have loved what we are doing. We all miss you, Sam.

Perhaps the best is yet to come. Someone once said that musicians don't stop playing because they get old. They get old because they stop playing.

Stormin' Norman Seldin

Appendix I
Discography

The following is a discography of all recordings either recorded or produced by Norman Seldin.

***Selsom* label** (45 RPM Singles)

Label number	Artist	Song Title	Release date
???	Naturals	One Mint Julep	1964
	Naturals	???	
100/101	Valtairs	Soul	1964
	Valtairs	Strangers Way	
102/103	Shondells	Why Do Fools Fall In Love	1965
	Shondells	Upsetter Of Her Heart	
104/105	Uniques / Nicky Addeo	Fool # 2	1965
	Uniques / Nicky Addeo	Over The Rainbow	
106/107*	Valtairs	The Ko Ko Mo	1965
	Valtairs	Moonlight In Vermont	
	** Some copies have 106 on both sides.*		
107/108	Motifs	Molly	1965
	Motifs	If I Gave You Love	
109/110	Jaywalkers	My Own Thing Going	1965
	Jaywalkers	I Do	
356	Shells	A Toast To Your Birthday	1967
	Shells	Can't Take It	

***Johnson* label** (45 RPM Singles)

Label number	Artist	Song Title	Release date
737	Soul Set	Surfin' Boogaloo	1967
	Soul Set	Love Love Love	
738	Soul Set	Baby You'll Get It	1967
	Soul Set	For Your Love	
739	Soul Set	With My Baby Behind Me	1968
	Soul Set	I Don't Want Her But I Need Her	
740	Soul Set	I'm Gonna Love You	1968
	Soul Set	Here Comes The Judge	

Vinyl LP's

Johnson J-1001 1967
"The Soul Set Featuring Norman Seldin – Live From The Village Purple Onion"

Side A
Medley: Don't Fight It / Day Tripper
Medley: Georgy Girl / Poinciana
Filet Au Soul
If I Were A Carpenter
Baby You'll Get It
Soul Set Theme

Side B
Love, Love, Love
Old Man River
Knock On Wood
Monkey Time
Good News
Show Me

Pandoras Box P-1000
"Norman Seldin And The Joyful Noyze" 1972

Side A
It's Time To Move On
It Ain't No Joke
Mean Woman Blues
A Winter Night
Search Through Your Tomorrows

Side B
Days Of Love
I Met A Stranger
Walkin' My Blues Away
Nowhere

Ivory 1001
Stormin' Norman – Rock 'N Roll Plus ca 1984

Artists include: Norman Seldin, Billy Ryan, Clarence Clemons, Max Weinberg, Danny Federici, Roy Bittan, Garry Tallent, Southside Johnny Lyon and others.

Side A
I Wanna Rock 'N' Roll
Monopoly Woman
Everything I Do Is For You
Metronome
I'm Blowin' Away
Vatican Rag

Side B
Misery Loves Company
One For Another
Dance Party
Stormin's Ragtime
Bourbon St. Honeymoon
White People

CD's

Joyful Noyze 2000
"Idyll Point" 1997
Stormin' Norman Seldin

Dreams Of A Misty Romance
Thanks For Being Here
Oklahoma City 1995
Inside Emotions
Favorite Songs Medley:
Vincent - Rhapsody On A Theme Of Paganini - I'll Be Seeing You - When You Wish Upon A Star
Melody's Symphony - 4 Hands For Jamey
Old Mill Rag
Turbo's Ragtime

Ivory International 2000
"House Special" 2000
Stormin' Norman & Steel Breeze

I Need You
Puppet On A String
Would You
Can't Go Down Without A Fight
Little Boy
The Island Song
Big Time Lady
Mean Woman Blues
I Had A Dream
Jersey Boy
Shake Rattle & Roll
Hideaway
I Got The Blues
The Island Song (Bonus Dance Mix)

Ivory 204 [Double CD]
"Asbury Park Then And Now" 2008
Stormin' Norman & Friends

Disc 1

1. Misery Loves Company
2. I Wanna Rock 'N' Roll
3. Monopoly Woman
4. Everything I Do
5. Bourbon Street Honeymoon
6. One For Another
7. Dance Party
8. Metronome
9. Molly
10. If I Gave You Love
11. Love Love Love
12. Surfin' Boogaloo
13. With My Baby Behind Me
14. I Don't Want Her
15. Stormin's Ragtime
16. Time To Move On
17. It Ain't No Joke
18. A Winter Night
19. Search Thru Your Tomorrows
20. Days Of Love
21. Walkin' My Blues Away

TRACKS 1-8: Stormin' Norman & Friends with Garry Tallent, Danny Federici, Clarence Clemons, Billy Ryan, Max Weinberg, Jody Linscott, Jude Johnstone, Roy Bittan, Artie Bressler, Southside Johnny. TRACKS 9-10: The Motifs. TRACKS 11-14: The Soul Set. TRACKS 16-21: Norman Seldin & The Joyful Noyze featuring Clarence Clemons, Barry Lynn, Hal Hollander, Ron Allard, Bob Danylchuk, Nicky Addeo.

Disc 2

1. Gloria
2. Zoom
3. When I Fall In Love
4. My Love For You Will Never Die
5. When I Woke Up This Morning
6. My Hero
7. Nessun Dorma
8. Over The Rainbow
9. Fool Number Two
10. Strangers Way
11. Soul
12. The Ko Ko Mo
13. Moonlight In Vermont
14. I Got My Own thing Going
15. Pretty Girls Everywhere
16. I'm Your Lover Man
17. Jersey Boy
18. Would You
19. Shake Rattle & Roll
20. I Need You
21. Puppet On A String
22. Little Boy
23. Dreams Of A Misty Romance
24. Melody's Symphony/4 Hands For Jamey

TRACKS 1-4: Barbaroso & Historians (Nicky Addeo lead). TRACK 5: Barbaroso & Historians (Ray Dahrouge lead). TRACK 6: Nicky Addeo & Nite Owls. TRACK 7: Nicky Addeo from the Opera Turandot. TRACKS 8-9: The Uniques featuring Nicky Addeo. TRACKS 10-13: The Valtairs featuring Harry Ray. TRACK 14: The Jaywalkers. TRACKS 15-16: Tony Maples. TRACKS 17-22: Stormin' Norman & Steel Breeze. TRACKS 23-24: Norman Seldin.

Index

Recordings

General Index

A

B

C

D

E

F

G

H

I

J

K

L

M

N

S

T

U

V

W

Y

Z

Made in the USA
Columbia, SC
07 January 2022